BIOCOMPUTERS

BIOCOMPUTERS

The next generation from Japan

Edited by

Tsuguchika Kaminuma

Hitachi Information Systems Research Institute

Gen Matsumoto

Analog Information Research Laboratory
Electrotechnical Institute
and
Biodevices Research Group
Ministry of International Trade and Industry

Translated by
Norman D. Cook
Department of Neuropsychology
University Hospital, Zurich

Chapman and Hall

LONDON · NEW YORK · TOKYO · MELBOURNE · MADRAS

UK	Chapman and Hall, 2-6 Boundary Row, London SE1 8HN
USA	Chapman and Hall, 29 West 35th Street, New York NY10001
JAPAN	Chapman and Hall Japan, Thomson Publishing Japan, Hirakawacho Nemoto Building, 7F, 1-7-11 Hirakawa-cho, Chiyoda-ku, Tokyo 102
AUSTRALIA	Chapman and Hall Australia, Thomas Nelson Australia, 102 Dodds Street, South Melbourne, Victoria 3205
INDIA	Chapman and Hall India, R. Seshadri, 32 Second Main Road, CIT East, Madras 600 035

First edition 1991

© 1988 Tsuguchika Kaminuma and Gen Matsumoto *et al.* This book was originally published by Kinokuniya Company Ltd in the Japanese language. English translation rights are arranged with Kinokuniya Company Ltd, Tokyo.

© 1991 Chapman and Hall

Typeset in Photina 10/12pt by Thomson Press (India) Ltd, New Delhi
Printed in Great Britain by T.J. Press (Padstow) Ltd, Padstow, Cornwall

ISBN 0 412 35770 4

British Library Cataloguing in Publication Data
Biocomputers: the next generation from Japan.
1. Computer systems. Development
I. Kaminuma, Tsuguchika II. Matsumoto, Gen 004
ISBN 0-412-35770-4

Library of Congress Cataloging-in-Publication Data
Baiokonpyuta. English
Biocomputers: the next generation from Japan/edited by Tsuguchika Kaninuma, Gen
Matsumoto; translated by Norman Cook.
1st ed.
p. cm. – (Champman and Hall computing)
Translation of: Baiokonpyuta.
Includes bibliographical references and index.
ISBN 0-412-35770-4
1. Molecular electronics. 2. Biosensors. 3. Conscious automata.
I. Kaminuma, Tsuguchika, 1940 – II. Matsumoto, Gen. III. Title.
IV. Series.
TK7874.B3413   1991
621.39–dc20

90-1937
CIP

Contents

List of contributors

Masuo Aizawa, Tokyo University of Engineering
Shozo Fujiwara, NEC Fundamental Research Institute
Noboru Hakkyou, Hitachi Energy Research Institute
Masao Itoh, Tokyo University Medical School
Yasuo Kagawa, Jichi Medical University
Tsuguchika Kaminuma, Hitachi Information Systems Research Institute
Gen Matsumoto, Analog Information Research Laboratory of the Electrotechnical Institute; and Biodevices Research Group of the Ministry of International Trade and Industry (MITI)
Joji Miwa, NEC Fundamental Research Institute
Yoh Tabuse, NEC Fundamental Research Institute

Translator's preface

The editors of *Biocomputers*, Tsuguchika Kaminuma and Gen Matsumoto, shun the 'sixth generation' label for the biocomputing revolution and prefer to emphasize the fact that certain qualitative changes in the nature of computing are underway. Nevertheless, as imprecise as such generational categories are, it is likely that the 'sixth' label will stick – merely as a convenient marker to identify the leap from a silicon-based technology to the various carbon-based organic technologies which are at the heart of biocomputing. There are of course various criteria upon which to determine the 'generation' of a particular computer configuration, but the so-called Fifth Generation Project in Japan has firmly attached the 'fifth' label to silicon-based inference machines having limited parallel processing capabilities. Further growth in those directions is likely, but the inauguration of a new generation requires a qualitative change to justify the new label. A switch to components which contain organic molecules would certainly justify the 'sixth' label.

On the other hand, 'neurocomputing' does not fall obviously within any particular generation. It is, broadly, an attempt to mimic or simulate in computers the kinds of operations that real brains perform. As such, neurocomputing can be done on computers of the third to sixth generations, whether serial or parallel, silicon- or carbon-based. Neurocomputing does, however, have deep connections with biocomputing in so far as the hardware and/or software design of neurocomputers is explicitly based upon principles of organization found to work in living brains. For this reason, neurocomputing – in the sense used by Kaminuma and Matsumoto – is often referred to as a field within biocomputing.

Particularly as silicon-based dedicated neurocomputers are developed for neural net style computing (the connectionist machines), the structural similarities between neurocomputers and third or fourth generation computers will be overshadowed by their functional differences. The structural gap between neurocomputers and biocomputers will remain, however, in so far as neurocomputers are silicon computers which have architectural or software principles borrowed from the brain, whereas biocomputers will have at least some organic hardware similarities with living nervous systems. In other words, regardless of whether or not biocomputing is synonymous with the sixth generation, biocomputing is conceptually a large step beyond the most optimistic ideas about successful fifth generation machines.

There is another sense in which biocomputing can be thought of as a new generation of computing. As mentioned by several authors in the chapters that follow, massive parallel processing, which will make rapid pattern recognition and manipulation of a large volume of analog data possible, is generally thought to be one of the principal strengths of the information processing done by the right cerebral hemisphere in man. If the fifth generation computers, with their logical, symbolic and language processing capabilities, can be thought of as artificial 'left hemispheres', certainly biocomputers can be considered to be artificial 'right hemispheres'.

Even assuming the success of these computing projects in capturing the essentials of left and right hemisphere functions, what will remain for neuro-science and computing to achieve will be (a) an understanding and (b) the technological implementation of mechanisms for the integration of those two 'hemispheres' or modes of information processing. It is a remarkable fact that the largest nerve tract in the human brain, the corpus callosum, connects the two cerebral hemispheres. It is also known to show more rapid evolutionary enlargement than even the cerebral cortex. These anatomical facts suggest that the coordinated interaction of the left and right sides of the nervous system across this tract is not a triviality, but may well be an important issue in the unravelling of the 'brain code' (Cook, 1986). Similarly, the task of getting fifth and sixth generation systems (or, alternatively, silicon- and carbon-based components) to 'talk' with one another is likely to require a significant effort.

Interesting developments within the realm of fifth generation computing continue to be reported. New expert systems, particularly in scientific fields, are appearing regularly, PROLOG has become a relatively popular programming language (Mizoguchi, 1990), natural language processing is becoming far more sophisticated, and machine translation systems are now available at the personal computer level in Japan (Nagao, 1989). As noted by Kaminuma and Matsumoto, however, these developments alone have not – and probably cannot – cross the threshold into creativity and higher-level cognitive processing.

Whatever the actual mechanisms used by the human brain in integrating and synthesizing the information of the two cerebral hemispheres and in achieving higher-level cognition, it is clear that the coordination of symbolic processes (language) with analogical data processing is not a topic that can be relegated to a mere footnote in neuroscience or be considered as a minor, single-channel connection between the fifth and sixth generation computers. There is apparently room for the development of one further generation (the seventh?) before we have computers which realistically mimic the integrated functioning of the bilateral human brain.

In any case, at least one 'generation' following the fifth generation computers is well on its way and is best described with the word 'biocomputer'. The discoveries and insights which underlie biocomputing have originated in universities and private industry throughout the world, but interest and capital investment is rapidly intensifying in Japan. This is evident in the Japanese media – with many books and magazines devoted to topics on neural nets, neurocomputing and biocomputing. More significantly, however, following the organization of the fifth generation project by the Ministry of International Trade and Industry (MITI), the same governmental agency has again organized two ten-year research projects aiming in the direction of biocomputing. The first to be funded was a biodevice project and the second is the biocomputer project to be funded for a decade starting in 1990. Progress in these and other fields of computing continues to occur at a rapid pace throughout the world; the present book represents an up-to-date view of current interest in Japan by nine senior figures in this field.

Among the various themes which recur in the chapters of this book, the following are particularly noteworthy. (i) There is a structural and functional unit of the cerebral cortex which is larger than the single neuron – that is, the cortical column containing several hundred to several thousand neurons. (ii) Simulated neural nets which also contain only several hundreds of artificial 'neurons' can already perform useful computations in physiologically semi-realistic ways. (iii) The sixth generation of computers must embody not only the logical inference mechanisms of fifth generation computers, they must also embody 'right hemisphere-like' capabilities – including analog data processing, creativity, emotion and perhaps even the subconscious mind.

Taken together, these themes suggest an interesting possibility in the development of a biologically-motivated computer architecture. That is, consider a neurocomputer which has linked coprocessors – where one of the two processors is specialized for the (left hemisphere-like) logical, symbolic operations, on the one hand, and the other is specialized for the (right hemisphere-like) processing of the context, higher-order implications, and logically less-precise connotations of the information simultaneously processed in the other processor. Such a linked coprocessor architecture would mimic the overwhelmingly-dominant bilateral organization of the animal (and, most importantly, the human) nervous system and would deal at a relatively microscopic level with the problem of the coordination between two complementary modes of thought. In such a view, the first task in developing a neurocomputer which mimics the human brain is the design of coprocessors with complementary functions, and only subsequently the linking together of large numbers of such coprocessors. In other words, before attacking the n-processor problem for massive parallel processing, the design of complementary coprocessors should be attacked – and then the n-coprocessor problem addressed.

The tone of the book is somewhat pessimistic with regard to the future of computing using silicon components without massive parallelism, but the editors are particularly optimistic about both the technological capacities and the humanistic applications of biocomputing once new carbon-based technologies are more fully developed. More speculatively, but ultimately of even greater interest, is the editors' contention that biocomputing is inherently linked to the technology of producing 'artificial life'. In other words, the deeper understanding of cellular mechanisms which will allow the exploitation of the molecules of life in biocomputers will inevitably be used to manipulate life forms to a far greater extent than is now possible in biotechnology. This kind of 'artificial intelligence' holds much greater potential for exploring and possibly altering the evolution of biological forms and is perhaps a more controversial topic and perilous adventure than biocomputers themselves.

Norman D. Cook, Zurich

Preface

The words 'biocomputer' and 'biocomputing' have recently come into use both in the life sciences and the computer sciences. Being involved in such research, we have felt the need to explain what is meant by 'biocomputing', and how 'biocomputers' differ from previous computers. Some enthusiasts ask if biocomputers are the 'sixth generation' computers to follow the fifth generation still under development. Frankly, we do not believe such labels are particularly meaningful since so many questions remain unanswered about the future directions in which biocomputers will be developed. The mechanisms implied by the 'bio' in biocomputing certainly are those found in biological organisms, particularly those in brains and nervous systems, but we still do not understand the underlying engineering principles of brains and do not know methods for their technological exploitation.

We nevertheless do know that one of the major trends in science and technology today is aimed at the biocomputer. Briefly, the biocomputer is a computer which contains characteristics of both current computers and living organisms. Three major approaches toward the construction of biocomputers are in evidence (Kaminuma, 1985a, 1985b).

1. The study of the mechanisms of biology, particularly those of the living brain, and the use of those results in the redesign of the software and of the hardware architecture of computers based upon semiconductor technology.
2. The development of biocomponents which are similar to and/or made of biological macromolecules, then the development of biochips which make use of those components, and ultimately the construction of biocomputers.
3. The development of techniques for artificially creating life, and then the utilization of the mechanisms of ontogeny or evolution in the development of computers with artificial intelligence or, perhaps, ultra-human intelligence.

In response to the first approach to biocomputing, the objection could be raised that it does not differ significantly from a variety of previous approaches which have been suggested over previous decades, such as bionics. With regard to the second approach, it could be argued that biochips and even biocomputers might be possible, but that does not necessarily mean that such machines will be significantly more powerful than today's computers. And in response to the 'artificial life' approach, it might well be said that as a consequence of our profound ignorance of what life is, such developments will remain impossible for the rest of this century and well beyond – and indeed very real ethical, if not technological, problems must be faced.

Why, in any case, must we incorporate biological and even brain characteristics into today's computers? The answer is that we believe that it is desirable for a host of reasons to produce computers with capabilities vastly superior to those of current computers, and that one road toward improvements of this kind is the close imitation of biological systems which display those capabilities. Such capabilities include fine-grained mechanical control, much sharper and faster pattern recognition, the capacity for flexible and intelligent interaction with human beings, and high-level reasoning capabilities which even surpass the best human specialists.

It might, of course, be asked whether or not such functions could be attained in current large-scale computer projects – such as those in progress in supercomputing and parallel processing logical inference computers (the so-called fifth generation computers). The answer is both yes and no. Since computer capabilities are all relative to the processing of other systems, it is hard to imagine that, in principle, there are any functions which absolutely can or cannot be achieved within any given technology. Nevertheless, of all the research and development plans of current projects, none are aiming at realization of cognitive functions comparable to human intelligence, or at the flexible and detailed information processing of living organisms. Moreover, none are devoted to implementing uniquely biological functions, such as the ability to discover and fix defects or identify and correct mistakes. Moreover, the quintessentially biological functions of living forms, that is, autonomy, self-organization, self-replication and development – as witnessed both in evolution and in individual ontogeny – are completely absent from current computing machines.

In a word, biocomputing is aimed at the technological realization of various biological characteristics which are missing in today's computers. But can such an attempt succeed as an extension of modern semiconductor technology? Or will it be necessary to use fundamentally new techniques for constructing artificial biological systems – techniques for incorporating biological structures and, in some cases, for making use of biological materials. If the latter is the case, then it will be necessary to employ so-called bioengineering techniques which differ fundamentally from present-day electronics techniques. In such a scenario, biocomputing will be a discipline which touches on a wide range of scientific fields. It cannot be said that all the targets of such a wide-reaching discipline fall within the realm of current engineering. But it can be said that there is now some enthusiasm for initiating such research and we believe that, at the very least, the scientific foundations for such research are now being laid.

The 20th century has been an era during which the fundamental laws of physics have been clarified. Those insights have greatly influenced not only the other natural sciences (chemistry and biology), but also the applied sciences of engineering and medicine. Notably, one of the physicists who helped build the foundations of quantum physics, Erwin Schrödinger, spoke of the possibility of new natural laws which were unknown to physics, but which might be involved in the processes of life in his well-known book *What is Life?*, published in 1944. Influenced by that book, many young physicists turned away from basic physics – where many of the fundamental questions concerning the foundations of physical reality had already been answered – and contributed significantly to the building of the foundations of molecular biology.

The more the basic mechanisms of life were clarified, however, the more it was apparent that there were no forces or laws unknown to the physicist. Instead, the mysteries of life were found to reside in the information system now known as the genetic code. Instead of the discovery of unknown 'vital forces', laws were discovered concerning the higher-order informational structure of molecules. In order to understand the dynamic properties of life, biological structures needed to be studied not only as physical objects, but also as informational processes (a view emphasized by Satoshi Watanabe in *Life and Freedom*).

Information science has progressed together with developments in computer science, but such progress has been primarily in mathematical logic and communications engineering rather than in natural science. For information science to develop as a true science, it is essential that it join hands with the life sciences. In so doing, such research will necessarily become the scientific foundations for bicomputing. We anticipate that, in the near future, exchanges between the computer sciences and the life sciences will deepen within a broad scientific discipline of information science.

Biocomputers will be the technological fruit born from the natural fusion of such scientific disciplines. For this reason, we believe that biocomputers are conceptually completely different from the technological developments of all previous computers of whatever 'generation'. Biocomputing involves both fundamental and applied research, and is likely to have a large influence on the directions of a vast range of endeavours in science and technology.

This book is divided into four parts. In Part One, a brief history of computing is given, followed by an explanation of current and new computers. In Part Two, the concepts and developments in the life sciences which form the basis for biocomputers are introduced. In Part Three, we explore ideas concerning biocomputers in relation to the concepts described in Part Two. There we discuss possibilities for so-called biochip computers, neurocomputers and computers with creative intelligence. In the final section, Part Four, we propose a research plan and develop ideas concerning the possible impact of biocomputing. Parts One and Four were written by the editors, and Parts Two and Three were written by various distinguished contributors – as well as by the editors.

We wish to emphasize that particularly Parts One and Four strongly reflect the personal opinions of the editors concerning developments in biocomputing, and those opinions are not necessarily shared by the authors of the other chapters. In other words, each author is to some degree developing his own ideas concerning biocomputers – as indeed we hope the reader will do.

Our main purpose in undertaking the writing of this book has been to communicate to a wide audience – and particularly to young researchers – the recent developments in and the interaction between computing and the life sciences. If we succeed in stimulating the reader's intellectual curiosity and perhaps even stimulate new research activity, we will be delighted.

Finally, we would like to express our thanks to the many people who have allowed us to use diagrams and photographs for this book, and to Mr. Hiroshi Mizuno of Kinokuniya, who has patiently worked behind the scenes on our behalf.

Tsuguchika Kaminuma and Gen Matsumoto, Tokyo

Part One

Birth of a new discipline: biocomputing

1

Progress in computing

1.1 FROM THE SCIENTIFIC ELITE TO THE COMMON HOUSEHOLD

It has been almost 40 years since the appearance of the first 'digital electronic calculating machine' – what we now refer to simply as the calculator or the computer. It is 'digital' because it works essentially with integers, 1, 2, 3, . . . , and not with the multitude of values between integers. The abacus is also a digital tool, but it performs calculations with the human hand, whereas the computer works by means of the flow of electrons.

Calculations in a computer are performed by means of a series of arithmetical procedures known as a 'program'. Since any program must have already been read into and stored in computer memory, calculations can be carried out automatically, provided that data are also given. In essence, it can be said that computers are automatic calculators with stored programs.

The machines we call computers have the following characteristics:

1. they are machines designed fundamentally to do calculations;
2. they are digital;
3. they contain programs;
4. they work electronically.

These fundamental characteristics of computers have not changed since the birth of electronic calculating machines. In this respect, the evolution of the computer has been very much like that of automobiles and aeroplanes. The cars that fill the highways of the world are functionally the same as the original Fords built at the beginning of this century; faster and more reliable, to be sure, but functionally nearly identical to the earliest prototypes. Even the modern jumbo jet is, in principle, unchanged from the Wright brothers' original biplane.

Unlike the car and plane, however, man's conception of the computer has changed quite dramatically. We no longer expect it simply to calculate, help us with numerical chores and store large volumes of data; we expect it to be intelligent.

1.1.1 Computers 30 years ago

Computers were first introduced into Japanese universities and businesses around 1960. Those who were students at that time are already well into their 50s; at least some of them were the first generation of students who studied and used computers. Today, those same people are active in various parts of society and constitute the first generation of executives who were convinced that computers are an essential tool in all aspects of modern life.

It is significant therefore that the image of the computer which that first generation had was that of the troublesome calculator capable of dealing only with 0s and 1s. In the early days, in order to use a computer, one first had to learn how to convert numbers into their binary form: on its own a thankless task. Next in order to make the computer do a calculation, it was necessary to express the commands (program) in binary. To most people, such work was a totally uninteresting, distasteful chore, so that those who chose to work with computers were a breed apart. Finally, the data and program needed to be changed into punch-card form – paper cards of a defined shape with holes in them indicating the 0s and 1s – so that a card-reading machine in the computer room could handle them. Results were printed out on line-printer paper.

It is probably fair to say that this is still the image that people of that generation have in the back of their minds when they think of computers! But the modern image of the computer – as understood by the following generations of students in computer science – has changed considerably. Surveys in Japan show that while university students want a car of their own more than any other material possession and secondary school students want stereo equipment, it is primary school children who want computers. The trauma-inducing binary computer has become a child's toy!

1.1.2 The idea of a computer network

In the summer of 1985, the Nintendo Corporation, having sold more than 4 million machines for video games, announced a plan to allow the networking of these family computer systems via a simple adaptor and the national telephone network. Through this network, it would become possible for children to communicate with mainframe computers and enjoy games and puzzles made available to the network. Moreover, using the same equipment, it would be possible to chat directly with other homes – sending and receiving music and pictures. At the heart of this plan was the mainframe computer of the newly privatized Nippon Telegraph and Telephone Company (NTT). This networking plan was not unique, but one of many for both domestic and international use. The era of the widespread dissemination of information had arrived – and was not confined to communications among scientists on specialized topics. Computer networks now link countless numbers of people with similar hobby, business or professional interests.

1.2 FACTORS IN THE CHANGING IMAGE OF THE COMPUTER

The most important factor in improving the general conception of the computer has been developments in computer software. The process of writing software no longer demands dealing with zeros and ones. For example, the language which continues to be popular in scientific fields, FORTRAN, and that which children use on personal computers, BASIC, make use of several hundred English words to instruct the computer what to do. The meaning of at least some parts of a typical program is often obvious even to the non-programmer. For business programming, COBOL is still in wide use, and a more sophisticated language called C is growing in popularity both for serious and hobby programming. In artificial intelligence, LISP and PROLOG are dominant. But in whatever language programming is done, it uses an artificial jargon employing specific rules of expression to describe the commands to be carried out by the computer. All such high-level languages are an improvement over binary code, but programming remains an exacting science, where even a misplaced comma is not forgiven. The significance of high-level languages lies in the fact that they make programming possible to virtually anyone with the interest. Computers are therefore not solely tools for use by those who think in binary!

Moreover, as every child who has played an arcade game knows, there is in fact no need to learn even these high-level programming languages in order to be able to use a computer. It often suffices to follow the instructions on the screen and respond accordingly. To be sure, there is a deeper and friendlier relationship between computers and today's technokids than there was between yesterday's users struggling with punch-cards and line printers. Today, it is possible to communicate one's intent to the computer by typing on a keyboard or manipulating a joystick or mouse – allowing for an easy interactive conversation between computer and user. So, in addition to the emergence of programming languages which make programming possible without a professional commitment of time and energy, there is also now a breed of usable off-the-shelf software which is largely self-explanatory. It is this conversational relationship which has been the second great step in modern computing.

The third factor in the progress of computers has been the miniaturization of the memory circuits which hold programs and data, and of the circuits carrying out the logical calculations at the heart of all computers. Originally, vast quantities of vacuum tubes and wires were used, but that expensive and unwieldy hardware has given way to much smaller equipment. Vacuum tubes had of course long been used in radios, and were an important part of all electronic circuits, but after the Second World War, Shockley and co-workers at Bell Labs invented the transistor. By means of their application in radios, Sony opened the door to the solid-state (semiconductor) era. From that time, the word transistor has come to mean miniaturization – and for a brief time in Japan, small and attractive girls were said to have 'transistor glamour'. Thereafter, it became nothing more than common sense to know that radios were constructed of transistor circuits and 'transistor' eventually lost its 'miniaturization' meaning.

As was the case with radios, the early vacuum tube computers gave way to transistorized computers and the long march of miniaturization was begun. What has made this possible is a technique called lithography, which allows the 'baking' of a complex circuit onto a silicon wafer. In this manner, it became

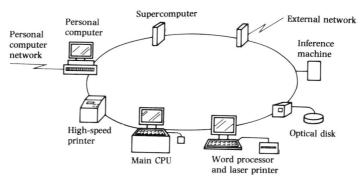

Figure 1.1 In local area network workstations of the future, it should be possible to interconnect all kinds of computers – supercomputers, word-processors, personal computers, inference machines, and so on (Kaminuma, 1982–6)

possible to produce complex circuitry over only a few square millimetres. Such circuitry is called an 'integrated circuit' or simply a 'chip'. Depending upon the density of the circuitry in the chips, they are referred to as simple integrated circuits (ICs), large-scale integrated circuits (LSIs), or very large-scale integrated circuits (VLSIs). A single chip which contains the entire 'heart' of a computer is called a 'microprocessor' or 'microprocessing unit' (MPU).

As a direct consequence of the development of MPUs, the size and cost of computers were greatly reduced, and their mass production became feasible. Naturally, a computer which was built around a microprocessor came to be known as a microcomputer. Because microcomputers then became accessible to individuals, they were later called 'personal computers' – but, in terms of their structure and function, they are still essentially microcomputers. Owing to developments in the technology of the components peripheral to the MPU, home computers, games machines, word processors and other dedicated mass-market systems have emerged. The microprocessor has been used, however, not only in such electronic gadgets which are clearly computers, but also as a small, but important, part of a wide variety of machines. They are often used in measuring equipment and in control apparatus, and have contributed to the greater functionality and 'intelligence' of many household electrical appliances.

In this way, the microprocessor has played a leading role in the still-progressing electronics revolution. Together with communications technology, it is a part of the fundamental technology of 'the information society'. The importance of the microchip can be understood from the simple fact that it is the basic unit, the currency of modern industry. It is already the case that the nature of modern society cannot be discussed without mentioning the computer. This phenomenon is not confined to the West, but is almost as true in Eastern Europe and mainland China as well – where the introduction of microelectronic technology has become a matter of high priority.

The emergence of microprocessors has brought possibilities not even foreseen by their developers. That is, it has opened the road for the design of new types of machines almost at will. Until the advent of the microprocessor, such a possibility was open only to research institutes within major organizations with sufficient capital and personnel. Now, by means of the recombination of ready-made microprocessors, a functionally new and unique computer can be devised within a modestly funded university department.

The fourth factor which has contributed to the evolution of computing is its combination with communications equipment. Such equipment is usually first associated with international communications and contact with far outposts in wilderness areas. Clearly, satellite communications and long-distance telephone communications are good examples. Indeed, what was first developed were ways of making use of mainframe computers from distant locations. Next came networks in which several mainframes were linked together, and these were followed by the emergence of software called 'electronic mail', whereby a new means of communication was employed to allow researchers to communicate not by telephone or telex, but directly from computer to computer over the telephone lines. And most recently there has followed personal computer networks which allow virtually anyone to participate in global computer communications.

There are also computer networks – within a single building, campus or factory. These so-called local area networks (LANs) employ high-speed, high-volume communications circuits which allow rapid communication among numerous computers and peripheral equipment.

It is noteworthy also that computers have been developed which have architectures specific to the needs of LANs. These are generally workstations which contain a central processing unit, display equipment, magnetic storage media and communications apparatus all working together. To allow several people to work on the same system, terminals are connected to the central computer; even when physically distributed among a variety of locations, numerous comparable systems can work together sharing peripheral equipment, data and software. What makes such systems possible are communications techniques for high-speed data transfer. Once they were developed, LAN systems took the meaning out of counting computers individually, for the whole system in such cases is greater than the sum of its parts.

What is of importance in such a system are the functions of which it is capable as a whole. Even if the individual components are simple, the entire system can take on a high-level complexity. By joining such LAN workstations together, still higher-level complexity can be achieved (Figure 1.1). The possibilities for hierarchical networking are exciting, but genuine difficulties lie in the co-ordinated organization of such networks.

The development of computer networks through which computers are joined by communications equipment is reminiscent of the process of formation of the complex neural circuits needed for the brain to control, for example, the hand. The concept of a high-level 'information society' implies the extension of such artificial nerves into all possible social spaces, allowing for the sending and receiving of information to and from all corners of society. In some respects, the possibilities for the development of this kind of information system are virtually unlimited. Assuming that the brain is a complex, but essentially similar, information network, it may be that, as the complexity of current computer networks increases, these networks too will attain higher-level characteristics, something comparable to the consciousness which emerges in living brains.

1.3 THE TRANSFORMATION OF COMPUTERS INTO OMNIPOTENT MACHINES

As described so far, computers are as diverse as the variety of talents which they can display. The diversity of computers can be understood in two senses. The first is the copy-cat nature of computers – the ability of computers to mimic other equipment, such as the typewriter, and/or to control the activities of other equipment. The second aspect of computer diversity concerns the new potentials which are born when computers are combined with other machines. The first topic will be dealt with in greater detail in the chapter which follows, but here we discuss the second topic.

When a computer is added to, combined with or embedded within another piece of equipment, the 'calculating machine' aspect of the computer is hidden and the equipment displays its other talents. Of course, the importance of the computer as a calculating machine is well appreciated, and for this reason the design of number-crunching computers remains a topic of great research interest. So-called supercomputers are just such number-crunchers. For many years the Cray company has played a dominant role in this field, but many other general and specialized computer manufacturers have started to compete – including Hitachi, Fujitsu and NEC. In this way, there has been a resurgence of research and development on the mathematical functions which are at the heart of all computing. For all their speed and importance, however, the greatest attention in the market-place has been focused on the other fields where computers have even greater possibilities.

1.3.1 Word-processing machines

The word-processor has the internal structure of a computer, but in a dedicated machine of this kind, its functions have been limited on purpose to those needed for text manipulation – thus making it easier for the non-computer expert to use. Most personal computers can of course run software which allows them to work as word-processors, but, as a rule, dedicated machines have greater capabilities as word-processors.

Therefore, although they are in principle the same kind of machine, in terms of actual operations and functions, they are quite different. In the future, since the text produced by personal computers will be used in other ways, today's word-processors will probably become computer terminals and a new generation of word-processing machines with the ability to understand and even produce speech will undoubtedly emerge. As such developments proceed, the distinction between the general computer and the word-processor will gradually disappear.

What has gained increasing importance in the world of business has been the ability to edit and print not only text, but also photographs and drawings. Moreover, functions for referring to encyclopaedic information stored on optical disks will increase in importance. The technological advances which are required here are an ability for the computer to 'read' visual images in such a way that it can match the human eye and the ability to produce high resolution output in a compact space. With such capabilities, the world of book and magazine publishing would be revolutionized. This realm is often referred to as computer-aided production (CAP) and desk-top publishing (DTP).

1.3.2 Computer graphics

Word-processors are of considerable help in dealing with text – whether English or Japanese – but the handling of drawings, pictures and photographs by means of computer relies upon computer techniques known as computer graphics. Of course, computers do not produce pictures of their own accord. The fundamental information must be supplied by people, and the computer can then produce the relevant picture through digitization. For this reason, computer graphics is fundamentally a technique for converting visual information from one form to another. For example, to draw a circle on a computer display requires at least a background colour, a foreground colour and the information on the position of the circle. It will suffice to have data on the location of the centre of the circle and its radius. Of course, the computer must have stored within it a definition of a circle – and similar information is required for other geometrical shapes.

Since we inhabit a three-dimensional world, the representation of a computer model for a 3-D shape is most naturally expressed in three dimensions. But since the computer display is of course two-dimensional, the technical problem remains of how the 3-D description should be converted into two dimensions for graphical display. Such techniques are already in widespread use in the realm of molecular graphics and the modelling of other objects of scientific study, in the design of dynamic structures, such as cars and aeroplanes, in electronic circuit design, in the design of advertisements and so on. Of particular importance has been the design of machine equipment by means of computer – so-called computer-aided design (CAD).

In general, the volume of information concerning any two- or three-dimensional object is orders of magnitude greater than the volume of symbolic information describing the same object, and there are many more degrees of freedom in its expression. At the processing speeds of today's computers, therefore, it is not yet possible to work freely with visual objects. High-speed parallel processors are required.

1.3.3 Control systems and robots

The term 'control' generally means action following a defined course to deal with an object in a defined way. Vehicle transport is a typical example of such control. Similarly, the human brain controls with great precision the movement of motor organs, for example, to play sports and musical instruments. Important industrial examples of control are seen in the control of chemical processes and nuclear reactors.

In 'control systems', it is necessary to measure the state of the controlled object and, depending upon the desired goal state, to alter the state of the object. The calculations required to compare the current state with the goal state are inevitably quite complex, despite the fact that similar 'control' of the human hand is something we achieve quite easily. For example, to take a cup off a desk, we calculate the position of the cup relative to the desk on the basis of perceptual information, and make the essential arm and hand movements. Inside a nuclear reactor, it is necessary for a computer system to determine the state of the nuclear rods and control their movement to accelerate or decelerate the nuclear reaction. In the control of aeroplane flight, a course must be selected for flying, while maintaining the aeroplane's safety to its destination in the most economical way feasible. In other words, the essential role of a control system is to receive observational information and, in the light of the previously determined goal state, to undertake the necessary operations of the effector mechanisms. In this sense, 'control systems' are essentially 'information systems' and are suitable for control by computer.

Computers used in control processes are not, however, placed quietly on desks or in air-conditioned computer rooms, but are incorporated within other machines, a portion of which may be mobile and exposed to the various fluctuations of the external world. One familiar example is the microprocessor used in cars to maintain engine performance and fuel consumption at an optimal level. Industrial robots are another example. But even in the case of such robots doing essentially human jobs and having human appearance, it is not true that they have high-level intelligence. They are competent performers when given a predetermined goal state to pursue and a limited range of situations with which to deal, but their adaptability is extremely limited. The need is for robots which have motor mechanisms with the flexibility of human and biological systems.

Recently, Bell Labs have reported the development of a robot hand capable of catching a ping-pong ball in a paper cup – and similar developments have been obtained at Toshiba and Hitachi in Japan (Figure 1.2). Such applications may seem light-hearted, but similar computer algorithms are an essential part of the American Strategic Defense Initiative and missile research. In any case, current robots of this kind still leave considerable scope for improvement – both in terms of information processing and of motor flexibility, the field known as 'mechatronics'.

Figure 1.2 The movements needed to play ping-pong provide a suitable research theme for high-level robotic functions. A robot at Bell Labs can catch a ping-pong ball in a cup. Shown here is a robot developed at Toshiba for returning the ping-pong ball by hitting it with a paddle

1.3.4 Sensors and pattern recognition

Biological sensors are superior to their silicon counterparts primarily in pattern recognition. For example, a human being could look at a TV screen and tell immediately whether the display was a human face or a building – but this is not a trivial task for a computer. Although a low-resolution depiction of a human face might suffice to allow the human eye to recognize the particular face, a computer might not succeed at all.

The rapid processing of a large volume of sensory information and distinguishing among various patterns is called pattern recognition. In reading, we are capable not only of identifying certain configurations as letters and words, but also of associating them with their symbolic content. Although it is clear that pattern recognition in living organisms involves the coordination of the sensory apparatus of the brain, the precise mechanisms remain unknown. In designing aeroplanes, man has always relied heavily on insights from bird flight, but even without full elucidation of the mechanisms of bird flight, the design of aeroplanes has been possible by borrowing various technical hints about wings, propellers and body balance.

In the realm of pattern recognition, however, even that technological approach has not yet been truly successful. Only a few developments in limited fields have succeeded – automatic reading of postal codes, leucocyte separation techniques and fingerprint identification. Outside the realm of visual pattern recognition, one of the long-standing dreams has been the possibility of voice recognition. Voice recognition and distinguishing among various human voices has reached a certain level of real-world application and the idea of computers having 'ears' is no longer science fiction. It is important to note, however, that successful voice recognition does not necessarily mean that computers can transform spoken speech into written words.

For example, it is easy to imagine the process of translation as the conversion of one set of symbols with certain regularities into a second series of symbols with similar regularities. In such a case, it should be possible mechanically to produce a corresponding text without consideration of the meaning of the symbols, that is, semantics. For this reason, developments in machine translation have outstripped those in natural language understanding.

Children are sometimes able to read words without understanding their meaning. Adults too sometimes have such experiences with foreign languages. Like a TV camera and microphone connected to a computer, we can hear, read and repeat the words, but the meaning remains unclear. Similarly, sensors which measure humidity, atmospheric pressure, temperature, tastes and smells might respond to various conditions, but this will not necessarily give the computer the perceptual capabilities of real sense organs. This is the essence of the difference between 'sensation' and 'perception'. However, if we were able to process the information received by sensors in cleverer ways, a computer could attain perceptual capabilities equal to or perhaps exceeding those of biological organisms.

The number of keys on a typewriter or computer keyboard are finite and consequently are easily digitized and expressed as digital information. Similarly, the frequency range of noises heard by the human ear is limited, so sounds can be treated digitally. And if the field of vision and the resolution of the visual image is reduced, visual images also can be efficiently digitized. Clearly, the extra dimensions of visual processing make this more complex than auditory digitization. In hearing, often the temporal dimension is the only dimension of interest, but in vision there are the two dimensions of the visual image, as well as the added dimension of depth, with the need for varying focal lengths. Despite some such problems in both vision and audition, the real problems for computers do not lie in the digitization process itself, but rather immediately thereafter.

Visual and auditory information which is not initially in mathematical form is called analog information. For many years, pattern processing of such analog information has been the hardest part of digital computing. One problem here is that, in digitizing analog information, the volume of data increases tremendously and any subsequent processing of the information is greatly slowed down.

As a consequence, in order to solve the problem of pattern recognition, two other developments must occur. First, greatly improved sensors are needed. Next we need high-speed computational capabilities to deal effectively with the larger volume of data. Even these two improvements, however, are not enough. The greatest problem remains: what kinds of computation need to be performed on the data, once captured and digitized? Biological organisms already have this ability stored within them, but its technological realization remains problematic.

1.4 SIMILARITIES BETWEEN BIOLOGICAL DEVELOPMENT AND COMPUTER PROGRESS

1.4.1 'Evolution' by means of differentiation and unification

It is clear that computers have already moved away from the single 'omnipotent machine' and towards remarkably differentiated 'specialist' machines depending upon their intended uses. This course of development clearly mimics the morphological development commonly seen in living organisms. By a repeated process of differentiation and complication, biological organisms gradually acquire higher-level functions. In fact, the evolution of all life forms on earth is thought to have originated in a single or small number of primitive life forms many millions of years ago.

Living organisms are of course made up from cells. In the case of animals, the single cell which is a fertilized egg replicates to form an entire organism – an organism which may exhibit the behavioural complexity of human beings. The emergence of life from one primitive life form and its systematic differentiation is known as the phylogenetic development within evolution. The growth of an individual organism, on the other hand, is referred to as ontogenetic development. What is characteristic of both kinds of development is the simultaneous differentiation of cells and individuals, together with their unification into a single, coherent organism. Differentiation is the process of, for example, one cell becoming a muscle cell, another becoming a blood cell, etc. It is the process of the organism's many cells attaining their unique structures and functions. For the whole organism, there gradually emerges a unique individual with unique characteristics. Simultaneously, these differentiated cells (or organisms) develop complex relations which other cells (organisms) and, in so doing, the astoundingly complex order of the biological world is formed.

In the short history of computing, as well, a similar 'evolution' by means of differentiation and unification can be seen. That is, by means of the specialization of computers, particular functions have been acquired and their structures have become greatly complicated – gradually leading to higher-level functions. Just as the mitochondria have many properties which suggest an autonomous existence within living cells, in computers many subcomponents themselves have the properties of computers. For example, it is not uncommon for the magnetic disk drives, communications boards and video displays to contain microprocessors. Just as the brain is a computer keeping harmony within the entire system, each of whose components has considerable autonomy and computer-like abilities, so computer systems also have sub-computers with different specialized functions.

1.4.2 The evolution of biological organisms and the progress of computers

It is not a matter of mere chance that there are deep similarities between the progress in computing and the evolution of life. They have in common the feature of being information machines which store programs. They differ primarily in having either a program which is supplied externally or a program which exists internally and functions autonomously. Their similarities mean that they have the possibility for virtually unlimited transformations and development.

A computer is, in essence, a machine which is as simple as the Turing machine. Similarly, the essence of the mechanisms of life is the reading of the genetic information found in the DNA chain – an elegant implementation of the Turing machine. Given some obvious similarities between biological evolution and computer progress, the next point of interest is where the evolution of life and the development of computers will begin to interact and to influence each other. The likelihood that this stage in natural and artificial evolution will someday arise, and that we are at the threshold of developments of this kind, is indeed the main theme of this book. The concept of the biocomputer is the natural growth of the inevitable intersection between natural evolution spurred on by the laws of biology and computer progress spurred on by the human imagination.

2

Tomorrow's computers

2.1 THE MATURATION OF COMPUTER TECHNOLOGY

2.1.1 Can the computers of the 21st century be predicted?

How will the computer, having achieved a permanent place in modern society, develop as we enter the 21st century? Firm predictions are not easily made, the main reason for which is that the growth of a technology which has permeated society to this degree will not proceed in ways unrelated to changes in society itself. And predicting the precise nature of social changes is a task which is all but impossible.

For all his genius, the man who is usually considered to be the father of computing, John von Neumann, did not anticipate the significance of computers for the 20th century. Even once the problems of the construction of computers had been largely solved, the specialists involved in the early production of real, functioning computers did not predict the magnitude of the demand which was to follow only years later. Predicting the course of a dynamic process is not easy, but it is nevertheless true that current computer technology, which is based on large-scale integration techniques, has reached a certain level of maturity and has begun to show a related stability. This does not mean that the world of computing has lost its dynamism, but that the scope and pace of future developments – at least those of silicon-based computers – can be anticipated with some certainty.

2.1.2 The boom in personal computers

The youngsters who enthusiastically built their own computers in garages at home are among the true initiators of the boom in personal computers – clever people who could see the potential of a yet-unknown market, and who made themselves rich in the process. Equally clever teenagers have since developed software products which have dominated the software market. Such success stories indicate both the youth and the potential of the computer industry itself and are also a good indication of the ease with which virtually anyone could get their hands on the relevant technology.

In 1985, dedicated word-processors for less than $800 appeared in the market-place. This price for such a sophisticated piece of equipment suggests that computer technology has come to the front-line of competition in the market place – just as televisions and calculators did before them. It is noteworthy that the price of the computer chips which are at the heart of these machines has already become a negligible part of the final product's price. This is true not only of word-processors, but also of many industrial products which have microprocessors within them.

Moreover, personal computers which have the capabilities of the mini computers and even mainframe computers of several years ago are now easily afforded by individuals. In some respects, computers have matured to a level where more functions and capabilities are supplied by the computer manu facturers than the relatively naive consumer has demanded. For this reason alone, prediction of tomorrow's computers based solely on technological factors is quite impossible. Keeping this difficulty in mind, we will nevertheless try to outline the likely direction of computer developments in the near future.

Let us begin therefore with current complaints concerning today's computers. Even admitting that the technology has matured, if we sit down to use a computer we will find several things unsatisfactory about it. We can assume that we were all agreed that efficiency and economy in performing any task are important. Moreover, when we find one task possible with a computer, we naturally seek to do other tasks with it. This is simply human nature. The computer is a machine with obvious potential and there are unlimited directions in which further development is possible, but here we will look only at its fundamental functions and review the current status of computing.

2.2 THE PROBLEMS WITH CURRENT COMPUTERS

2.2.1 The difficulty of writing programs

In order to make a computer work, a program is required. Recently, word-processors and games machines which do not demand or even allow the user to write programs have increased in number, but the developers of such machines certainly did write programs to make those machines perform as they do. So despite the convenience to the end-user, it remains the case that programs must be written for every conceivable task that computers are put to.

There is, however, no reason to belittle the task of computer programming. On the contrary, programming is of crucial importance – to the extent that the phrase 'software crisis' has come into use to indicate the world-wide lack of capable programmers. Computer hardware and software companies have made considerable efforts to improve the productivity of their programmers by writing programs which themselves write programs, once general indications of what is required have been supplied. Some significant progress in this direction has recently been made, but the problem of programming has not by any means been solved.

2.2.2 The problem of speed

There exist certain physical limitations on the processing speed of computers, which derive from factors such as the speed of light, but there is no limit to demands for increased speed. It seems that crying 'Faster!' is a fundamental human need. Even if there is no logical necessity for further increases in speed, improvements in processing speed are likely to continue to the practical limits. However, particularly for the processing of various forms of analog data, dynamic visual displays in real-time and large-scale scientific and technical simulations, today's computers cannot meet the processing speeds which are genuinely necessary. And this remains one of the main motivations behind the developments in supercomputing. Even in the world of scientific supercomputers, one would be quite mistaken to think that the demands of speed have already been met.

2.2.3 The problem of memory size

The place where data are stored in a computer is called its memory, and its capacity is called memory size. There are two kinds of memory – main memory, which is capable of rapid communication with the CPU, and peripheral memory, which is slower, but can hold much larger volumes of information. How much memory can be used by any one computer is determined by the computer's basic word-length. Personal computers are generally 8-bit or 16-bit machines, whereas larger computers usually work with a word-length of 32 bits. In main memory, primarily one kind of semiconductor memory chip is used: dynamic random access memory. Already in one such chip, circuits containing several million transistors are being made. This technology allows individual memory chips of several square millimetres to contain 1 million bits of information (one 'megabit'). Pushing back the frontiers of memory storage has continued to be one of the areas of the severest competition in the integrated circuit semiconductor industry. In contrast, peripheral memory equipment includes floppy disks and hard disks. A single floppy disk can hold up to several million bytes, whereas a hard disk in minicomputers can hold several hundred times more. Growth here has been rapid, but needs are greater still.

2.2.4 The challenge of miniaturization

As mentioned earlier, developments in semiconductor integrated circuit technology have greatly contributed to the reduced size of computers. It is often remarked that ENIAC, the earliest functional ancestor of modern computers was made of vacuum tubes, weighed 13 tonnes, and filled an entire room – and yet its capabilities fell far short of those available in today's smallest hand-held computers.

It is still the case, however, that many of the business computer systems in use today take up considerable physical space. Although the ratio of capabilities to physical size has greatly improved, not all computers fit neatly on desk-tops. Furthermore, although memory and data processing components involving semiconductors have become smaller, most display monitors still employ the bulky cathode ray tube used in television sets and little progress has been made in making them more compact. Similarly, improvements in resolution have been rather modest.

It is also important to note that, relative to the magnitude of potential health problems (eye strain, etc.) of current display apparatus, improvements have been extremely slow. In comparison with the remarkable progress in the computer itself, those in peripheral equipment; such as display units, equipment for recording analog information and printers are almost used leisurely. This lack of progress has clearly been an impediment to the dissemination of computer technology. If peripheral equipment can also become compact and low-cost, computer systems with more capabilities will more easily be built, so increasing the infiltration of computers into society.

2.2.5 The problem of processing analog information

For many years, it has been said that computers are good at handling numbers and symbols, but not good at handling analog information, such as auditory sounds and visual patterns. It has also been argued that computers are less capable of handling analog information because the internal structure of the computer itself is essentially binary digital, dealing only with 0s and 1s. Such arguments are not mistaken, but they do not go to the heart of the problem. In fact, the technology for digital recording of analog data has developed remarkably. Some of those developments are already familiar to us in the form of digital recording of music, digital cameras, voice synthesis chips and so on.

Nevertheless, in comparison with the technology for handling numbers and symbols, developments in the technology of analog information have lagged behind, as have processing techniques for pattern recognition – which is arguably the single most characteristic feature of biological analog data processing. Consider, for example, the fact that, based upon a variety of perceptual memories of a certain visual scene, melody or fragrance, human beings are able to recall similarities among vastly different situations. From a certain fragrance, the visual image of a certain flower can be remembered – as well as the place, the sound of the wind, the people there, the emotions felt for those people – all in a momentary association of analog recall!

Today it is possible to store a huge volume of melodies or pictures on an optical disk, but it remains impossible to call up directly in a mechanical recorder the analog information of a melody which 'resembles' another melody, or a drawing which reminds one of a certain photograph. As is apparent in the previous example, human memory is multi-dimensional and has many complex cross references. It is a dynamic, searchable memory with a huge number of 'vertical' and 'horizontal' connections among a variety of sources of analog information – visual, auditory, olfactory, somatosensory, gustatory and even emotional.

Computers with comparable capabilities do not exist today and will not be easily built in the near future. For today's computer, problems such as the matching of simple multi-dimensional visual arrays are not easily solved – for example, determination of whether or not a solid structure resembles a two-dimensional drawing is not a trivial problem for modern-day computers to solve.

Here, two notable technological problems remain:

1. storage of a large volume of multi-dimensional analog information;
2. given such a massive informational database, recognition of similarities or differences – in other words, pattern matching.

By means of optical disk technology, problem 1 is in the course of being solved, but problem 2 remains virtually untouched. It is of course true that it has been necessary to solve the mass storage problem before significant advances in accessing data could be made, but the pattern-matching dilemma is daunting.

2.2.6 The contradiction between ease of use and versatility

The latest generation of photocopy and fax machines have many more buttons than previously, reflecting an increase in the options available to users. Similarly, the number of computer applications which require only selection of appropriate key strokes from a menu displayed on the screen has greatly increased.

It remains the case, however, that ease of use and versatility (or freedom of choice) represent diametrically opposite tendencies. For example, most people are delighted with the automatic gear change in automobiles, but in racing cars which must be driven to their highest potential, manual gear-changing relying on human perceptions takes priority. Despite this, even in such fields there is a trend towards further automation, for example, in the reliance on computer systems in jet fighters. If it is this kind of limited mechanical operation, computerization of quite high-level operations is possible.

In everyday life, however, there is normally a high degree of freedom, particularly in work situations where creativity and decision-making play important roles. It would therefore be desirable to have computers with far more flexible abilities to make decisions and respond appropriately to somewhat vague human commands. They could then carry out a variety of human tasks. But if computers do not have intelligence at least equal to human intelligence, it is uncertain whether or not, in addition to carrying out mechanical operations, they would be able to interpret commands that are anything short of explicit. In many cases it is better to have a truly unintelligent computer which can be easily programmed to do work than it is to have a 'half-witted' almost-intelligent computer which sometimes understands and sometimes fails to understand.

For this reason, there are also limits on the amount of effort that should be spent giving computers flexibility. This limit is not a technological one, but one which must be decided on in the light of the nature of the work to be undertaken. In other words, even if a machine can do a variety of jobs, it is not necessarily the case that this will be beneficial to the user. As the scope of choice for the user increases, the burden on the user to make choices increases. In the opposite case, if the number of possible operations is reduced and simplified, the machine becomes functionally easier to understand and easier to use, but its flexibility will become correspondingly poorer. This 'double bind' is an inevitable part of current computer technology. Although it will become possible to achieve some balance between these opposing tendencies by means of technological innovations, a complete 'solution' is unlikely – even given considerable progress in computers and computing techniques.

2.2.7 The challenge of artificial intelligence

Giving intelligence to computers is the ultimate dream of every researcher in computing. A computer which has acquired some modicum of intelligence is said to have 'artificial intelligence' (AI).

At the outset of the computer age, this concept was often called 'artificial brains', but before long it was realized that no matter how fast a computer's calculations, it lacks the flexibility of organic brains, and the phrase 'artificial brains' was dropped in favour of 'silicon brains'. The artificial intelligence' label has of course been widely used in recent years. A large number of journalists and for too many academics have announced, in effect, that since such a large volume of fundamental research has now been completed in AI, the age of its flowering and practical application has arrived. That view is unfortunately quite mistaken.

For example, the deductive inference systems (that is, expert systems) which are representative of the current state of the art in AI (Figure 2.1) are, from their very inception, designed for practical applications of limited scope. Those systems are, methodologically, a great departure from the games and puzzles of the previous generation of so-called AI, but it is debatable whether or not they constitute anything approaching genuine intelligence.

A final verdict has not been reached on whether or not pattern matching should be included within AI research, but at the level of academic meetings and research conferences, the two are treated as distinct entities and the algorithms used in both fields are not commonly shared between them. Ultimately, of course, AI is defined as the methodologies in which people who consider themselves to be AI researchers are interested. But the image which AI evokes in the ordinary person is certainly that of a computer which has capabilities which one can easily and intuitively describe as intelligent. By that definition, the history of

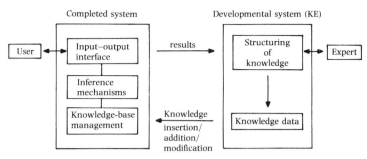

Figure 2.1 The fundamental structure of expert systems. In order to build a system such as that on the left, a developmental system (a knowledge engineering, KE system) is also required

AI is synonymous with the history of computing itself. Such a definition is arguably more precise than many of the definitions of academics trying to stake out a narrow territorial argument!

In fact, however, we still have a very limited understanding of the essence of human intelligence. Particularly unclear is the relationship between universal, general intelligence and specialized, narrow field intelligence. Moreover, the relationship between creativity and intelligence is not understood. For example, what relationship exists between the intelligence involved in a computer that can do machine translation and that of a computer that can play chess? Or, what is the cognitive link between a computer that can make medical diagnoses and one that can recognize handwriting? Finally, which is more intelligent: a program that predicts the higher-order configuration of a protein molecule from its first-order amino acid sequence or a program that can give advice on investments in the stock market? And will developments along one line have implications for developments along other lines? More generally, which, among the many types of research related to AI, will come to be regarded as truly fundamental, the basis for further developments in AI?

The fact that there are no simple answers to these questions is often expressed with the phrase: 'There is no fundamental general theory of AI' (or of pattern recognition, for that matter). But, despite such pessimism, solutions to these separate themes are gradually being found. In this sense, the intelligence of computers is certainly evolving. There is, in any case, no doubt but that AI is an important theme of research and development. The principal problems remaining are the selection of the avenues of research likely to prove fruitful. In other words, if a high level of 'general intelligence' in digital, serial computers is, as it now seems, impossible, what are the fields of application within which computers of limited intelligence are likely to prove of value? Indeed a variety of attempts aimed at tomorrow's computers is being undertaken in light of the dissatisfactions and criticisms of today's computers. Let us look now at a few of these developments.

2.3 RE-EVALUATING THE VON NEUMANN ARCHITECTURE

2.3.1 Three roads for revolutionizing computers

In order to revolutionize the current world of computers, three distinct roads are clearly visible:

1. changing the physical elements at the foundations of all computer components;
2. changing the architecture of computers;
3. devising new software and computing algorithms.

Combinations of these three possibilities are also likely.

Progress in computing thus far has been almost entirely in the realm of improvements in the hardware elements and in software innovations within the constraints of that hardware – not in architectural changes. Even when the hardware elements are changed, however, the basic functions remain the same, while the integration techniques alone are improved. In this respect, the development of higher-level capabilities in computers has been due to progress in developing algorithms and progress in their implementation as programs. Only very recently have significant efforts been made, not on these two approaches, but on the topic of computer architecture, that is, the basic design of computers.

2.3.2 What is a non–Von Neumann architecture?

Most current computers are designed along the lines of the Von Neumann architecture. In such a computer, the data and program (commands) are stored in computer memory and they are serially called up by the central processing unit (CPU). The results of computations are returned to memory locations and/or output to peripheral devices, such as printers or display monitors, which are external from the CPU.

A major strength of the Von Neumann architecture is the fact that the data handling is simple and control is therefore uncomplicated. Its main drawback is that when a large volume of calculations must be done, a bottleneck develops owing to the sequential processing architecture. A simple analogy here is instructive. Consider a bank with only one teller at work. If service is sufficiently quick and the number of customers sufficiently small, a queue of customers will not develop, but if the number of customers relative to the speed of service increases, a queue is inevitable. The solution in a bank is of course to have several tellers at work at separate windows in parallel. Depending upon the needs of the customers, however, even this solution may not suffice. For example, a customer may want to take money out of one account, buy foreign currency with some of it, and deposit the remainder in a different account. Such tasks cannot, in principle, be carried out in parallel.

In contrast, there are comparable tasks which could be performed in parallel – for example, it would be possible to make a deposit in account A, withdraw money from account B, and exchange dollars in cash for yen. If parallel processing techniques were employed here, first those tasks that could be processed in parallel would be separated, and processing in the separate routes could be interwined and separately controlled. In a bank, organization of such 'parallel processing' would simply be a matter of common sense, but in a computer, such control is not a trivial problem.

Because of the difficulties inherent in parallel processing, it has not been implemented in most general purpose computers, which remain today essentially Von Neumann–type machines. Fortunately, because of the great strides in microprocessors in general, it has become relatively easy to try out various computer architectures. For this reason alone, there is growing interest in various non–Von Neumann–style computers. It should be noted, however, that simply saying 'non–Von Neumann' does not give us any indication of what kind of architecture can or should be employed. To paraphrase Tolstoy, there is only one Von Neumann architecture, but there is a plethora of non–Von Neumann architectures. Moreover, among the parallel processing machines which have been proposed to date and which generally fall under the label 'non–Von Neumann', there are virtually none which depart radically from the basic ideas of Von Neumann. On the contrary, even parallel processors are often little more than 'multiple Von Neumann–style' processors. A truly non–Von Neumann, genuinely revolutionary computer architecture remains to be found.

2.4 RESEARCH ON NON–VON NEUMANN ARCHITECTURES

It is no insult to Von Neumann that the eyes of many researchers have turned towards non–Von Neumann architectures. In his defence, let it be said that perhaps the most serious student of non–Von Neumann architectures was in fact Von Neumann himself. He was a mathematician with the good sense of an engineer, and he thought deeply about a mathematical and engineering model of the brain and of the brain–computer analogy. In fact, during his later years from 1948 to 1953, he wrote extensively on such ideas. They included:

1. self-replicating automaton theory;
2. a mechanical model of the brain;
3. models of neuronal activation, thresholds and recovery;
4. a model of the above ideas expressed as non-linear partial differential equations;
5. a probability model which included non-deterministic and error functions.

Moreover, Von Neumann was one of the first to attempt a quantitative comparison of the human brain and computers (Table 2.1).

For a man such as Von Neumann, who attacked the brain–computer problem from so many angles, the so-called Von Neumann style of architecture must have seemed extremely simple – a transitory stage which would inevitably be superseded. If he had known that well into the 1990s one style of computing would still

Table 2.1 The first comparison of brains and computers (based Von Neumann, 1958)

	Logic devices			Memory devices			
	Cycle time	Number of devices	Integration per chip	Number of devices (per chip)	Integration	Heat dissipation–energy of logical operations (ergs)	Breakdown rate
Brain[a]	10^{-1}–10^{-2} s	10^{10}	–	10^{15}–10^{16}	–	3×10^{-3}	5×10^{-21}
Computing:[b]							
1940s	–	2×10^4	–	7×10^2	–	6×10^2	10^{-13}
1990	10^6–10^8 FLOPS	5×10^5	–	10^8	10^5–10^6	4×10^{-6}	15×10^{-22}
2000	10^{10}–10^{12} FLOPS	10^9	10^7	10^{10}	3.2×10^7	–	–
2010	10^{12}–10^{14} FLOPS	10^{11}	10^9	10^{12}–10^{13}	10^9	–	–

[a] The brain has more than 2 billion cells and more than 10 billion synapses. Cell density: 10^9/cm^3.

[b] The relation between the width of VLS and density of integration:

$1\ \mu m \longrightarrow 1\ Mbit \longrightarrow 4 \times 10^6$ elements

$0.2\ \mu m \longrightarrow 32\ Mbit \longrightarrow \sim 10^6$ elements

be a 'trunk artery' of computing after more than 40 years, he would undoubtedly have been surprised and would have greeted such news with mixed feelings!

In any case, let us look briefly at some current developments in parallel processing and non–Von Neumann computers.

2.5 SUPERCOMPUTERS

In whatever age and in whatever field, a man or a machine which surpasses the usual capabilities is of great interest. Inevitably, we attach the 'super' label and end up with supercars, superstars and supercomputers. Supercomputers are computers which outpace the common mainframe computers in virtually every category.

Historically, the supercomputer that has had the greatest impact is the Cray-1 – a supercomputer with a horseshoe design which allows a nimble technician to get inside. In addition to military uses, many Crays have been delivered to public research institutes and private businesses. Although Japanese supercomputers have recently laid claim to some of the fastest benchmark tests, in the world of computers and their rapid evolution, the Cray-1 had the distinction of maintaining its position as the world's fastest computer for some ten years – and for this reason the word 'Cray' is virtually synonymous with supercomputer (Figure 2.2).

While acknowledging the success of the Cray supercomputers, it is true that the supercomputer has been seen as a very unusual, specialized computer. Even IBM, the world's leading computer manufacturer, has never produced a supercomputer, undoubtedly because IBM saw that for most business data processing purposes (which account for the bulk of computer sales) a machine which is extremely fast for purely arithmetic calculations is unnecessary. The use of supercomputers has been limited to a relatively small number of scientific and technical purposes and, because of the narrow range of specialized uses, the

Figure 2.2 The Cray-2 supercomputer, consisting of 14 columns arranged in a horseshoe configuration. The computer contains four CPUs and 256 megawords of memory. Behind the computer are its cooling tanks

big computer manufacturers have generally not been interested in their development.

The current situation in computing has, however, begun to change. Considerable interest has been generated both in the production and the use of supercomputers. There are claims that supercomputers that are 1–10 million times faster than the Cray-1 will be developed within ten years. Clearly, the expectations for such machines are great: with such increases in processing power, calculations on black holes, research on nuclear fusion, weather predictions, aeroplane design, the design of new materials at the molecular level, and the elucidation of various biological phenomena and pathological conditions will advance dramatically. And these are not the only fields likely to be influenced. Economic predictions using large-scale world models, anticipation of marketplace changes and other applications in the social sciences and business world can be expected.

Of course, predictions concerning the demand and results of such a technology cannot be relied on, but there can be no doubt that, as the number of supercomputers dramatically increases, they will be put to many more uses in many more fields and a variety of new applications will emerge.

The ultimate target in the development of supercomputers is the same as that of the first computers – the performance of computations at the maximum speed possible. What methods have been devised for such a purpose? The first of course has been to increase the speed of the fundamental electronic components. The 'switch' which can be either on or off is at the heart of all digital computers and the rapidity of its operation is a crucial factor in computer speed. To maximize that basic hardware property, a variety of alloy semiconductors have been employed, including gallium arsenide components and Josephson components.

The second method is to increase the efficiency of data flow between the CPU and memory storage units. In order to avoid using slowly operating peripheral storage units, the trend is towards increasing the storage capacity of the CPU itself.

A third method is to break up the computational work and relegate various processes to multiple CPUs (and memory); this is essentially a method for improving computational techniques by means of parallel processing. For this purpose, current supercomputers commonly employ a so-called pipeline architecture, thus allowing different computational tasks to be done by different CPUs which are connected linearly. In terms of human work, this corresponds to an assembly line where the flow of different jobs is along a single assembly line. Each individual receives the work done before him, completes his own task and hands the work on to whoever is next in line. As a result of such an assembly line formation, it is generally the case that the hands of all employees are busy at all times (except at the very start and end of work). Therefore, the time required by an assembly line team is, roughly, inversely proportional to the number of people in the line. Of course, it is presumed that the flow of work proceeds evenly and does not accumulate at any one site. Today's state-of-the-art supercomputers employ ten or more such pipelines working in parallel.

As mentioned above, whether or not this technique works efficiently depends entirely on the nature of the work itself and the division of labour employed. The breaking up of the computational procedure is a problem of programming and various innovations can be exploited to attain improvements here, but the fundamental nature of the work itself often cannot be altered significantly. For example, in various types of image processing which require massive parallel data input and output, current supercomputers are not terribly effective. As a consequence, there are big differences in the arrangement and connectivity of CPUs and memory chips, depending upon the work which the computer is expected to do.

2.6 MASSIVELY PARALLEL MACHINES

The pipeline architecture is an assembly line style manufacturing process employing people with different talents. It is possible to consider an architecture which calls for the cooperation of people with similar abilities. For example, the HEP computer from Denelcore has up to 16 fundamental computer systems, and the processing speed is inversely proportional to the number of systems in use. This architecture was, in its time, remarkable, but the essential software proved difficult to write and the firm ceased trading in 1985.

Certainly, the use of the same kind of processors placed in a symmetrical configuration is an easier issue for both design and control than would be an asymmetrical configuration of processors with different capabilities. Possibilities for expansion are greater as well. Provided that the problem of control is well worked out, it would be enough for each individual processor to be assigned extremely simple tasks. In fact, in line with the rapid development of microprocessors, some of the systems which are drawing the greatest attention in the world today are multiprocessor machines which have been shown to have supercomputer-like performance. Notable among such developments is the work of G. Fox and colleagues at the California Institute of Technology. They succeeded in producing a machine with a performance like that of Cray-1 by means of the parallel connection of 64 Intel 8086 and 8087 boards, each of which has capabilities similar to those of the familiar IBM personal computer.

In Japan, the work of Chikara Seino and colleagues at Waseda University has been of particular interest. They have built parallel processing PAX-series machines which employ 32, 64, 128 (and so on!) microprocessors (Kawaii, 1985). It is possible that future developments along those lines will lead to the connection of 1 million or more processors. Such extremely large multiprocessor systems can be joined in a tree structure where each processor is influenced only by processors that are peripheral to it – an architecture which has also been called a 'cellular automaton machine'. Examples of these systems include the

DADO and NON–VON machines developed at Columbia University and the CAM (cellular automation machine) developed at MIT.

This kind of non–Von Neumann architecture with rich possibilities for expandability is one 'ideal', but it is difficult to determine today how far such systems will succeed in solving real computational problems. The bankruptcy of Denelcore is only the tip of the iceberg of failed parallel processing machines. Moreover, it is likely that, with specialized functions, some such machines will prove suitable for some tasks and unsuitable for others. In any case, what has made experimentation with parallel processing machines possible is the rapid progress in microprocessors, together with rapid decreases in CPU prices. In this respect, research into parallel architectures is today in full bloom.

So, just how fast are computers which employ pipelining and parallel processing? To give precise answers to this question, we need various yardsticks with which to measure computer speeds. One of the frequently employed measures is the number of floating point operations per second (or FLOPS). One million (10^6) FLOPS is of course a MFLOP, 10^9 FLOPS is called a gigaflop (GFLOP) and 10^{12} FLOPS is called a teraflop (TFLOP).

It is worth mentioning here that the actual speed of computer calculations is heavily influenced by the content of the work to be done, the style of the programming and the set-up of the machine itself. As a consequence, it is often difficult to make accurate comparisons among different machines – just as it is difficult to make meaningful comparisons of automobiles solely on the basis of top speeds.

In very general terms, however, it can be said that current small computers work in the MFLOPS range, typical mainframe computers work in the several tens of MFLOPS range, and the Cray-1 works at speeds of about 100 MFLOPS. The more recent Cray-2 and supercomputers from Hitachi, Fujitu and NEC work at speeds ranging from several hundred MFLOPS to 1 GFLOPS. It is noteworthy that the MITI project for 'High-Speed Scientific Computers' is aiming at the construction of computers which, over the ten-year period starting in 1990, will achieve 10 GLOPS. For computer operations at this speed, it is presumed that highly parallel processing will be needed.

2.7 INFERENCE MACHINES

Most machines in use in current AI research, i.e. deductive inference systems, are programmed in the so-called declarative, as distinct from the procedural, languages, such as LISP and PROLOG. It is well-known, however, that LISP runs quite slowly on the machines most favoured by AI researchers in the 1970s: the PDP-10 and PDP-20 computers from DEC. Indeed, at that time, one of us (TK) had the opportunity to make comparisons of various medical diagnosis systems, including the MYCIN system of Shortliffe at Stanford University, the EXPERT system of Krikofsky and Weiss at Rutgers, and the Digitalin systems of Solovsky at

MIT. Remarkable as they were, one's overwhelming impression when seeing these systems at work was the slowness of the response to queries. Indeed, this has been one of the main motivations for many researchers in AI: working on the development of specialized machines which can run LISP-like functional languages more quickly.

There is, however, one important lesson that is soon learned when trying to develop an expert system in a narrow specialist field. That lesson is the fact that the rules of experience upon which mechanical logical operations must rely are almost non-existent. Some AI researchers call this the problem of 'knowledge representation' and others view it as a problem of 'knowledge acquisition', but those labels miss the point. In fact, with the exception of the world of games and mathematics – where the ground-rules are explicit and generally unalterable – there simply is very little knowledge which is absolutely certain and can be encoded in a symbolic form. For this reason alone, no matter how improved the programming technique and how fast the processing in a specialist expert system, the belief that genuine artificial intelligence has been achieved or is on the verge of being achieved is too optimistic.

Nevertheless, despite such well-grounded pessimism about current expert systems, considerable competition in the development of AI systems began in the early 1980s – spurred on, no doubt, by the Japanese Fifth Generation Project. It seems that the optimists had at that time won the day, but let us remember that in computer folklore there is the familiar phrase: 'When you've got nothing constructive to do, build hardware!'

Whatever the case may be, at the Institute for New Generation Computer Technology (ICOT), which has been the driving force in the Fifth Generation Project, two very interesting machines have been developed. They are the Parallel Serial Inference (PSI) Machine, which is a dedicated PROLOG computer, and the relational database machine called DELTA. Using those machines, work is still in progress on the transformation of the Von Neumann–style PSI machine into a parallel inference machine (PIM) and on the transformation of DELTA into a parallel database machine (PDM) (Fuchi and Hirose, 1984). Outside the Fifth Generation Project, as well, many parallel processing machines are under development for dedicated use in AI.

In order to make use of the characteristic features of declarative languages such as LISP and PROLOG, it is thought that non–Von Neumann–style architectures, such as 'data flow machines' and 'reduction machines' are desirable. Considerable efforts in these directions are now being made. In machines of this kind, the measure of processing speed commonly used is the number of logical inferences per second (LIPS). The PSI machine performs at a speed similar to the DEC mainframe computers – at around 300 000 LIPS (300 KLIPS). ICOT is striving ultimately to produce a machine capable of several hundred million LIPS. It is thought that high-speed parallel inference machines of this kind (Figure 2.3), which handle the data stored in truly massive knowledge bases, will make large-scale knowledge processing feasible.

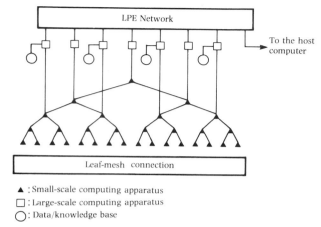

▲ : Small-scale computing apparatus
☐ : Large-scale computing apparatus
◯ : Data/knowledge base

Figure 2.3 A non–Von Neumann computer architecture suggested by Shaw (1987)

2.8 IMAGE PROCESSING AND OPTICAL COMPUTERS

The field of image processing has long awaited the emergence of parallel processors. Let us consider a simple example. Coherent (in phase) laser light can be made to pass through two convex lenses as a broad parallel beam. If we place an object of varying light intensity in front of the first lens, from the second lens will emerge the original image with its orientation reversed.

In principle, what has happened is that the original image has undergone a

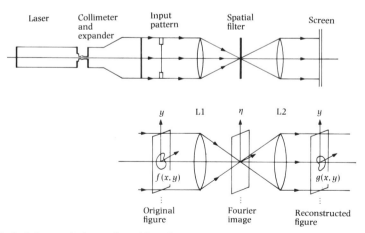

Figure 2.4 Coherent light produced by a laser (upper) and processed in an optical system (lower). The spatial filter performs a convolution calculation on the original image. An original image, its Fourier transform and convolution are shown in Figure 2.5

two-dimensional Fourier transformation. That image is brought to the focal point and then undergoes a reverse Fourier transformation. Although it is reversed left-to-right and top-to-bottom, the original image is reconstructed in all its detail (Figure 2.4). Indeed, it is well known that if a function undergoes both a forward and a reverse Fourier transformation, the original function will be obtained.

Cooley and Tukey discovered a method to perform one-dimensional Fourier transforms rapidly, using digital data, but in two dimensions the volume of calculations becomes tremendous. In an optical system, however, it is noteworthy that such a 2-D transformation is achieved with ease as light passes through a medium.

Based upon the same principles and some innovations in optics, it is possible to perform correlational computations, convolutions and spatial filtering on two-dimensional visual images (Figure 2.5). Applications of these techniques include

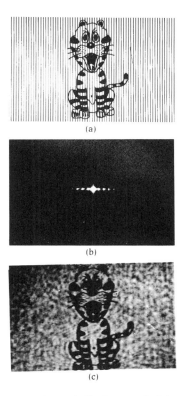

(a)

(b)

(c)

Figure 2.5 If a laser light system is used, the image of picture **(a)** is transformed into a diffraction pattern **(b)** in an instant. Conversely, an image **(c)** similar to the original **(a)** with the vertical lines removed can be reproduced. (This example is taken from the work of Isamu Suzuki and Katsumi Ohara done in Kaminuma's research laboratory at Chuo University.)

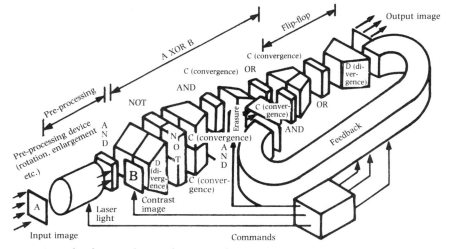

Figure 2.6 The design of part of an optical computer (a parallel digital operator from Jun'ya Seko, 1981)

simple object recognition and automated defect detection. The drawback of such ultrafast optical systems is that they have very little processing flexibility. Attempts are now being made here to add logical functions which would provide the flexibility of parallel processing to the speed of optical computing (Figure 2.6).

Even if we indulge in the use of a phrase as attractive as 'optical computing', it remains the case that current computers cannot be replaced entirely with optical components. Optical processing will probably find widespread use as subsystems in today's computers or be used as peripheral sensors and interface units. In other words, it seems quite unlikely that optical computers will supplant more traditional computer systems for many years to come. Nevertheless, in terms of speed and for use in parallel processing, optical components are extremely good (Figure 2.7).

Moreover, research is quite advanced in optical computing – not as the basic CPU for computers, but as visual sensors which might someday replace the TV camera, and of course as memory media. The former topic will be discussed in a later chapter, but it is worth noting that one of the first development goals in the field of biodevices is the optical sensor. For example, one line of research is the application of the photoelectric conversion properties of the protein rhodopsin extracted from micro-organisms in sensor devices. Of interest also is the so-called 'hole-burning' effect in optical memory systems. The above discussion has been concerned primarily with analog information processing systems using, for example, lasers, but there are also exciting developments in the visual image processing of parallel processors which utilize digital LSI techniques.

One well-known system is the so-called LINKS system developed at Osaka University for use in film-making. When making a moving picture with LINKS,

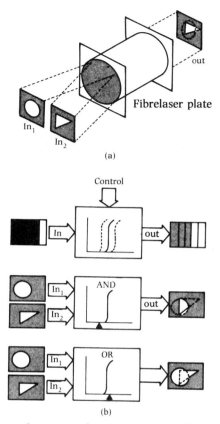

Figure 2.7 Using an optical system such as in **(a)**, it is possible to perform basic computer operations, such as A/D conversion, logical AND, and logical OR (Seko, 1981)

multiple (64 or 128) microprocessors are utilized to process portions of the visual image independently and the entire process is controlled by a master processor. Similar dedicated parallel processor machines have been designed for image displays in computer-aided design and computer-aided manufacturing. NEC has managed to develop LSI techniques for image processing which put the various computational algorithms needed for visual image analysis on a single high-speed chip.

3

Expectations from the life sciences

3.1 WHAT IS A BIOCOMPUTER?

Now that we have completed a brief introduction of computing today, we can proceed to discuss various aspects of the issue at hand, biocomputing. Although the words 'biocomputing' and 'biocomputers' are not infrequently used today, they are used with a variety of meanings. Indeed, those of us working in this field are often asked to explain simply and briefly in what ways biocomputers differ from usual computers.

It is, unfortunately, not simple to respond to such requests. Depending upon the aspects of biology and computing that are emphasized, the meaning will clearly differ. Indeed, as with the term 'artificial intelligence', 'biocomputing' has become a seductive and fashionable catch-phrase, but it is hard to pin down. Perhaps as a consequence of the lack of a single, clear-cut definition, some have expressed doubts about biocomputers, saying that the word exists, but no real and tangible biocomputing entity yet exists. In this respect, biocomputing is certainly a phantom technology.

It is, however, true that a biological computer of a completely different nature from today's electronic computers already exists in the form of the fundamental phenomenon of life. That is, we know that protein is produced by means of the flow of information from the nucleic acids, and that the brains and nervous systems of animal organisms are the multicellular manifestations of that information flow.

The single most noteworthy fact emerging from the increased tempo of the life sciences since the 1950s is that living organisms have a computer-like control mechanism. In a word, life is a chemical machine and is regulated by extremely computer-like central control processes. No mysticism and no ghost in the machine are needed. What is most remarkable is that, on the contrary, complex, diverse and 'mysterious' life activities ranging from the bacterium to the human spirit emerge from the simple mechanical structures of molecular biology.

The ultimate aim of life science research is the complete elucidation of this biochemical puzzle. The dream of computer engineers, on the other hand, is to reduce the distance between today's electronic computers and nature's living 'computers'. In other words, to build a computer with some of the features of a living organism. As a consequence, the ultimate aims of both the life sciences and the computer sciences are inextricably intertwined.

In this light, biocomputing can be understood as the technological field which will soon emerge from the intersection of developments in the life sciences and computer technology. It cannot therefore be said that biocomputers are of the same general nature as supercomputers with new devices appended to them, or the same as the logical inference machines of the Fifth Generation Project, or even the same as optical computers. Already the technological targets for these latter forms of computer have been clearly formulated at a conceptual level – even if their actual implementation remains incomplete. In contrast, with regard to the biocomputer, all aspects of their subcomponent devices, architecture and programming are still undergoing extensive debate. Moreover, such research themes are not confined solely to computer technology or electronics, but extend to nearly every field of the life sciences. Biocomputing is, in other words, a broad and unexplored technological continent – we are aware of its existence, but are uncertain of its scope and riches.

In order to explore an unknown land, both a map and a base camp are essential. Indeed, for the exploration of Antarctica, developed nations have established bases and have for many years taken measurements, explored and surveyed the region. Biocomputing is a technological continent which, in the latter part of this century, has begun to show its face and its immense potential. For several years yet, what will be required is the construction of a complete, if yet imperfect, map and a base camp or perhaps a bridgehead. The construction of these will serve as a concrete target for research and development. The contents of this technological continent will undoubtedly gradually become clear once two main objectives have been fulfilled.

3.2 THE HONEYMOON BETWEEN THE LIFE SCIENCES AND THE COMPUTER SCIENCES

Before we enter into discussion of what biocomputing may become, we should look briefly as the history of the exchange between the life sciences and the computer sciences (Table 3.1). What needs to be clarified at this juncture is how the biocomputer, which has properties of living organisms, differs from previous ideas concerning cybernetics and bionics.

3.2.1 The birth of cybernetics

Exchanges between scientists in the life sciences and computing were particularly active in America and Britain at the time of the Second World War and contributed heavily to current concepts in computing. That era is well depicted in Norbert Wiener's memoirs, *I am a Mathematician* (1956). Wiener had been an electrical engineer at MIT since the 1930s, working on a kind of analog

Table 3.1 Exchanges between the computer sciences and the life sciences

Computer sciences	1940–60 / Post-1960 (exchanges)	Life sciences
1940		1940
1946 ENIAC	1943 Neural model of McCulloch and Pitts	
1948 Von Neumann's automation	1948 Wiener's cybernetics / Automatic control mechanisms / Artificial brain	
1950 Death of Von Neumann		1950
First AI boom	1957 Control logic DP	1953 Double helix model of DNA
1960	Post-1960	1960 Remarkable progress in molecular biology
IBM 360	Body-imaging techniques	
Pattern recognition	X-ray CT / NMR CT	1965 Discovery of mechanism of genetic switch / Elucidation of genetic code
	Positron CT	
1970 Re-evaluation of knowledge systems		1970 Use of the techniques of molecular biology in developmental and neurosciences
Expert systems		1972 Recombinant DNA
Microprocessors		1975 Monoclonal antibody production
Graphics		
VLSI		
1980 Workstations	Biochip / LB membranes / Molecular circuit devices	1980
1982 Second AI boom / Fifth Generation Project / Parallel architectures	...	1982 Determination of complete cell structure of C. elegans
1986 AI chips	Biocomputers	
Neural computers		

computer called a 'differential calculus' machine, under the supervision of V. Busch. Eventually, Wiener became interested in the differences and similarities between electrical circuits and nervous systems, and he organized a conference at Princeton University for mathematicians, computer scientists, communications technologists and neurophysiologists to examine similarities between these two realms. At the conference various fundamental concepts were debated – including the 'bit' as the basic informational unit, 'memory' as stored information, feedback control and so on. Wiener recalled this conference as the birth of both communications and control theory in machines and living organisms i.e. the birth of cybernetics.

3.2.2 Models of the nervous system and the perceptron

Soon after the Princeton conference, two other American physiologists, Warren McCulloch and William Pitts, published a paper in which they advocated an extremely simple model of the nervous system (1943). As will be discussed in Chapter 6, in that model, the neuron is seen as a unit which receives many simultaneous inputs and, by summing the on/off (0/1) states of those input signals, each neuron has a single output value of 0 or 1, depending on whether or not it has exceeded some predefined threshold.

This perceptron model has two important features:

. The signals that flow within such a net have a binary character, 0 or 1, on or off.
. The circuitry has a linear, deterministic character.

Using this simple device, they then showed that the fundamental logic circuits for AND, OR and NOT operations can be built. This meant that, if the brain makes use of this kind of model, then it should, in general, work in a way identical to electrical circuitry.

Starting from that very general argument, concrete suggestions concerning the similarities and dissimilarities between the brain and electrical circuits have been developed. Mathematical models of neural nets have become of interest to neurophysiologists, computer technologists and mathematicians. In fact, a circuit model capable of learning based upon a feedback mechanism – the so-called perceptron – was then advocated by Rosenblatt and colleagues (Rosenblatt, 1959; Caianiello, 1961; Minsky and Papert, 1969; Figure 3.1).

3.2.3 The Turing machine and automatons

Unfortunately, with the passing of time, the pace of physiological research – with its emphasis on experiment – and that of theorists gradually got out of step and the dialogue that had begun was abandoned. From the theorist's point of view, neural networks were, at heart, a kind of calculating machine. That image of a machine to aid mathematicians was inextricably linked with an imaginary

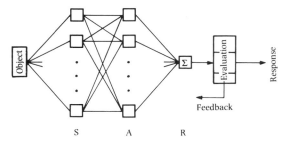

Figure 3.1 The structure of the perceptron, as advocated by Rosenblatt in 1957. An object is represented in the layer of sensory units (S), which is connected to a layer of association units (A). The response unit (R) sends a signal, which results in a response if it is above a certain threshold value, or results in feedback to the A layer if it is below the threshold value. The feedback mechanism is a kind of learning circuit (adapted from Minsky and Papert, 1969)

machine for clarifying the theoretical structure and possibilities for calculations rather than an actual physical object. Best known of such imaginary machines was the Turing machine, advocated by the Briton, Alan Turing (Figure 3.2) The Turing machine consisted of a central control unit containing a finite number of internal states, a 'head' for input and output, and an infinitely long tape which can read states one bit at a time and write new bits. It is said that Von Neumann developed his more concrete ideas about computer architecture in light of Turing's theoretical machine.

The American mathematician, Alan Church, showed that a Turing machine can compute any calculable function, and argued that the contrary – that is, that any uncalculable function could not be calculated by the Turing machine – was also true. This hypothesis is today still thought to hold true. One of Church's disciples, S.C. Cooling, began mathematical research on the time series phenomenon of neuronal potential pulses and was responsible for the birth of

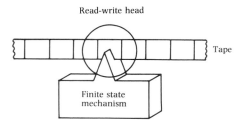

Figure 3.2 The 'Turing machine' – a hypothetical computer devised by Turing – comprising an infinitely long tape and a mechanism with a finite number of states. The tape moves along the head mechanism one unit at a time, reading in the finite signal there and writing out a new signal (adapted from Figure 3.16 of Birkhoff and Bartee, 1970)

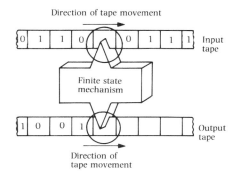

Figure 3.3 The automaton. The head of a mechanism, taking a finite number of states, reads from and writes to moving tapes, thus altering its internal states (adapted from Figure 3.2 of Birkhoff and Bartee, 1970)

automaton theory'. Von Neumann's later computer research was ultimately based upon this automaton research (Figure 3.3).

Although many experimental physiologists had participated in the development of concepts related to feedback and the perceptron, they no longer entered the discussion when it came to formal logical models, such as the Turing machine and automatons or statistical thermodynamic models of neural nets.

From the theorist's point of view, progress in experimental work was seen as being slower than a snail and the arrival of stimulating results which could provoke new ideas was far too infrequent. To wait for the results of experimentalists before engaging in theoretical discussion would be to wait at least until the end of the individual's own research life. That was the feeling among many theoreticians. Even if they ran the risk of sometimes being off target, they felt that theoretical work needed to be pursued on the basis of sometimes incomplete experimental findings.

In this way, the honeymoon between computer researchers and those in the neurosciences came to an end at some time in the 1950s – the physiologists despairing of the lack of biological realism in the theoreticians' speculations and the theoreticians despairing of the slowness of empirical research.

3.3 PROGRESS DURING A LULL

Paradoxically, the 1950s is when the word 'bionics' was coined and enjoyed some fashionableness. Bionics was the technological attempt to re-create certain of biology's superior functions – the first amorous glance that the technologist cast upon living organisms! Bionics became a word that invited particularly mechanical engineers into research on the flexible control dynamics found in biological systems. Despite the invitation, however, there were practically no concrete hints for computer developments arising from such biological research.

On the contrary, the contribution of electronics to biology and medicine has bee much greater. The emergence of various disciplines that make use of compute technology, such as biomedical engineering, medical technology, bioelectron engineering and medical electronic engineering, has been a major stepping stor into modern medical therapy.

3.3.1 Computer tomography and expert systems

Two particularly noteworthy technologies have emerged from application sophisticated electronic/computer apparatus to medical problems. One is con puterized tomography (CT); the other is medical expert systems.

CT is, in essence, a kind of imaging technology which allows the constructic of two-dimensional pictures of the internal organs of living systems by means of high-energy scanning technique. The principle behind CT is called numeric radon conversion and was understood theoretically in 1917. Combining th mathematical understanding with the high speed of computers and with wel known X-ray measuring technology was not possible until the 1970s whe computer technology became sufficiently mature. Now generally known as X-ra CT scanning, medical equipment of this kind is widespread all over the worl

Following developments in CT scanning, those techniques have been combine with nuclear magnetic resonance (NMR) and positron emission tomograph (PET) to produce new, non-invasive diagnostic techniques for obtaining visu images of internal organs without entering the body. These new techniques hav already become indispensable for diagnosing structural and functional abnorn alities lying even at difficult locations, such as within the skull. Not surprisingl in the hands of researchers they have become important tools in investigating tl functions of the brain.

It has now become a realistic expectation that, in combination wit measurements of the brain's magnetic field using the SQUID apparatus ar traditional EEG techniques for measuring changes in the electrical potential at tl surface of the brain, it will become possible to make detailed observations on tl dynamic internal states of the living brain. The importance of combine technologies in brain research deserves some emphasis. Each of the techniqu currently in use has theoretical and methodological advantages, but each alor does not produce sufficient detail concerning the relationship between brai structure and brain function. For example, the EEG allows excellent tim resolution, while PET scans provide good spatial resolution. MEG recordings a much less affected by the skull, and therefore attain greater spatial resolution, bu demand expensive and cumbersome equipment. Future developments whic exploit the strengths of each of these techniques will undoubtedly become or of the basic technologies contributing to neurocomputing.

We have already mentioned expert systems and their contribution to medic science, and we will not pursue that topic further. However, we want to point o the fact that expert systems have not been a simple outgrowth of pure AI, bu have emerged from the contact between computer research and biomedical research.

The above discussion has focused not on developments in basic computer research, but more on applied fields. There have also been important developments in research in the functions of biological signalling and in mathematical models of biological phenomena. Such research is important at the interface between biomedicine and electronics – the field known as biomedical electronics. Here, some success has been achieved in the automation of the analysis of the electrocardiogram. Thus far, however, the actual mechanism of generating the heart waveform has been treated as a 'black box'. The analysis is therefore of an extremely phenomenological nature, where correspondences are simply drawn between identifiable ECG waveforms and known conditions of the heart. In other words, a fundamental understanding of heart physiology and therefore of the relationship between the ECG and heart failure is not yet achieved. Expert systems which can analyse the ECG and make diagnoses do not therefore penetrate to the essence of the cardiac abnormality in making their decisions: they deal with the macroscopic, inexact and often difficult to quantify findings of the ECG.

3.3.2 Various models of life phenomena

Norbert Wiener studied mathematical models for explaining abnormalities of the heartbeat and for analysing brain waves (EEG). Those techniques were developed as mathematics applied to probabilistic processes, non-linear oscillation theory, and so on, but it is difficult to say whether or not they had real impact on biomedicine or medicine itself.

Other developments have included mathematical models of life phenomena – such as Turing's morphogenesis model (1952), Zeeman's (1977) and Thom's (1975) catastrophe models of heart and brain activity, Haken's synergistics model (1989), Eigen's game model (Eigen and Winkler, 1975) and a return to analysis of the ECG by M. Gelfart and others. These models have not, however, yet left the realm of intellectual games. In other words, despite their manifest potentiality, they have not deepened our understanding of life processes.

It must be said that, up until the late 1960s, relative to the volume of published academic studies, theorists have contributed surprisingly little to developments in biology, but the one outstanding exception has been the group of theorists responsible for the elucidation of the genetic code – notably, George Gamow and Francis Crick. Furthermore, making extensive use of current computers, theorists who have clarified the linear structure (sequence) and higher-order configuration of macromolecules over the last two decades have contributed profoundly to our understanding of life phenomena.

In other words, theory has been of vital importance only to the fields of molecular biology and genetics (discussed below), but has provided little or no insight into the macroscopic phenomena of life. Such models do not go beyond descriptions of various interesting phenomena. This is perhaps not so much an indication of the shortcomings of theorists, as an indication of the complexity and multi-levelled, hierarchical structure of the mechanisms of life.

The talented physicist, F. Dyson, has described this situation as follows (1979):

> The lectures concerning 'general automaton theory' in volume 5 of Von Neumann's collected works were given in 1948. The central theme of the lectures was about the structural complexity of a self-replicable automaton. Unfortunately, he died before completing this theory, but the double helix model of DNA was discovered shortly thereafter in 1953 by Watson and Crick and was followed by the discovery of the four factors necessary for the self-replication of DNA – that is, the DNA, the RNA and the DNA–RNA polymerases [enzymes]. This biochemical system was surely the self-replicating mechanism that Von Neumann had predicted.
>
> Today, the cellular differentiation of [multicellular] high-level organisms and replication are topics of great interest. One approach to them may be the elaboration of Von Neumann's self-replicating automaton theory to the various kinds of cells. It may be necessary to consider the switch mechanism by which the fertilized sex cells become multicellular organisms.
>
> With the death of Von Neumann, it may be that we will not be wise enough to reach the correct answer using his idiosyncratic approach. In that case, we may be forced to wait for relevant experimental results from research in developmental biology.

3.4 HORIZONS IN THE LIFE SCIENCES

In certain respects, the life sciences are less than 40 years old, which is to say that the principle of DNA as a linear tape program which can be mechanistically read has been established over the last four decades. From the perspective of biocomputing, those developments, as remarkable as they are, can be summarized in a few paragraphs.

1. The control information (program) of living organisms viewed as informational machines is called the genetic information, which is recorded in the genetic code as a double helical nucleic acid containing four nucleotide bases: adenine (A), guanine (G), cytosine (C) and thymine (T).
2. The sequential base information recorded in the DNA is copied to an intermediary tape message – the messenger RNA (mRNA) – in the process known as transcription. RNA also has four nucleotide base pairs, but differs from the DNA in that thymine is replaced by uracil (U).
3. The information of the intermediary mRNA tape allows for the alignment of transfer RNA (tRNA) molecules in a protein complex known as the ribosome. This mechanism corresponds to the read–write head of the Turing machine (Figure 3.4). There are a variety of tRNAs, each of which is attached to a related amino acid; the binding together of these amino acids leads to the formation of a peptide chain, i.e. a linear sequence of amino acids.

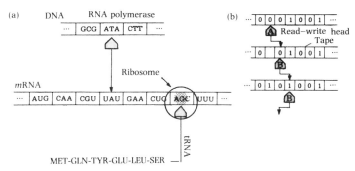

Figure 3.4 The manifestation of the DNA information in living organisms **(a)** and its similarity with the reversible Turing machine **(b)**

4. The essence of the above 'translation' process is that a sequence of three consecutive nucleotide bases in the mRNA determines a single amino acid in the peptide sequence. Since the transcription process from DNA to RNA involves a one-to-one correspondence between nucleotide bases, it is clear that there are three consecutive nucleotides in the DNA (referred to as a 'codon') code for a single amino acid (Figure 3.4).

5. Amino acid chains of this type take on a 3-D configuration by folding back upon themselves and, in some cases, by forming complexes of several such chains. These are called proteins. The nature of the 3-D folding of an amino acid chain depends upon the precise sequence of amino acids, temperature and the strength of the acidic or alkaline solution in which it is immersed.

6. Proteins are not only important subcomponents of living structures, but they are also one of the factors which control responses to external stimuli. Cells also contain carbohydrates, sugars and fats – all of which can act as energy sources. The cell membrane, consisting of a double layer of lipid molecules, has embedded within it important protein molecules which control the flow of ions in and out of the cell.

7. The cell with semipermeable membrane is the unit structure of living organisms. The DNA tape exists in the cellular nucleus as a tightly wound thread, forming one or several chromosomes. When a cell divides, the chromosomes themselves must first replicate.

8. In multicellular animal organisms, growth occurs by the repeated division of cells, starting with the fertilized egg. Some cells will die in the course of development as a means of selecting certain structures out of a much larger number of possibilities. Today, the mechanisms of the formation, death, differentiation, fusion, movement and communication (as between neurons over their axons and dendrites) are not well understood. Pursuit of these topics is the essence of current research in developmental biology.

9. There have been several remarkable discoveries concerning the brain and nervous system. They include the fact that a group of small molecules and

peptides, known collectively as the neurotransmitters, are involved in connecting nerve cells across synapses. Of equal importance is the fact that learning may alter synaptic connections, and that the cerebellum (at least) has connections and control mechanisms similar to those of the perceptron.

It can be seen that these fundamental principles of life processes have many properties that are 'computer-like' and, moreover, have been shown to be essentially mechanistic. It may well be that the 'internal perspective' of living brains – that is, consciousness – will remain outside the scope of scientific manipulation, but the living organisms themselves can be said to be machines in the same way that automobiles are machines.

3.4.1 Future topics in the life sciences

The converse of the simplicity and comprehensibility of the fundamental structures involved in life processes is their extreme dynamic complexity. First of all, the DNA tape, where the life 'program' is written, is known to undergo various dynamic changes – in the evolution of species, in the growth of an individual organism, and in the very process of transcribing DNA information into a useful RNA form. Secondly, the higher we ascend in the evolutionary ladder, the greater is the redundancy of the DNA. It is estimated that in man some 98% of the DNA is informationally meaningless. Moreover, although the relationship between the DNA nucleotide base sequence and the protein amino acid sequence is understood, no other aspect of the DNA 'program' can now be read. For example, it is not known how a given gene (the nucleotide base sequence corresponding to a specific protein) is switched on to begin its work (Figure 3.5).

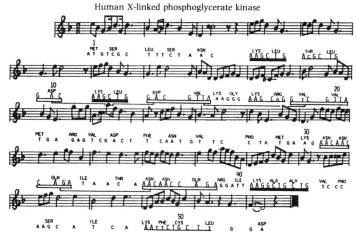

Figure 3.5 The transformation of the amino acid base sequence of the first 52 codons of the human phosphoglyceride kinase gene into a musical score (Ohno and Ohno, 1986)

By means of bacterial experiments and powerful reasoning, F. Jacob and J. Monod were able to clarify how specific *in vivo* chemical reactions control the on–off digital operations of the DNA tape, but a general switch mechanism is not known. As Dyson has pointed out, the rearrangement of the DNA tape during growth and morphogenesis and the mechanism of the reading 'switch' may hold the key to the design of multicellular organisms. At the present time, however, little is understood on this topic.

Thirdly, little is known about the influences of the environment on living organisms. To be sure, there is fragmentary knowledge indicating that the environment has a large influence on the growth and functioning of the brain and nervous system of the higher animals, but detailed mechanisms remain to be clarified. In any case, it is clear that computers which receive no influence from their environment contrast sharply with the case of living organisms.

For these reasons, the central topics in the life sciences have gradually shifted away from pure biochemistry and molecular biology and towards ontogeny/morphogenesis and the nervous system/brain. Moreover, the mechanisms of protein production from DNA information (which has been the central theme of molecular biology) has become an applied science – an industrial means of production. This is the heart of so-called genetic engineering which has been behind the boom in biotechnology throughout the 1980s.

3.5 THE BEGINNINGS OF NEW EXCHANGES

3.5.1 A time for dialogue

Even if it is not the case that progress in molecular biology has led to the elucidation of all the complex mechanisms in life, it is certainly true that, in comparison with the knowledge available at the time of the birth of computing, a great many fundamental facts for our understanding of the mechanisms of life as a chemical computer have been established. Moreover, the arrival of biotechnology has opened the road to the artificial design and synthesis of proteins for research purposes.

In this way, the dialogue between researchers in the life sciences and the computing sciences has been re-ignited. What are the characteristics of the new dialogue and how does it differ from the dialogue concerning cybernetics and bionics? The first thing that can be said is that the scope of the dialogue has greatly increased. Previously, the dialogue was predominantly between physiologists, representing the life sciences, and mechanical and electronic engineers specializing in measurement and control, representing the computer sciences – with a few mathematicians thrown in for good measure!

Today, specialists in molecular biology, biochemistry and genetics talk with specialists in physics, chemistry and semiconductor technology concerning protein design, molecular assembly techniques, the structure of molecular and biodevices, protein–lipid membrane formation on semiconductors, and even molecular Turing machines. Moreover, the number of chances is steadily increasing for biologists, computer scientists and theoreticians from various fields to talk as equals with one another concerning research on the development of multicellular organisms and the morphogenesis of the nervous system.

Previously, the dialogue between researchers in different fields had been predominantly the discussion of analogies. The interest of engineers was to make a model which exhibits phenomena analogous to those of living organisms or, at best, to simulate life phenomena. Researchers in the life sciences (particularly medical people) saw computer scientists as people who could build useful tools to help with medical work, but they considered computer scientists not so much as scientists as assistants. Such an attitude was not a strong foundation on which to build.

3.5.2 The biocomputer as the ultimate aim

However, in order to develop entirely new kinds of computers and to research from first principles the workings of the brain and the formation of the nervous system or whole organisms, the relationship between the tool-makers and the tool-users must change fundamentally. Physicists, chemists and computer scientists have now become genuinely interested in research in this field. In other words, provided that the appropriate guidance by management can be given, the strengths of the researchers responsible for the progress in computing can be utilized in research on tomorrow's problems in biology. Moreover, there is every possibility that we will arrive in an era where products of industrial significance can be achieved.

In any case, the era of discussing analogies has come to an end. Just as biomedical people have improved their own results by employing computers and just as researchers on the fundamentals of computing have combined measuring techniques from what was originally physics engineering (X-ray diffraction, NMR, electron microscopy and so on) and molecular biological and biochemical techniques (gene recombination, monoclonal antibody techniques, 2-D electrophoresis and so on), now both groups can directly attack questions concerning life phenomena. This is not a case of the invasion of the life sciences by the computer sciences. On the contrary, owing to progress in the life sciences, the characteristics of various biological structures as information machines have been clarified and the distance between 'biological thinking' and fundamental research in computing has decreased. The convergence between these two broad disciplines is not, therefore, a transient fashion. On the contrary, it is only natural that, with the passage of time, the fusion between them will continue to deepen and expand.

Viewed in this way, the biocomputer can be understood as the ultimate, if, perhaps, only symbolic, aim of the fusion of the life and computing sciences. Research in biocomputers also promises possibilities for a new dimension in science – a science of artificially constructed living organisms.

Simultaneously, learning about diverse and subtle biological mechanisms, extending from self-replicating enzymes to protein synthesis, the development of the nervous system and perhaps reaching to the activity of the human psyche, will be essential for developments in computer devices, architecture and programming. Biocomputer research is not, therefore, a single pathway of technological development, and it is not in direct competition with any existing research project in the race to develop a specific technological artifact.

3.6 BIOCOMPUTING AS A NEW TECHNOLOGICAL CONTINENT

In our perception of biocomputing, the biocomputer will emerge as the inevitable result of a connection between the life and computing sciences – a new technological continent. It will probably be one of the fundamental technologies of the 21st century (Kaminuma, 1985). If this is to be so, we should decide during the present century how we can, we would like to build a bridgehead on that continent.

First of all, it can be said that such a technological field must be built upon current technologies. No matter how revolutionary a new technology is, it does not start from scratch. Inevitably, it will rely in part on certain older technologies.

Secondly, even if considerable time is required to reach the ultimate target, there must be other possible results which can be achieved in the meantime. It cannot be an all or nothing attempt to land on the moon: there must be realistic, technologically exploitable way-stations from which significant developments are possible. Indeed, if such realistic subgoals cannot be achieved during the research project, it will be difficult to maintain the morale and motivation of the research team.

Thirdly, for both scientists and engineers, the research theme must be of fundamental interest. To state this point more strongly, the theme must be one for which research results could lead to the winning of a Nobel Prize. This is prerequisite for maintaining the interest of outstanding researchers. In other words, it is desirable that, as in the development of semiconductors and lasers, the fundamental research is rich in possibilities.

Fourthly, if possible, the theme should relate to the predicted future needs and problems of current technology. For example, problems for modern computing, such as the weakness of pattern recognition and the physical limitations for large-scale integration, should be addressed.

3.6.1 Themes for future technology

If the technological field is selected in light of the above conditions, the following themes come to mind.

1. Organic thin membranes and lithography. This topic includes the techniques for constructing membranes with unidirectionally oriented molecules and their subsequent applications. Joining silicon semiconductors and organic thin membranes which include natural or artificially designed proteins would be a topic of high priority.

2. Molecular devices. According to Carter's vision, molecular devices could be electronic circuit devices controlled at the molecular level. For this purpose, research is needed into the (semi-)conductivity of organic molecules. The most exciting ideas in this field are those advocated by Carter, but the possibility of working devices remains to be proven.
3. Research in development and morphogenesis. This research is essential as a means of fully investigating the phenomenon of growth and development, using various primitive life forms, such as the tapeworm, snail and leech.
4. The structure and function of the brain and nervous system. This includes research on simple animals, such as the squid, and more complex animals, including the mouse, cat, dog and monkey, to elucidate the mechanisms of sensory, motor and cognitive systems. The development of non-invasive experimental techniques will also allow human experimentation.
5. Bio-architecture. On the basis of the results obtained in research such as that mentioned above, biological architectures – from the molecular level to that of the brain – will be elucidated. On the basis of those results on the hierarchical control of living organisms, the design of new computer and component architectures should be possible.
6. The combined technology of the nervous system and the computer. This theme ranges from the microtechnology of culturing neurons directly on semiconductor silicon to the macrotechnology of joining the signals of computers and nervous systems together.

Among these research themes, there are some which are already considerably developed, some which have been partially developed for practical purposes, and others for which today only the words exist and actual developments are meagre. In any case, biocomputing is a new technology, and a clear conception of what it includes and excludes will emerge gradually during the years to come.

Part Two

New developments in the life sciences

4

Bioenergetics and biodevices

4.1 ATP AND THE CONVERSION OF BIOLOGICAL ENERGY

In order to stay alive, living organisms must continually use energy. The energy conversion process itself and the materials used are, however, very unlike the electric motors of trains or the combustion engines of automobiles. The fuel is protein molecules composed of amino acids, each of which has a minute molecular structure with a 5–10 nm diameter. Although muscle tissue is a visible, macroscopic energy conversion apparatus, the basic unit of muscle tissue is a molecule called actomyosin – sometimes referred to as a 'molecular machine'. The immediate energy source for this device is the chemical energy found in adenosine triphosphate (ATP) (Figure 4.1).

It is now well known that energy is obtained by the cell by 'cutting' the three phosphates away from the ATP molecule. As illustrated in Figure 4.2, the separation of the phosphates in a water solution converts ATP into energy by means of various molecular biodevices, the structures and functions of which have been elucidated over the last 30 years.

At the extreme right of Figure 4.2 are shown the various ways in which the energy obtained from ATP is ultimately used. Kinetic energy is the mechanical energy released by the contraction of muscles, due to the breakdown of ATP to ADP (Figure 4.1). Energy can also be released as heat, light or sound, or the energy can be utilized in various processes of biochemical synthesis.

Unlike the electrical phenomena in computers – which are due to the flow of electrons – the electrical phenomena occurring in living organisms are all due to the flow of positive ions across biological membranes. The flow of information among neurons thus depends upon the maintenance of an appropriate balance of ions on the two sides of the neuronal membrane. This also is achieved by the breakdown of ATP by the so-called Na^+-K^+-ATPase enzyme, which carries K^+ ions in and Na^+ ions out of the cell.

Although each cell is involved in the synthesis of countless different molecules from a variety of molecular building blocks, all such kinds of molecular construction also occur through the utilization of ATP energy by the various synthetic enzymes (the so-called ligases). Moreover, the light emission from some living organisms, such as the firefly, is achieved by enzymes using ATP as their source of energy. As described in greater detail below, the various information

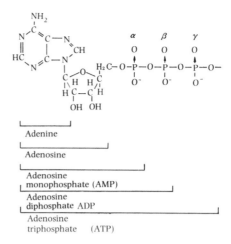

Figure 4.1 The structure of ATP. When the bond between the β and γ phosphates is broken, breaking down ATP into ADP and inorganic phosphate, energy is released. This energy is used by the actomyosin of muscle tissue, the ATPase of the ion transport system of neurons (the source of electrical activity) and various synthetic enzymes. Of particular importance is the fact that the information processing of living organisms relies upon ATP – the raw material from which AMP (an intracellular secondary transmitter, see Figures 4.8 and 4.9) and DNA (the central information storage mechanism of the cell; see Figure 4.5) are built

transmission devices in living organisms are also mobilized by ATP molecules.

In brief, ATP is needed for the emergence and functionality of the various biodevices found in the living cell. Those that synthesize the ATP itself are the H^+-transporting ATPases F_0 and F_1. When the supply of ATP decreases, it is synthesized again from ADP and inorganic phosphate (Pi); the energy released by the oxidation of sugar and fats is used during respiration. Both respiration and nutrition are functions devoted to the regeneration of ATP molecules.

4.2 DIRECT MEASUREMENT OF ENERGY METABOLISM

As shown in the upper part of Figure 4.2, because of the minute size of the biodevices involved, the flow of energy from the breakdown of ATP is not as easily observable as the energy release from a combustion engine. Modern techniques, however, allow a direct measurement of the energy conversion process at several distinct stages in the ATP cycle. For example, the metabolism of the phosphates in ATP can be measured using the so-called nuclear magnetic resonance (NMR) technique (Figure 4.3).

The flow of blood to the tissues of the body is the supply route for oxygen and nutritional compounds – both of which are needed to maintain ATP levels. When ATP supplies dwindle, blood flow must increase and, unlike the molecular events in the cell, the macroscopic flow of blood is easily measured. It is then possible to

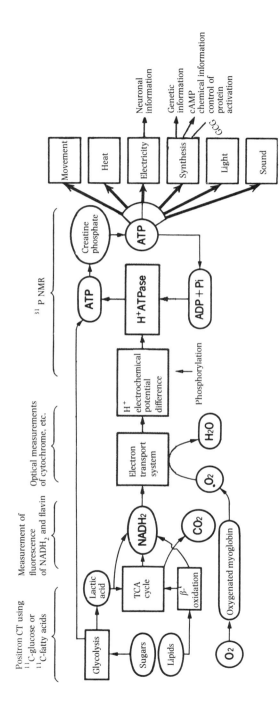

Figure 4.2 The flow of energy in living cells and the means of direct measurement (Kagawa, 1985)

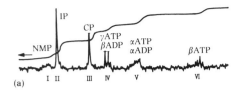

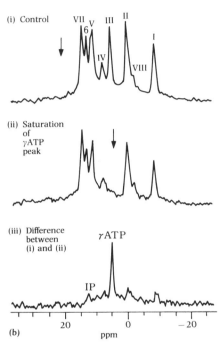

Figure 4.3 (a) ^{31}P NMR spectra of the acidolytic fraction of the rat heart at 36.4 MHz. The various peaks have the following meanings: I monophosphoric acid ester of AMP; II inorganic phosphoric acid; III creatinic acid; IV the γ phosphate of ATP and the β phosphate of ADP; V the α phosphate of ATP and ADP; VI the β phosphate of ATP **(b)** Measurement of the rate of kidney ATP synthesis using ^{31}P NMR (the saturation-transfer method, Koretsky *et al.*, 1983). (i) The control NMR spectra. The coil used for NMR measurements is embedded around the rat kidney and measurements made at 97.3 MHz. The peak numbers are as follows: I βATP (Figure 4.1); II αATP plus NAD(H); III γATP; IV CP; V urinary inorganic P and P-monoester; VI intracellular inorganic P; VII P-monoester; VIII unknown. (ii) NMR spectra in which the γATP peak has disappeared. The arrow indicates the location of the missing peak. (iii) The difference spectra of (i) and (ii). A difference in the size of the inorganic phosphate peak (IP) is seen. From this it can be calculated that the constant of inorganic phosphoric acid incorporation into ATP is 0.12 ± 0.03 s

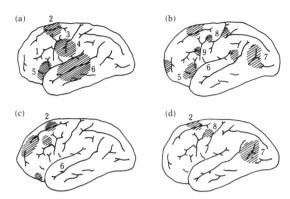

Figure 4.4 Cerebral cortical activity and increases in blood flow of the left hemisphere (Ingvar *et al.*, 1977). The shaded areas indicate blood flow increases of 20% or more: **(a)** during speech; **(b)** during silent reading; **(c)** during silent counting; **(d)** during visual tracking of a moving object. The brain areas indicated with numbers are as follows: 1 prefrontal area; 2 motor association area; 3 motor area (mouth and tongue); 4 primary somatosensory area; 5 Broca's area (motor area involved in speech); 6 primary auditory area of the temporal lobe; 7 primary and secondary visual areas; 8 motor cortex; 9 motor cortex of frontal lobe near the region controlling eye movements

know the level of activity of ATP consumption indirectly by measuring the changes in blood flow. Figure 4.4 illustrates the metabolic activity of the 'living computer' called the human cerebrum by using radioactive isotopes. The collaboration of various areas of the brain, as indicated by their simultaneous increases in blood flow, is shown during many cognitive functions such as hearing, seeing and speaking. Although the neurons of the brain can be viewed as individual devices, each neuron can itself also be viewed as containing many biodevices. It is these smaller biodevices with which we will be concerned in the present chapter.

4.3 THE DEVICES AND CIRCUITS OF BIOENERGETICS

It is possible to think of a living organism as an energy and information processing apparatus with the ability to self-replicate. An apparatus such as a silicon computer can process energy and information because of devices and circuits which supply energy from an external energy source. In the living cell, various forms of energy are converted within the cell itself and utilized for various purposes.

Regardless of the actual materials of the devices, a 'flow diagram' of information and energy can be drawn. In the thermodynamics of circuit networks which view the energy and information of living organisms as a unified flow diagram from the perspective of irreversible thermodynamics (Oster *et al.*, 1980), both the devices and the flow are treated as analogous to electrical circuits. However, living organisms consist of biodevices which are completely different from those of resistors and copper wires. Let us therefore look at the special features of living organisms from the perspective of the 'hardware' of the individual devices.

4.4 THE ULTIMATE INTEGRATION OF BIODEVICES

The attention of many researchers has been drawn to biodevices because of the extremely high level of integration found there. All of the devices needed to sustain life are found in miniscule bacteria measuring less than 1 μm across (10^{-6} metre). The individual molecules are of the order of approximately 10^{-9} metre in diameter. Even the relatively large, so-called macromolecules – the proteins and nucleic acids – which are the main biodevices – have diameters of the order of 10^{-8} metre (Figure 4.5).

If we consider the fact that already the 1 μm unit poses severe problems in current LSI manufacturing processes using silicon-based components, the extremely high density of biodevices is apparent. It can in fact easily be calculated that the density of integration in living 3-D biodevices is some 10^{6}–10^{12} times greater than that possible in current computer technology.

In biodevices, the central memory 'device' is the DNA molecule. DNA is built of four nucleotide bases, adenine (A), guanine (G), thymine (T) and cytosine (C). At the time of DNA synthesis, energy is released from ATP to allow the energy-consuming task of building a larger molecule. The DNA is normally found as two intertwined chains of these nucleotides – where G is bound to C and A to T. At the time of replication, however, the DNA unwinds and separates into its two chains, and each chain replicates the other chain by collecting the corresponding nucleotides (Figure 4.6).

Since one bit of information corresponds to one pair of nucleotides (AT or GC), the density of integration in terms of molecular weight corresponds to one bit per 10^{-21} gram. It is worth emphasizing that all the genetic information of biology is determined by the sequence of A, G, C and T in DNA. This means that, in man, there are some 5 600 000 000 bits (base pairs) of such information.

4.5 THE SPECIFICITY AND SENSITIVITY OF BIODEVICES

Practical biodevices in use today include biosensors and bioreactors, and in all cases these devices make use of the specific functions of organic molecules. Their specificity is due to the molecular structure of the device.

As illustrated in Figure 4.7, enzymes and other macromolecules have specific 3-D structures owing to the configuration of the ligands within them. In the case of an enzyme, the ligands react with the bonded substrate molecule and can decompose the substrate or bind it to another molecule – as suggested in Figure 4.7. This ability to distinguish among different molecules is a molecular 'recognition' capability which allows a given enzyme to 'choose' and bind one

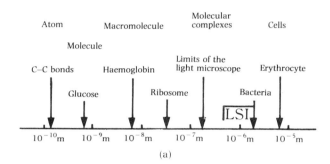

(a)

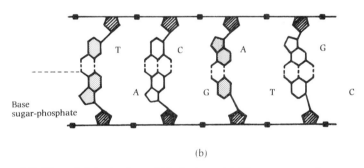

(b)

Figure 4.5 The miniaturization of biodevices. **(a)** The extreme of integration in living information processing systems: the size of biological molecules and cells. **(b)** the memory capacity of DNA: DNA is composed of the base pairs AT and GC, and contains two bits of information per 10^{-21} gram

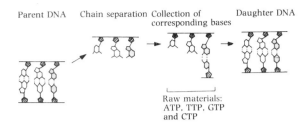

Figure 4.6 DNA replication

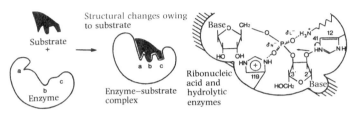

Figure 4.7 The high specificity and sensitivity of macromolecules (biodevices). Enzymes, receptors and carriers are involved

molecule but not another. Since the higher-order structure of a macromolecule which undergoes processing by an enzyme is changed by the bonds formed, information can be transmitted in this way.

It is well known that living organisms transmit information by means of chemical transmitter substances and hormones using molecular recognition capabilities of this type. Hormones are released in extremely small quantities into the bloodstream along with countless other substances. They bind to specific receptors located on the cell membrane of target organs or in the cellular cytoplasm itself. There they have their unique actions as hormones. In general, the separation constant of the hormone is small, so that the sensitivity of the cell to the presence of the hormone is high. To take an extreme case, an insect pheromone can be perceived by an insect antenna at a distance of several kilometres – owing to the presence of a few of the relevant hormone molecules.

Biosensors can directly determine the level of an extremely small dose of a substance without any pre-treatment of the substance. Since even the most sophisticated physico-chemical analysis equipment requires such pre-treatment in order to amplify the effect of the relevant substance, biosensors are superior both in terms of specificity and sensitivity. Because of this great disparity between artificial and natural biosensors, considerable efforts are being made to replace other equipment by nature's biosensors. Moreover, since biosensors can not only produce a specific effect without side-effects, but also require only a small activation energy, they are useful for moderate and low energy conditions.

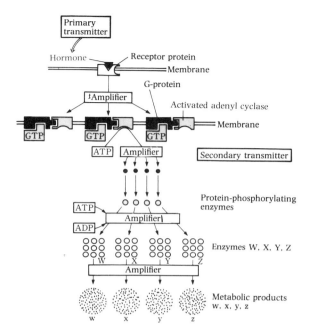

Figure 4.8 A mechanism for amplifying information in cells (after Alberts *et al.*, 1983)

4.6 AMPLIFIERS USING BIODEVICES

A cell can undertake many varieties of reaction as the direct result of a single hormone molecule. An example of this type is illustrated in Figure 4.8.

First a single molecule of the hormone called glucagon (a primary information transmitter) binds to a hormone receptor on the cell membrane, thus altering its higher-order structure. This change results in activation of a G-protein, which in turn activates adenyl cyclase, resulting in the formation of the secondary information transmitter, cyclic AMP, from ATP.

The phosphorylating enzyme activated by the cyclic AMP phosphorylates many enzymes which make ATP. In this way, one enzyme can produce a countless number of substrate molecules. Over a series of stages like this, the amplification of information can be achieved. This waterfall phenomenon is often referred to as a 'cascade', and is at the heart of biochemical amplification phenomena.

The phosphorylation of enzymes due to proteins activated by cyclic AMP is known to be a complex phenomenon. As shown in Figure 4.9, in certain kinds of enzyme, the phosphorylation due to ATP occurs at two different sites, resulting in maintenance of the activated state for a definite period after which it becomes dephosphorylated and again undergoes phosphorylation. Because of this time lag, information can be transmitted only during a certain period, and the molecule

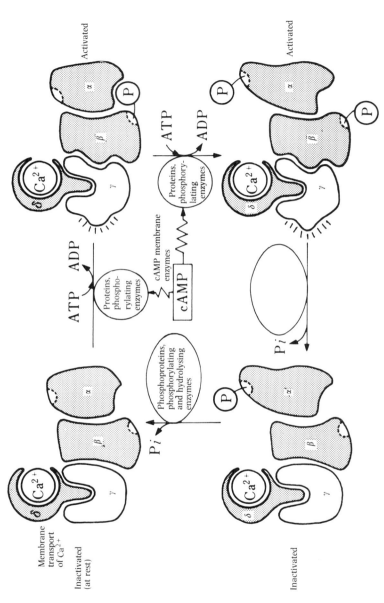

Figure 4.9 A mechanism for producing a time lag in the activation and transmission of information by means of the phosphorylation of protein (after Alberts *et al.*, 1983)

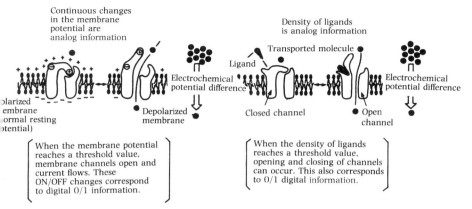

Continuous changes in the membrane potential are analog information

Density of ligands is analog information

Transported molecule

Ligand

Electrochemical potential difference

Electrochemical potential difference

Polarized membrane (normal resting potential)

Depolarized membrane

Closed channel

Open channel

When the membrane potential reaches a threshold value, membrane channels open and current flows. These ON/OFF changes correspond to digital 0/1 information.

When the density of ligands reaches a threshold value, opening and closing of channels can occur. This also corresponds to 0/1 digital information.

Figure 4.10 An analog-digital converter (operating when a threshold is crossed for opening an ion channel gate owing to voltage or ion concentration changes). Today it is possible to make single channel recordings using microelectrodes. On the left the opening of a channel gate by applying voltage to the membrane is shown. On the right is shown closing of the gate by ligand bonding

then returns to its original state. If this type of cyclic mechanism did not exist, the cell would not be able to respond to the signals which follow immediately thereafter.

4.7 AN ANALOG-DIGITAL CONVERTER USING A BIODEVICE

The energy and information that enter the cell – concentrations of substances, membrane potentials, light, and so on – are largely analog data. But the high-level information processing by living organisms is more accurately and more conveniently carried out if the data are converted into digital form – either as the base pairs of DNA or neuronal impulses. Therefore, among the various information processing devices in living cells, there exist analog-digital converters of minute dimensions.

Figure 4.10 shows a channel which opens depending upon voltage changes and a channel which opens depending upon the presence of a specific substance. If the membrane potential or the concentration of transmitter substance (both of which are analog values) reaches a certain value, the structure of the membrane channel changes and ions can flow into the cell according to the electrochemical potential difference on the two sides of the membrane. The electrostatic potential or concentration which is the trigger for opening and closing the channel is called the trigger and is the mechanism by which an analog value is converted into a digital value.

The mechanism which opens and closes the various kinds of channel is called a 'gate' and the portion which detects the potential or concentration is called the 'sensor', but these terms have slightly different meanings from those found in electronics. It is worth noting that the fine structure of these channels is already known in detail at the molecular level.

For any sensory organ, stimuli bring about physico-chemical changes in the cell membrane at the sensory receptor membrane. In most cases, those changes are analogical changes which are in direct proportion to the strength of the stimulus (that is, corresponding to the sum total of applied physico-chemical energy). However, in the transmission of the information from the sensory organs to the CNS along sensory nerves, the information is converted to a pulse – digitized to a '0' or '1'. This is known as 'coding'. The information concerning the sensory stimulus – regardless of whether it was originally light, sound, chemical potential or mechanical change – is represented as a frequency of neuronal impulses.

The nature of the impulse which is transmitted along nerve fibres is illustrated in Figure 4.11. Note that the action potential which is transmitted along a nerve fibre (axon) is not a fast impulse, such as an electron in an electrical wire; the impulse exists as a slowly moving change in the concentration of Na^+ ions flowing into the axon and K^+ ions flowing out. If the membrane has even slight permeability, K^+ ions will leak out of the axon and if, as a result, the charge on the inside of the axon becomes -80 millivolt, the leakage out of K^+ ions and the flow in owing to the negative potential will be balanced and a state of equilibrium achieved. This is the resting potential.

If the cell is then stimulated or the nearby Na^+ channels are opened, first the Na^+ channels are opened (Figure 4.10) and Na^+ ions flow into the cell (Figure 4.11). This is the cause of the action potential. Na^+ channels spontaneously close after they have opened, so that the outflow of K^+ ions will restore the membrane potential. This, in effect, causes a 'pulse' which is transmitted to neighbouring regions down the axon. Excitation of muscle cells is due to ligand-

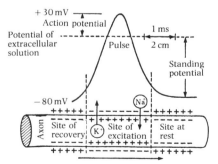

Transmission of axonal excitation

Figure 4.11 The action potential of the neuron caused by the flow of Na^+ and K^+ ions across the membrane (Kagawa, 1968)

dependent channel activity, but the channel mechanisms are fundamentally similar to those during neuronal activity.

4.8 ORGANIC CURRENTS

In computers, electrons flow in electrical wires, whereas in living organisms, the current is due to the flow of ions through membranes. Moreover, the transmission in nerve or muscle, as shown in Figure 4.11, is the transmission of ion channel opening and closing (excitation), so that the actual speed of transmission does not exceed several centimetres per second.

Although the flow of Na^+, K^+ and Ca^{2+} ions is the means of information transmission in nerve and muscle cells, the flow of H^+ ions is the mechanism in prokaryotic organisms, and is the means of ATP synthesis and energy conversion in almost all cells. Ultimately, that which we call respiration is the process of removing hydrogen from organic molecules and, in so doing, obtaining the energy released when water is formed in combination with oxygen.

As illustrated in Figure 4.12, the respiration process is a kind of organic fuel battery. Unlike industrial batteries, where the energy is taken away along electrical wires as a flow of negatively charged electrons, in living organisms the energy is obtained as the flow of positively charged protons.

In order to mobilize protons (H^+), in addition to electrical work corresponding to a change in voltage ($\Delta \Psi$), osmotic pressure work must be done against a concentration gradient. The electrochemical potential difference of hydrogen atoms ($\Delta \bar{\mu} H^+$) emerges from these two kinds of work. As shown in Figure 4.13, two devices known as F_0 and F_1 bring about ATP synthesis by utilizing the flow of

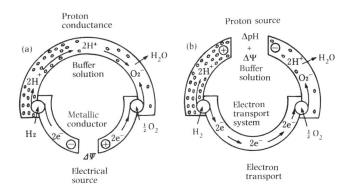

Figure 4.12 A hydrogen-enzyme battery and the electromotive force. **(a)** In a conventional battery, electrons are mobilized from a metallic conductor by means of a potential difference. **(b)** In an energy conversion system made of living membranes, H^+ ions are mobilized and flow across permeable membranes – that is, there is 'proticity' rather than electricity

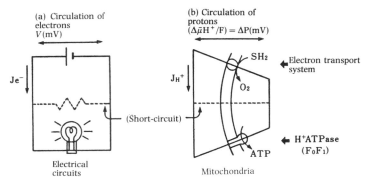

Figure 4.13 A comparison of the flow of electrons and the flow of protons

ions. Here we have compared this circulation of hydrogen ions with the circulation of electrons occurring in electrical circuits. In the biological system shown in Figure 4.13, the flow is between the two sides of the cell membrane and there are no electrical wire-like structures.

How then do the devices of the electron transport system, illustrated in Figures 4.12 and 4.13, actually transport electrons? Again, electrical wires are not used. Polysaccharides undergoing reduction are located within the cell membrane and accept electrons between molecules as they collide owing to thermodynamic movement. As shown in Figure 4.14, electrons flow from electron transport substances with low oxidation–reduction potential to those

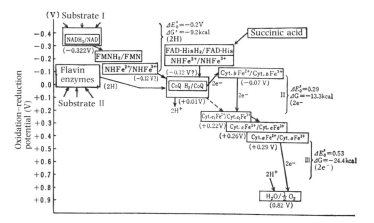

Figure 4.14 The electron transport system and the oxygen reduction potential (Kagawa, 1985). In an actual oxygen reduction potential, the elements are unevenly distributed within the cell membrane. Not only can the concentration not be determined, but the conditions of the membrane potential, etc. can also change, so that the situation is much more complex than that of the reactions in a simple solution

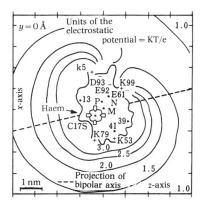

Figure 4.15 The isoelectronic potential lines around the reduced cytochrome *c* molecule (from the horse). The thick lines indicate the surface of the molecule, and the numbers indicate the ligand numbers from the N terminal. K indicates lycine, E glutamic acid, M methionine, D asparginic acid. The electric field is indicated by the thin solid lines (Koppenol and Margoliash, 1982)

with higher potentials – resulting eventually in the formation of water from H^+ and oxygen. Clearly, the acceptance of electrons between the electron transport substances can occur only between quite specific molecules.

One class of protein which accepts electrons is cytochrome. It includes an iron-containing haem group and donates and accepts an electron in the $Fe^{3+} + e^- \rightarrow Fe^{2+}$ reaction. Figure 4.15 shows an example of a cytochrome molecule, cytochrome *c*. Since this molecule exposes only 0.6% of the pi-electrons of haem at the molecular surface, electrons are not exchanged simply because of the oxidation or reduction of an electron transport protein caused by thermal collisions. As illustrated in Figure 4.15, oxidation–reduction occurs only when a protein with precisely the opposite potential surface docks at the correct position.

All other proteins are similar in this regard. In a neutral water solution, since the structural amino acids of cytochrome, such as glutamic acid and asparaginic acid, have negative COO^- ligands, while ligase and others have NH^{3+} electrostatically positive ligands, complex isoelectric boundaries are produced. As an electron transporting device of great specificity, cytochrome is a molecule of great interest.

4.9 ENZYMES FOR ATP SYNTHESIS

ATP, the ultimate energy source for all biological activity, is produced by organic devices called the ATP synthesis enzymes, making use of an electrochemical potential difference of hydrogen ions (Figures 4.2 and 4.13). Because this enzyme is mobilized by H^+ ions, it is called an H^+-ATPase. Its two main portions are called F_0 and F_1 (Figure 4.16). These two portions are also included in the cellular membrane of bacteria, in the mitochondria (a source of energy in respiration), and

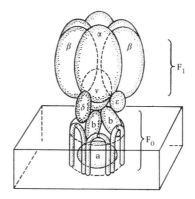

Figure 4.16 The enzyme which synthesizes ATP (also referred to as H^+-ATPase and F_0F_1) (Kagawa, 1982). The F_0 portion is embedded in the cell membrane, through which the H^+ ions pass. The F_1 portion breaks up the ATP and release the H^+ ion.

in chloroplasts (active in photosynthesis). Although the ATPase synthesis system is known from the glycolysis cycle which does not use F_0 and F_1, the total volume of ATP produced in that way is only a small fraction of that produced using F_0 and F_1.

Pushed by the electrochemical potential differences, hydrogen ions pass through F_0 and when they reach F_1 their energy is utilized. ADP and Pi behind the α and β subunits (Figure 4.16) are converted into ATP, which is released from F_1.

By means of modern genetic recombination techniques, the amino acid sequences of the main portions of human, *E. coli* and heat-resistant bacterial F_1 portions are now fully known. Moreover, it has been possible to deduce with some certainty which amino acid ligand approaches and reacts with what portion of the ATP. One possible structure of this interaction is illustrated in Figure 4.17.

In ATP synthesis, magnesium forms a complex with ATP, and structures with specific configurations (δ, β, γ and ATP-Mg) are formed. When phosphoric acid becomes bound to ADP-Mg (bottom left of Figure 4.17), the O^- of ADP undergoes reduction. At the position where the electrochemical potential difference of hydrogen ions is felt (the upper part of Figure 4.17), even if only the voltage part of the potential difference is felt, ATP synthesis occurs. As can be seen from this brief description, the mechanisms by which ATP is applied in living organisms are rapidly being clarified.

4.10 THE FUTURE OF BIODEVICES

The activity of living organisms consists of the conversion of energy and the transmission and processing of information. As is also apparent from the direct relationship with thermodynamic entropy, the amount of information is

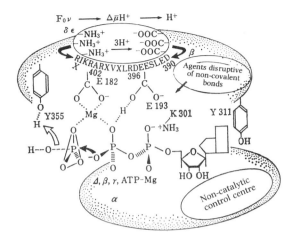

Figure 4.17 ATP synthesis at the border of the α and β subunits (Kagawa, 1984)

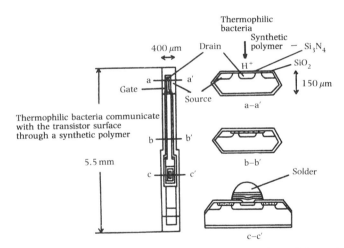

Figure 4.18 An ATP biosensor. A heat-resistant ATPase is bound to an ion-selective electric field effect transistor. By means of H^+ release, ATP is measured

inseparable from the volume of energy metabolism. Indeed, great advances have already been made in the theoretical understanding of information processing systems and energy conversion systems in terms of network thermodynamics.

It is therefore worth emphasizing that, in the pursuit of the analogy between the computer and living information processing systems, it is essential to give due consideration to the energy conversion system which mobilizes information. However, in light of the fact that most biological 'devices' are principally proteins and have ATP as their source of energy, they are fundamentally different from LSI chips which demand external energy sources to drive their electrical circuitry. This is a significant advantage for organic information systems to have over inorganic ones. In contrast, the greatest defect of biochemical devices is their instability, but even this problem might be resolved by using heat-resistant bacteria. Already the gene responsible has been isolated and analysed (Kagawa *et al.*, 1984) and the protein engineering techniques required for producing protein for desired effects are already well known (Ulmer, 1983).

Finally, the slowness of information transfer in living organisms might be resolved by a combination of transistors and biodevices. Already many biosensors exploit the specificity of biodevices, and successes in converting them into electrical signals have also been reported (Karube *et al.*, 1987; Tahata, 1983). Figure 4.18 illustrates an ATP biosensor obtained by connecting a heat-sensitive bacterial ATPase to the surface of a transistor (Karube *et al.*, 1987). In the near future, we can expect many developments along these lines – ranging from extremely sensitive biosensors to complex biodevices capable of carrying out processes now achieved only in the biological world.

5

Information processing in biological organisms

5.1 DEVELOPMENTAL BIOLOGY AND COMPUTER RESEARCH

The purpose of this chapter is to introduce current ideas in developmental biology, using the nematode as our main example. Before jumping to the front line of such research, let us briefly consider the significance of developmental biology from the perspective of biocomputing.

Both living organisms and computers are information machines which operate on the basis of internally stored programs, but the differences between these systems are also quite large. In the case of living organisms, self-assembly following an internal program occurs and the nervous system and brain formed in this way function as an autonomous information machine. Unlike traditional computers which must be 'driven' from the outside, the nervous system has somehow incorporated within it rules on how to function. This aspect of living systems has drawn the attention and curiosity of computer scientists for obvious reasons.

The functions of a ready-made information machine are, however, deeply related to their developmental progress. In the case of biological entities for which there is no external blueprint, the design plan is entirely internal and is thought to undergo changes both in the evolution of species and in the development of individuals. For example, the wiring of the sensory nervous system of mammals is at least approximately determined genetically, but this is further refined after birth by the environment. This has indeed been clarified in experimental work using cats raised in environments containing only vertical stripes. The actual structure of the brain is altered from the normal morphology simply as a consequence of this environmental manipulation.

It is also thought that non-genetic factors play an extremely large role in the workings of the mind and the development of intelligence in man. It will remain difficult to obtain a true understanding of human intelligence until we know how much is determined genetically, how much by the physico-chemical environment, and how much by cultural and psychological factors. For example, for the higher-level acts of will and creativity, our thoughts are given emphasis or direction by value judgements and aesthetic considerations, but if we do not have an understanding of the process by which such 'emphasis' and 'direction develops, we will probably be unable to design an intelligent machine capable o such high-level cognition.

Of course, there is little hope if we jump immediately into the most difficult o problems. What we can do, however, is to take one step in this direction by using a simple living organism. For this purpose, it is necessary to select an organism which will allow analysis at the molecular level, at the developmental level and a the behavioural level. At the outset, what is of particular importance is the developmental and morphogenetic aspects of the organism.

5.1.1 The choice of research materials

In developmental biology, the sea urchin and the newt have long been objects o study, but both are, unfortunately, still too complex to be appropriate for research at the molecular and genetic levels. Following the establishment of molecular biology as a discipline in the 1960s, however, organisms such as the *Drosophila* fly have become the focus of much genetic research because of certain characteristic features of their chromosomal structure. As a consequence, they have also been used in developmental research and detailed study of the functions of the nervous system. On the other hand, the nematode – which was the principal material for study in developmental biology during the 1800s and early 1900s – has again become the focus of intense research, now at the molecular and genetic level. The man who is responsible for establishing the genetics of the nematode is S. Brenner of the MRC Molecular Biology Unit at Cambridge University.

It is of some interest to understand how the nematode became the centre of so much research in developmental biology. Prior to Brenner's work, *Drosophila* had been used in the great majority of genetic experiments. *Drosophila* had the advantage as a research material of already having been studied and a crude genetic map had been drawn up. In Japan, excellent research had already been done on the mutations and mosaic patterns of *Drosophila* by Horida and colleagues. More recently, Gehring and co-workers at Basel University had determined the base sequence of the arthromeres of *Drosophila* and developed the concept of the 'homeobox'.

In contrast, the nematode was not well known as a research material in molecular biology, even among biologists. What, then, were the reasons for focusing on this animal? In Brenner's own research proposal, he stated the case as follows:

> We want to study the developmental process of multicellular organisms. For this purpose, we want to choose the simplest organism which shows cellular differentiation. We plan to apply techniques for genetic analysis which have already been established in microbiology. For this reason, a multicellular organism is needed which has a short life-cycle, is easily cultured, has a small number of cells that can be obtained in large numbers, as is the case with unicellular micro-organisms, and moreover for which genetic study will be

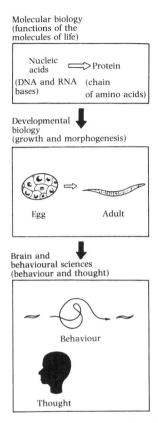

Molecular biology
(functions of the
molecules of life)

Nucleic acids ⟹ Protein

(DNA and RNA bases) (chain of amino acids)

Developmental biology
(growth and morphogenesis)

Egg   Adult

Brain and behavioural sciences
(behaviour and thought)

Behaviour

Thought

Figure 5.1 From genetic information to the brain. Molecular biology has shown that the program of life is written in the nucleic acids, the sequential information which determines the amino acid sequence and therefore the function of the proteins. How an egg divides to form the many organs of a multicellular organism remains, however, unknown. Once this secret has been revealed the secrets of the living organism as a computer will be known (Lewin, 1984)

possible. We believe that *C. elegans* (a variety of nematode) is such an organism.

This research strategy received bitter comments from other researchers – among whom was even one of the discoverers of the DNA double helix, James Watson (Lewin, 1984), but time has vindicated Brenner and his colleagues. One of Brenner's objectives was to trace the three-dimensional growth and differentiation of cells during the developmental process and to discover the rules whereby equipotential cells take on different roles within a multicellular organism (Figure 5.1). As will be discussed below, the wiring of the nervous system and the distribution of all the cells in the nematode have been determined, and work on the 3-D grouping of the cells has been pursued principally by von Ehrenstein's group at the Max Planck Institute.

5.1.2 From molecule to brain

Setting aside questions of the history of research on *Nematoda*, it is of some interest that the aims of Brenner's research and the language used to express those aims are virtually identical with those of certain computer researchers. In fact, Brenner's own scholarship in computing is deep. Born in South Africa, he was a childhood friend of MIT AI researcher Seymour Papert, the original developer of the computer language called LOGO. The mathematician David Marr invited Brenner to his laboratory in Cambridge and, together with the physicist J Whyte, wrote the operating system called MODULA-1. Marr then studied at MIT and became famous for his modelling of the cerebellum and visual cortex.

Brenner himself was interested in computer graphics and has had long standing contacts with S. Leventhal of Columbia University. Since the mid 1970s, he has applied molecular graphics techniques learned from Leventhal to nematode research. Inevitably, someone as active in molecular biology and computing as Brenner would eventually become involved in biocomputer research. In 1986, he was invited to the NEC Fundamental Research Laboratories to give a talk. Below, we have summarized some of the more salient points of that lecture.

5.2 BRENNER'S THOUGHTS ON THE PHENOMENON OF LIFE SEEN AS A COMPUTER

My own interests in computers date back to the early 1950s when I read Von Neumann's paper entitled 'Self-regulating automatons' and later his work on probabilistic logic and reliability. At that time, Kendrew had recently used the EDSAC computer for crystallographic analysis of myoglobin – a monster of a machine containing some 15 000 vacuum tubes.

There are certainly similarities between computers and living organisms, but the outstanding question for biologists is: how does the genetic information which is the program contained within living organisms, actually control behaviour? It is very difficult to draw a straight line from genes to behaviour and it is known that a mere micron (10^{-6} metre) of genetic information in *E. coli* contains codes for chemical reactions which have more than 4000 individual steps. Moreover, owing to feedback mechanisms, still more complex relations are implied. In computer language, it is as if the living cell were not a supply machine, but worked in response to demand.

On the other hand, it is clear that living organisms have very orderly structure. For example, the proteins produced by certain viruses can form a regular duodecahedron. How is such perfect geometrical information encoded in the genetic program? When the amino acid sequence of that protein is studied, it is found to have a repeating structure appropriate for such geometrical shape. The rules for such structures, as seen at the molecular level, are undoubtedly present at higher levels, for example, at the cellular level, as well.

In general, when trying to clarify the ways in which living organisms compute, we encounter two major problems. The first is how genes construct living organisms. The second is how does behaviour emerge from the neuron network which has been constructed by the genes.

To attack these biological design problems, there are two noteworthy methods. One is to physically destroy one of the component parts. For example, a portion of the neuronal wiring or cells of a part of the growing embryo can be selectively destroyed by laser. The other method is to induce mutations, thereby altering the original genetic plan. Both approaches have their advantages and disadvantages.

Thus far, we have been talking as if the design of living organisms was created by a designer, but is this correct? In general, living beings are extremely opportunistic and are not 'perfect'. They do not seem to embody general rules or to be susceptible to application of mathematical equations. They are the inheritance of the process of evolution and often contain structures which have completely lost all biological significance. How then are we to distinguish between the inessential structures and the structures which carry out vital functions? Moreover, the workings of genes are not really like computer programs in that the genes appear to be referred to when needed, as in a look-up table.

Great care is needed in research on the technological simulation of living organisms. Whether or not it will be possible to simulate entire nervous systems depends on our definition of simulation. One often hears of simulations of the movement of animals, such as the snake-like movement of nematodes. The true solution to the problem of accurate simulations means the rules of generation which produce behaviour. To accomplish that, the answers must have coherency and consistency and clearly define the boundary conditions. In other words, a superficial mimicking of the final output of behaviour will not suffice; it will be necessary to obtain a true understanding of the system's internal mechanisms.

One current theme of interest is the relationship between the primary structure of proteins and their functions. Since there has been rapid progress in techniques for sequence analysis for both proteins and nucleic acids, this is a field from which exciting developments can be expected. A database and analysis program is currently being developed for use on personal computers, so that ideas on the relationship between primary structure and function can be easily tested. The program is called MOBY DIC (the *MO*lecular *Biolog*Y *DIC*tionary) and is being written in *C*. It is not yet a powerful program, but will eventually be of interest when networked with many users.

Living organisms, even if they can be validly considered as 'biocomputers', are opportunistic in nature and have bottom-up, not top-down, control structures. Indeed, this is the fundamental perspective shared by most molecular biologists – a faith that elucidation of molecular details will lead to fundamental insights into the control of living systems – and ultimately insights into how to construct a biocomputer.

5.3 INVESTIGATIONS WITH NEMATODES

It is often said that the information processing animal nervous system includes many superior features, such as pattern recognition and parallel processing, which are not found in current information processing machines. For this reason, much research is currently devoted to the construction of devices and computers which apply the logic and mechanisms exemplified by living information processing machines. We must ask, however, if our current understanding of the information processing of living organisms is sufficient to allow applications at this stage. It is certainly true that aspects of the basic mechanisms of nerve excitatory transmission and the measurement of molecules involved therein have advanced remarkably. But large problems remain regarding the development of the nervous system and the information processing mechanisms employed by the mature nervous system.

Information processing occurs in neural networks made up of specific nerve cell types joined together. Research into the development of the nervous system, that is, the foundations of neural networks, is synonymous with trying to elucidate the design thinking which underlies the nervous system. The two central themes within neuroscience, in general, can therefore be said to be the understanding of neural network development and the understanding of the information processing mechanisms of the mature networks themselves.

These are not, however, two independent themes. It goes without saying that mature neural networks can function only once they have passed through their formative stages of development. It is therefore extremely unlikely that a true understanding of the mechanisms of information processing can be understood if we ignore the construction and morphogenesis of the nervous system on the basis of its design plans. For this reason, if we are considering the application of our knowledge in the neurosciences to the development of biodevices and biocomputers, our first challenge is the understanding of the basic design plans according to which living nervous systems are constructed. This is indeed the fundamental justification for studying extremely simple multicellular organisms – not because their own behaviour is of particular interest, but because only in such a simple system is it likely that a clear relationship between genetic structure, neural structure and behaviour can be discovered.

The nervous system, which is but one part of the somatic structure, also grows under the control of the genetic information. Consequently, learning how the somatic structure of simple organisms develops through the expression of genetic information is directly related to what is, for us, a more interesting question: how the nervous system is formed. For obtaining an understanding of life phenomena

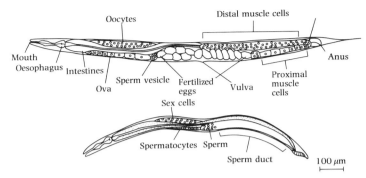

Figure 5.2 The structure of the adult *C. elegans*. The hermaphrodite adult is shown above (its dorsal side facing up), and below is shown the male (its ventral side facing up). Muscle and nervous tissue are not shown.

It is extremely important, however, to choose an experimental system which can be analysed easily and in detail. This also holds true with regard to research in the neurosciences. We do research on one species of *Nematoda, Caenorhabditis elegans* (*C. elegans*), which satisfies these conditions. Let us briefly outline the scope of our own research and current topics of interest in developmental biology.

5.4 WHAT IS *C. ELEGANS?*

Nematoda is a phylum of genuine higher-level, multicellular organisms (Figure 5.2). Its origins are ancient – going back to the Pre-Cambrian era some 500–1000 million years ago. There are free-living *Nematoda* that live off bacteria and organic material in the soil and parasitic *Nematoda* living directly off plant and animal organisms. Already some 15 000 varieties of *Nematoda* have been discovered and new varieties are discovered every year. It has been estimated that a total of 500 000 varieties may exist. Nematodes in the soil have been discovered virtually everywhere – sometimes in numbers near to 10 million individual organisms per cubic metre of soil. The actual number of nematodes is greater than that of any other animal phylum and is thought to constitute some 15% of the earth's biomass.

The species *C. elegans* has been the object of developmental and cellular biological research for more than 100 years and has contributed greatly to basic insights of biology, including the development of cell lines in ontogeny. In the 1970s, Brenner established analytic methods for *C. elegans*, subsequent to which it has become the focus of much research activity as a model for elucidating basic life phenomena which are unique to multicellular organisms. Today, as a result of combining morphological and genetic techniques, it has become an important research material for the study of problems such as cell differentiation and morphogenesis common to all higher organisms.

C. elegans has a body length of 1 mm, a body width of 0.1 mm and is one of the

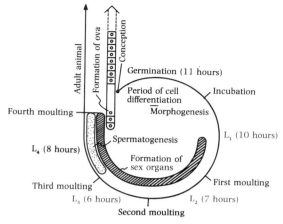

Figure 5.3 The life cycle of *C. elegans* (Brenner, 1974). In parentheses is shown the duration of each stage at 25 °C

free-living nematodes commonly found in the soil. It is normally hermaphroditic and rapidly self-fertilizing. Its basic structure can be observed under microscopes with × 5–50 enlargement. It is highly mobile and can be seen to move in an S-configuration by means of regular body oscillations.

The time required for reproduction of *C. elegans* is strongly influenced by the ambient temperature. At 16, 20 and 25 °C, it reproduces after 5, 3 and 2 days, respectively. Even in comparison with the highly prolific *Drosophila* fly, it reproduces quickly. The time required until maturity at 18, 20 and 25 °C is 19, 16 and 11 hours. After incubation of that duration, the animal undergoes moulting of the skin four times – phases referred to as L1, L2, L3 and L4 (Figure 5.3). Since some 300 offspring are born of a single hermaphrodite, under controlled conditions it is possible to produce a large mass of *Nematoda* in a short period.

The chromosomal structure of *C. elegans* is 5AA + XX, that is, five autosomal chromosomes and one sex chromosome. Owing to the non-splitting of the sex chromosome, male organisms appear with a frequency of 1 in 700. Using this male, it is relatively easy to study the detailed genetics of *C. elegans*. Mutations can be induced artificially using known mutagenic agents, and since nematodes proliferate by self-fertilization, a mutation produced in the sex cells of a parent (FO) results in the appearance of mutated phenotypes in the next generation (F2), even if it is a recessive gene – without the added confusions of cross-fertilization. As a consequence, homozygous mutations are naturally and easily produced (Figure 5.4).

Another merit of *C. elegans* as a research material is the fact that, since they self-fertilize, even mutations which cause gross behavioural abnormalities can be isolated and the mutant strain maintained indefinitely. In non-hermaphroditic

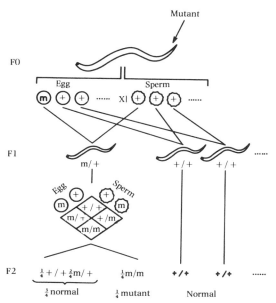

Figure 5.4 The separation of mutant forms of *C. elegans*. Since mutations induced in the F0 generation arise in half the male and half the female cells, a quarter of the descendants in F2 are dominant mutants. The figure shows a mutation arising in the female; *m* signifies the mutant gene; + is a normal gene

higher-level species, most mutations lead immediately to death and cannot therefore be studied. This feature of *C. elegans* is extremely important for its use in research on nervous systems. Thus far, such mutants have been isolated and used for research on motility, sexual behaviour and mechanical sensibility, as well as research on neurotransmitter abnormalities and study of the development of their minute central nervous systems.

It is also a merit of *C. elegans* that the larvae can be frozen and preserved for long periods in liquid nitrogen without being killed. A variety of mutants is therefore maintained easily and efficiently. Thus *C. elegans* has many advantages for genetic research and over the last ten years, some 700 of its 3000 genes have been studied in detail.

The body of both the mature and the immature *C. elegans* is nearly transparent and its structure is simple, so that its cells in a living state can be identified and followed under the normal light microscope. In fact, by making use of these properties, the cell division and movement of all cell lines during development – from conception to maturity – have already been clarified (Sulston *et al.*, 1983). The actual number of cells (or, in reality, the number of cellular nuclei, which is the more important figure because of the effects of cell fusion) is small – 959 cells in the hermaphrodite and 1031 in the male. The pattern of cell

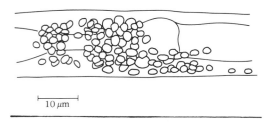

$\vdash\!\!-\!\!-\!\!-\!\!\dashv$
10 μm

Figure 5.5 The nerve plexus (brain) of *C. elegans*. The figure depicts the position of the nuclei of the nerve cells in the rostral nerve plexus. Dendrites and axons are not shown

division of each cell and its movement during development is known to be under tight control, and there is almost no individual variability among organisms in the spatial and temporal aspects of individual cell growth. The fate of each cell is predetermined. This difference between the strong genetic control of this small organism and the relatively large effects of the environment on higher organisms such as man must be kept in mind, but for the elucidation of the fundamental principles of the genetic control over development, the genetic determinism of *C. elegans* is ideal.

The body of *C. elegans* can be subdivided into various tissues and organs – skin, nervous system, muscular system, digestive organs, sexual organs and so on. The number of cells in each kind of tissue is known; for example, there are 143 cells in the sexual organs and 302 cells in the nervous system. Neurons and nerve fibres aggregate around the oesophagus and form a neural plexus (Figure 5.5) – which is the central nervous system or 'brain' of *C. elegans*. Ventral and caudal nerve tracts extend from this plexus to the body musculature – the former ending in the pre-anal ganglion. The sensory nerves extending anteriorly from the nerve plexus are connected to the rostral sensory organs around the mouth region. The entire nervous system has now been reconstructed by means of electron microscopical serial sections, and the position and connections of every neuron are known (Figure 5.6).

Most of the nerve cells are monopolar with few branches. In the entire nervous system, there are about 600 so-called gap junctions and 7000 chemical synapses. From the morphology, ultrastructure and chemical nature of these connections, 118 types of nerve cell have been identified: in contrast, five types are known for man. Moreover, multiple, rather than unique, functional types are common in *C. elegans*. For example, certain sensory nerves have synapses with muscle tissues, and certain neurosecretory cells also function as motor nerves.

Above all else, the detailed knowledge of *C. elegans* accentuates our ignorance about man, but it is believed that a thorough understanding of such a small organism will greatly help in obtaining a proper perspective on the scale of the difficulties in understanding the human nervous system.

Since genetic and morphological analysis of *C. elegans* can be done in great detail, research which combines the two most interesting fields in modern

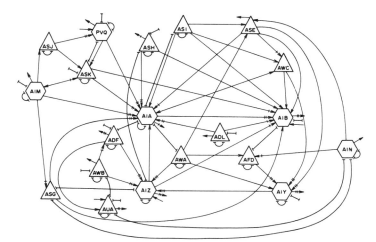

Figure 5.6 The neural network of *C. elegans* (after White *et al.*, 1986). Triangles depict sensory neurons; hexagons depict interneurons; arrowheads depict chemical synapses; T-symbols depict gap junctions

biology – developmental biology and neurobiology – has advanced rapidly. For the interested reader, the technical papers by Miwa, and Hedgecock and colleagues are strongly recommended (Miwa *et al.*, 1980; Schierenberg *et al.*, 1980; Hedgecock *et al.*, 1985; Yamaguchi *et al.*, 1983; Kaminuma, 1986).

5.5 CONCLUSIONS

Modelling the mechanisms of biological information processing can be done only once the fundamental biology of the relationship between gene structure and morphological development is understood. The deeper that understanding, the closer the modelling will actually correspond to the real biological objects which we are trying to understand for technological exploitation. For such progress within the realm of neurological information processing, much fundamental knowledge is needed concerning the formation of neural networks, the logic of the information processing carried out by neurons and so on. With regard to the functioning of neural networks, knowing how living organisms form them under the guidance of a limited number of genetic instructions is itself one of the central issues remaining for developmental biology.

 C. elegans is a superb model for morphological and genetic research, and has become the focus of attention as a model for understanding fundamental life phenomena which all multicellular animal species have in common.

6

The neural circuitry of the brain

Together with advances in brain research, the subtlety and complexity of the neural structures of the brain that have come to light are simply beyond description. The neurons, of which there are thought to be between 10 billion and 1 trillion in the human brain, are known to be the functional units of the brain. But the number of synapses per neuron – that is, the number of connections per functional unit – may reach 80 000, and the complexity of the mechanisms controlling its membrane activity is well beyond everyday experience. Neurons of this description are connected in complex ways to produce circuitry characteristic of the various locations in the brain.

In the functional units of the cerebral and cerebellar cortex (the columns), there are between 10^5 and 10^6 neurons, each of which is, on its own, capable of quite complex information processing. This type of localized neuronal circuitry is combined into several association regions and makes up large functional systems. These include large-scale systems within the brain which are responsible for perceptual, motor and autonomic functions, including emotions, sleep, memory and so on. The fundamental structure of these functional systems is similar among all animals, but the higher the organism in the evolutionary ladder, the more complex is its structure. Particularly in man, additional systems have emerged for higher-level mental functions, such as language and the ability for abstract thought and creativity, owing to the development of cerebral associative areas.

Brain research is currently progressing at the three distinct levels of system functions, networks and components – utilizing a variety of methods and techniques – but many unknowns remain at each level, and much can be anticipated from future research. In the present chapter, the current state of brain science will be outlined. Of most importance when considering brain science from the perspective of biocomputing are the principles concerned essentially with the informational processing of the brain at these three levels (Ito, 1980). In this chapter, we will attempt an overview of the current state of several areas of research in brain science from this standpoint.

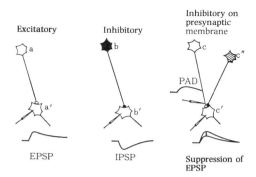

Figure 6.1 The three varieties of synapse. Owing to the electrical signal arriving at each kind of synapse, changes in the potential at the post-synaptic membrane are seen. EPSP: the excitatory post-synaptic potential. IPSP: the inhibitory post-synaptic potential

6.1 THE NEURON AS THE FUNCTIONAL UNIT OF THE BRAIN

6.1.1 Three varieties of synaptic effect

In the 1950s and 1960s, the first detailed research was carried out on the nature of signal generation in neurons and their mutual interactions occurring over synapses. It was then determined that there are three varieties of synapse in the brain: excitatory, inhibitory and presynaptic inhibitory (Figure 6.1). Many varieties of chemical substance bring about these effects: it has been estimated that at least several score of chemicals act as neurotransmitters, but from the perspective of signal transmission, we can confine ourselves to three main types.

Among these, the excitatory synapse has the effect of addition, the inhibitory synapse has the effect of subtraction and the presynaptic inhibitory synapse has the effect of logarithmic multiplication. Because of such effects, each neuron functions as a type of calculator and, in this respect, the neuron is very similar to a transistor. What is most strikingly different between silicon transistors and neurons is the very large number of synapses which any single neuron will have.

The cerebellar Purkinje cells are an example of cells with the largest number of excitatory synapses – some 80 000 – but all neurons form synapses with at least 10 000 other neurons. Through these synapses, neurons form complex connections with other neurons, the majority of which are from the neuronal axon and to neuronal dendrites. The excitatory and inhibitory input through most of these neurons synapse at the membrane of the neuronal dendrites and cell body, and combine to form a single potential which changes over time in an analog fashion. Depending upon the magnitude of that potential, an impulse signal is fired at the post-synaptic membrane of the neuron.

The axonal membrane can usually be treated simply in terms of electrical resistance and as a passive cable with volume conductance, but in fact local potential spikes are formed and a prolonged potential called the plateau potential is formed. It is thought to undergo even more complex changes. The role of these local processes occurring at the neuronal processes at the time of the neuronal signal generation is not well understood.

One important point concerning the excitatory and inhibitory effects of neuronal synapses is that, if an axon from a neuron branches and has effects on many other neurons, all such synapses have the same effect. For example, the pyramidal cells of the cerebral cortex always make excitatory connections with other cells, whereas the Purkinje cells of the cerebellar cortex always make inhibitory connections. For this reason, the pyramidal cells can be called excitatory cells, and the Purkinje cells are inhibitory ones. The synaptic effects of many different kinds of neurons in the brain and spinal cord are today being examined in great detail.

6.1.2 Reversible Synapses and Memory

One more important fact about synaptic actions is that they can be fixed, unchanging effects or they can change according to conditions and, moreover,

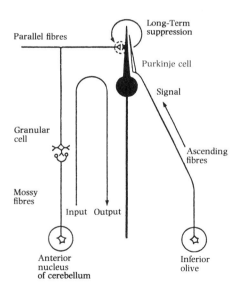

Figure 6.2 The reversible synapses of the cerebellar cortex. If signals arrive simultaneously along the ascending fibres and the horizontal fibres, the signal transmission from the horizontal fibres is suppressed – a condition which is maintained for a lengthy period

continue to change. The latter kind of synapse is called a reversible synapse – and four main varieties have been discovered over the last 15 years.

The first is the so-called long-term potentiation (amplifier), which was discovered in the hippocampal cortex. If a signal from such a synapse occurs, the efficiency of the transmission is raised, and is maintained at that level (Figure 6.1). The second kind is the long-term suppression type, which has been detected in the cerebellar cortex. In the cerebellar Purkinje cell, there are two kinds of excitatory inputs along parallel fibres and climbing fibres, but if these two kinds of signals are sent more or less simultaneously from the same Purkinje cell, the transmission efficiency between the parallel fibres and the Purkinje cell is suppressed over a prolonged period (Figure 6.2).

The third type is a facilitating synapse and has been discovered in the nerve ganglia of the sea hare. Its structure is such that, on top of one excitatory synapse, a second synapse exists and the serotonin (or similar substance) secreted from the latter synapse acts as a long-term potentiator of the transmission efficiency of the former, excitatory synapse.

The fourth kind of reversible synapse makes connections between the cerebral cortex and the so-called red nucleus of the midbrain. Owing to various changes in neuronal conditions, new synaptic connections produce a variety of firing phenomena. These plastic synapses work as kinds of memory devices, and have the important role of allowing neural networks to have self-organizational capabilities.

6.2 THE NEURAL CIRCUITRY OF THE BRAIN

6.2.1 The columnar structure of the cerebral cortex

Neurons such as those described above are connected in great numbers and in great complexity, forming a massive neural network throughout the brain. Complete elucidation of the structure of such a network is a daunting task. There are some 10^5 neurons in each cubic millimetre of cortex, the processes of which would stretch for about 15 kilometres. The total number of synapses present between neurons is 10^9, some 90% of which are formed by neuronal processes and most of which are excitatory.

Neurons of the cerebral cortex are of two main kinds – pyramidal cells and stellate cells – but about 60 subtypes have been identified. These include unusual types such as the recently discovered chandelier cells, which form many synapses at the 'exit' of the axon of pyramidal cells (Figure 6.3). It has long been thought that the connections among neurons of the cerebral cortex are largely orthogonal to the surface of the brain and form cylindrical units (the so-called cortical columns) with 0.3 mm diameters, but in recent years it has become clear that there also exist connections running parallel to the cerebral surface and that there are many synapses between cortical columns. A complete understanding of the neural circuitry of the cerebral cortex has not yet been achieved.

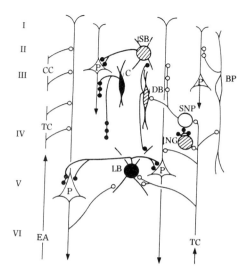

Figure 6.3 The neural circuitry of the cerebral neocortex. I–VI indicate the layers of cortex. TC are the connections from the thalamus; CC the input from the contralateral cortex across the corpus callosum; P pyramidal cells; SB small basket cells; LB large basket cells; C chandelier cells; DB double bogey cells; SNP spiny non-pyramidal cell; NG neuroglial cell; BP bipolar cell. Inhibitory cells are black or shaded (after Houser *et al.*, 1984)

6.2.2 The geometrical structure of the cerebellum

In comparison with the cerebral cortex, the neural circuitry of the cerebellar cortex is relatively simple and shows some beautifully geometrical structure (Ito, 1984). Its detailed anatcmy has been studied thoroughly (Figure 6.4), and several theoretical models of its fundamental circuitry have been advanced.

The cerebellar neural network consists of five types of neuron: Purkinje cells, basket cells, stellate cells, Golgi cells and granular cells. Of these, only the granular cells are excitatory, the rest being inhibitory. There are also two kinds of input fibres, the ascending fibres from the white matter beneath the cerebellar cortex and the mossy (descending) fibres. Both the ascending and the descending fibres form excitatory synapses on the Purkinje and granular cells, respectively. The axons of the granular cells form parallel fibres running along the surface of the cerebellum, and the parallel fibres form excitatory connections with Purkinje cells, basket cells, stellate cells and Golgi cells. It is also known that noradrenaline- and serotonin-containing fibres enter the cerebellar cortex and branch diffusely.

6.2.3 Theoretical models of neural nets

Signals that have entered the cerebellar cortex over the mossy descending fibres are intercepted by the granular cells and ultimately are output along the axons of

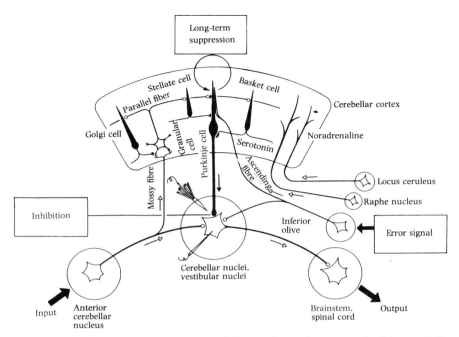

Figure 6.4 The neural circuitry of the cerebellum. The inhibitory signals of the cerebellar cortex modify the flow of signals passing through the cerebellar and vestibular nuclei. The error signals of the ascending fibres alter the emergence of these inhibitory signals

the Purkinje cells. This signal pathway in the cerebellar cortex includes long-term suppression-type reversible synapses, as described above (Figure 6.2). Therefore, because of interference with the signals from the ascending fibres, the flow of the signal along the mossy fibres – granular cells – Purkinje cells pathway is altered. Among the many synapses between granular and Purkinje cells, those interfering with the ascending fibre signals are suppressed and only those not interfered with remain. In other words, self-organization occurs by the 'removal' of mistaken connections relying upon the ascending fibre signals.

Theoretical discussion of these self-organizing functions was begun by David Marr in 1969, and developed as a simple perceptron model by Albis in 1971 (Figure 6.5). Of course it is not the case that the cerebellar cortex performs pattern recognition like the simple preceptron, but the perceptron is in fact modelled after the parallel distributed information processing circuitry of the cerebellar cortex. In the more realistic adaptive filter model of Fujita (1982) (Figure 6.6), the time factors of the input and output are modified by the ascending fibre signals, and this effect can be reproduced in computer simulations.

The structure of the neural circuitry of the hippocampus – part of the cerebral cortex, but a phylogenetically old and relatively simple part – is also well understood (Figure 6.7). The perforating fibres entering from outside the

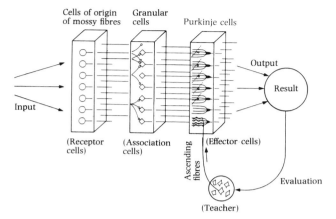

Figure 6.5 A simple perceptron model of the cerebellum. A comparison of the known cell types of the cerebellum and those of the perceptron are shown (in parentheses)

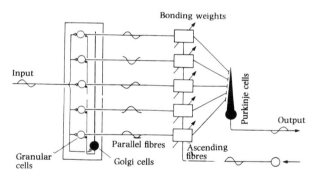

Figure 6.6 The adaptive filter model of the cerebellum. The sine waves show the time analog components of the signal carried by modulation of the frequency of neuronal impulses. At the horizontal fibres, small phase changes in the input signal emerge. The summed output of these cells controls the response of the Purkinje cells. The summation is influenced by the ascending fibres (after Fujita, 1982)

hippocampus form excitatory connections with the granule cells of the dentate gyrus, and the axons of the granule cells (that is, the ascending mossy fibres) next make excitatory connections with the pyramidal cells of the hippocampus. The signal is then sent from the hippocampus to other parts of the brain. In this way, a signal pathway is formed in the hippocampus through two excitatory synapses, and both of these synapses show long-term potentiation.

In the hippocampus there are also inhibitory neurons which receive excitatory synapses from pyramidal cells and form inhibitory synapses to other pyramidal

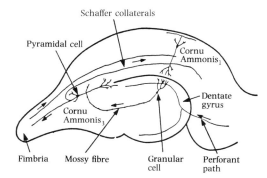

Figure 6.7 The neural circuitry of the hippocampal cortex

cells. Moreover, among the pyramidal cells, there are also those that send collateral axons to other pyramidal cells where they form excitatory connections. Despite knowledge of this kind concerning the hippocampus, there is not as yet a sufficiently convincing model of its neuronal circuitry.

6.3 FUNCTIONAL SYSTEMS OF THE BRAIN

6.3.1 Reflex systems which are at the foundations of movement

Elucidation of the structure of the circuitry of various functional systems of the brain and analysis of the signals generated by the neurons in such circuits is progressing, but because of the complexities involved there are few examples where a genuine understanding of the precise relationship between structure and function has been achieved.

That best understood is the reflex system which is the basis of the motor and autonomic systems. When a nervous signal is sent from sensory organs because of an external stimulus, it is sent to reflex centres of the spinal cord or brainstem. After undergoing a certain kind of information processing, an output signal is sent to the muscle or secretory gland, and an effect is then observed in the somatic structure. The body has many such reflexes and performs a variety of automatic regulatory responses without their entering consciousness. Reflex pathways are made up of the chained reactions of two or four neurons. For this reason, the nature of the information processing which can occur within them is relatively simple. There are also, however, reflexes with rhythm-generating mechanisms – such as the scratch reflex – and these can be complex.

6.3.2 The vestibulo-oculomotor reflex and cerebellar control

The cerebellar circuitry is inserted into various reflex pathways as a collateral pathway. That which shows this feature most clearly is the relationship between

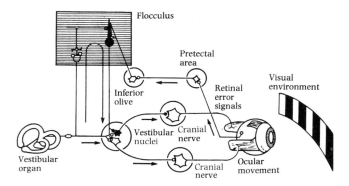

Figure 6.8 The circuitry of the vestibulo-ocular reflex and the cerebellum. The cerebellar circuitry is connected to the reflex circuitry, thus forming an inhibitory circuit

the pathways of the vestibular oculomotor reflex and a small region of the cerebellum known as the flocculus (Figure 6.8). This reflex moves the eyes in the direction opposite to the movement of the head and works to prevent 'blurring' of the image of the external world on the retina. When damage is done to this reflex mechanism, it becomes impossible, for example, to read while travelling in a train.

Structurally, the reflex consists of the actions of three neurons, and it requires accurate movements of the eyes to allow for eye movements which correspond directly to the movements of the head. In other words, if there is an over-response or an under-response, the reflex will not achieve its intended purpose. It is normally difficult to achieve such fine control of movements solely by means of reflexes. There are also changes with growth and development in the case of movement of the eyes, and the sensitivity of the vestibular organs to head movements cannot be said to be constant and unchanging. Moreover, there is no feedback from the eyes to the vestibular organs; rather this system is a kind of open-loop control system without the ability to correct errors in movement. It is therefore believed that the reason why the flocculus circuitry is 'inserted' into the vestibular reflex circuitry is to make up for the deficiencies of the reflex itself and to guarantee greater accuracy of the reflex.

The signals from the vestibular organs are sent to the flocculus through the mossy fibres and the Purkinje cells of the flocculus, which then send the signals to the interneuron of the reflex. Therefore, the pathway within the flocculus from the mossy fibres to granular cells to Purkinje cells works as a collateral pathway. If the characteristic transmission of the signal through the cerebellum changes, the motor characteristics of the reflex also change.

Moreover, visual signals are also sent to the flocculus along the ascending fibres. If the reflex is not working appropriately and an error signal is generated from the retina, it is thought that it is sent to the flocculus along ascending fibres and, at that time, the synapse between the parallel fibres and the Purkinje cells is suppressed. The vestibular signal flowing through the flocculus is then altered.

These workings of the flocculus closely resemble the concepts embodied in an adaptive control system. If we contrast the cerebellum with such a system in which the input and output are compared, an 'error difference' signal is obtained, and the dynamics of the control apparatus are modified according to that error. Study of the mechanisms of the cerebellum has made it clear that the means of transmitting the error signal is along the ascending fibres and that the flocculus is the apparatus for modifying the reflex dynamics.

A series of experimental findings supports these theoretical ideas. For example, if prism eyeglasses are worn, thereby reversing the left and right visual fields, the dynamics of the vestibulo-oculomotor reflex changes according to the nature of the retinal error message, which has been artificially made to be out of normal synchrony with head movements. Moreover, if damage is done to the flocculus in animals, these changes do not occur. In simulation experiments using the Fujita adaptive filter model, the adaptive functions of the vestibulo-ocular reflex are well reproduced.

The cerebellar cortex is divided into many long, thin regions which are functional units comparable to the cortical columns of the cerebral cortex. It is thought that each strip is included in a different reflex or other control system and is organized to ensure the accuracy and smoothness of control. The cerebellar actions are not limited to reflexes, but are probably an adaptive control centre in other adjustable collateral pathways, such as in the case of voluntary motor command signals sent to the brainstem or spinal cord. It is therefore likely that this mechanism is used during sports coaching and the training of subtle finger movements.

6.3.3 Future topics in the information processing of the cerebrum

The so-called basal ganglia of the cerebrum – the caudate nucleus, putamen and globus pallidus – constitute a motor control centre comparable to the cerebellum, and there are many other substructures, such as the substantia nigra and hypothalamic nuclei, which together make up the larger brain system. When focal damage is done to limited parts of the brain, various pathological states follow – such as Parkinson's disease, where the extremities shake and will not move as intended, and the disease called chorea, where the entire body makes involuntary movements and will not stop moving. Analysis of the signals generated by neurons and the neural circuitry involved in such diseases is already quite advanced, but clear-cut functional models, such as are now available for the adaptive control system of the cerebellum, have not yet been formulated.

The hippocampus, mentioned above, has long been thought to be an important part of the memory system of the brain. Recently, however, it has become clear that the hippocampus plays a particularly important role, not in all forms of memory, but in memory concerning combinations of places and objects. It remains

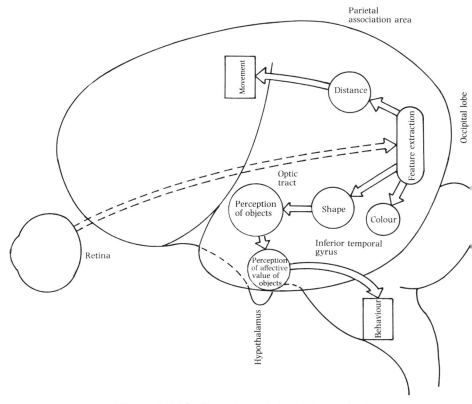

Figure 6.9 The flow of visual signals in the brain

to be clarified, however, how the memory system is constructed and how the hippocampal circuitry is constructed.

The higher mental functions of man ultimately depend upon the cerebral cortex. Brodman subdivided the cortex into some 52 areas according to differences in the fine structure, and it is gradually becoming clear that each of these areas serves different brain functions (Figure 6.9).

For example, visual signals are first sent to areas 17, 18 and 19, and are then passed on to area 21 for information processing of the shape of the perceived objects. In contrast, visual information is also sent to area 7, where spatial information concerning distance and depth of objects is processed. Signals for cutaneous sensations are initially sent to areas 1 and 3, and auditory signals are sent to areas 41 and 42. In *Homo sapiens*, around this auditory region there has developed a large language area which processes linguistic information. On the other hand, it is thought that movements are programmed in area 6, and that the signals which generate movement have their origins in area 4. It is believed that the so-called prefrontal area lying anterior of area 6 is where the programs for motor movement are actually formulated.

The details of the information processing in those areas are not currently understood. Moreover, the difference in functions of the left and right cerebral hemispheres in man have been the focus of much attention, but the fundamentals of the neural circuitry and the functional systems which produce such bilateralism remain unknown. Of primary importance here is to determine whether the functional differences between the cerebral hemispheres are due to differences in intrinsic neuronal circuitry or to interhemispheric communications.

6.4 THE FUTURE OF BRAIN SCIENCE

Many unknowns remain concerning the internal mechanisms which support the exquisite workings of the brain, and much effort is required to understand these. Today, three principal methods are used in brain research: clarification of the anatomical structures, analysis of neuronal activity in relation to animal behaviour, and study of the symptoms characteristically produced by localized brain lesions. As important as these three lines of research are, there is a growing need for the modelling of structures based upon firmly established anatomical facts, as well as additional hypothetical factors. The need for close cooperation between structural methods and experimental research, as has been achieved for the cerebellum, will increase as we approach questions of higher-level brain functions. In this sense, the challenge of biocomputing is the same as the challenge of brain research in general.

7

Thought and creativity

7.1 DEFINITIONS OF THOUGHT AND CREATIVITY

If we look up 'think' in a dictionary, we will find definitions such as 'to consider ideas in order to form an opinion'. If we then look up 'opinion', we will find 'a conclusion not dependent upon reasoning'. On the other hand, if we look up 'consider', we will find 'thinking in light of changing circumstances'. In other words, thinking is 'the process of drawing inferences not dependent upon reasoning on the basis of incomplete data and made in light of changing circumstances'.

The brains of vertebrate animals with central nervous systems can be thought of as devices which can convert, for example, the continual stream of the visual stimulations reflected by various external objects into meaningful concepts and then into a series of commands for behavioural responses. Improvements and refinements in this ability to deal meaningfully with external stimuli are what we call evolution, which itself can be thought of as a relatively slow process of creativity.

The dictionary definition of 'creativity' emphasizes the act of 'bringing into existence' that which did not previously exist – either the creation of something from nothing or from parts obtained elsewhere. In terms of the human brain, the act of finding meaningful elements in the stream of environmental stimuli is the receptive side of creativity, and building phrases and sentences from a lexicon of meaningful elements is the constructive side.

Analogy or the ability to determine the partial similarities between two objects is a logical leap at the foundations of pre-modern thought-processes. For all its weaknesses, it proved to be an effective thought mechanism in the development of the pre-modern world. And, before we dismiss it as irrelevant, let us recall that the mechanism of molecular recognition relies upon the cell's ability to recognize a partial similarity between a molecule's (that is, a protein's) three-dimensional structure and its own.

If pre-modern thinking can be characterized as the search for similarities between two differing objects, modern thought can be characterized as the tendency to discover the differences between similar objects. Creativity is the prudent combination of these two tendencies – the ability to discern which differences are significant (and therefore deny the commonality of two structurally similar objects), but also to discern which similarities reflect functional unity (and therefore affirm a previously unseen commonality).

7.2 THE PERCEPTION OF 'SAMENESS' AND 'NEWNESS' IN BIOLOGICAL ORGANISMS

In 1959, Lettvin, Maturana, McCulloch and Pitts discovered two neuron groups in the visual system of the frog which distinguish between retinal images of known and unknown objects in the external world (Lettvin *et al.*, 1959). They called these 'sameness' neurons and 'newness' neurons.

Objects which are already known are further divided into two groups by higher-level cells – between quickly moving small objects (prey) and slowly approaching large objects (predators). Once activated, these cells convert their input into output signals for attacking or escaping, respectively. To the frog, objects which lead to the same class of behaviour appear to be the same (Figure 7.1).

For example, if we consider the frog brain to be an apparatus for converting the visual image on the retina (Ω) into a response command (Γ), the conversion function can be expressed as $h:\Omega \to \Gamma'$. If, in response to each visual image $f \varepsilon \Omega$, a response $h(f)\varepsilon\Gamma$ is elicited, a sameness function to any image f can be written:

if $h(f) \equiv h(f')$,   then $f' \equiv f'$

It can then be said that the frog has an 'internal state' which corresponds to the number of such identities. The overall images which lead to the same response command have, to the frog, the same meaning. Moreover, all visual images

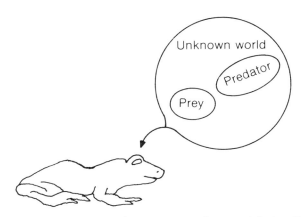

Figure 7.1 Newness neurons responding to new environmental stimuli, and sameness neurons responding to familiar stimuli, have been discovered in the frog brain. Familiar stimuli are further subdivided into predator and prey stimuli, leading to escape or attack behaviour

which are not converted into response commands also have the same meaning. The excitation of newness neurons can be seen as manifestations of the dissatisfaction of the frog, which cannot stop exploratory behaviour in search of unknown stimuli.

At a higher evolutionary level, it is thought that the right cerebral hemisphere of man sees the world as 'a Gestalt-like whole' – as a direct intuition – whereas the left hemisphere analyses the semantic units in the external world and converts them into a series of behavioural commands (algorithms of action). The newness and sameness neurons of the frog may, therefore, show the origins of the specializations of the right and left cerebral hemispheres, respectively.

7.3 THE MECHANISMS OF EXCLUSION

It is said that mathematics, music and games are creations of the freedom of human beings. In all three cases, they entail thinking in an artificial language with specific rules (a grammar) for manipulating a finite number of symbolic elements. A scientific paper, a musical score, a chess match and a baseball game are all 'written' following a relatively small number of rules. The same sentence will not appear twice, future sentences may have never appeared in the past and each game is unique. It is appropriate to note that the linguist Noam Chomsky called the self-generating functions of language an 'infinite creativity regulated by finite rules'.

Chess is a game which continues until a winning situation has been found, but let us consider the number of moves required on a chessboard where ten moves in any direction are allowed. If only 100 moves were required to reach victory and a new move were considered every second, it would take 10^{100} seconds to work out mentally all the possibilities. Since the age of the universe is thought to be only 10^{17} seconds (10 billion years), there would not be enough time to finish the game. Even using supercomputers capable of 10^{11} moves per second, the impossibility of the situation would not be significantly altered.

From the point of view of one of Japan's most famous Shogi (Japanese chess) players, Jugosei Ohyama, ten years of experience are required to be able to find winning strategies. All such strategies, he believes, are variations on that shown in Figure 7.2. The actual 'positions' involved, however, are rather uncertain, pre-verbal, often visual, analogical images which do not have a fixed configuration, but change over time. Let us say that they are formulated at an artistic stage of thinking – that is, the individual's own analogical representation of the world.

A countless number of books have been written on ways to win at chess, but virtually all such books have been predominantly about opening and closing moves. When it comes to the middle game, such books are less about 'the next move' and more about artistic, intuitive considerations. In any case, since no sure way of winning has been discovered, strictly speaking, they are books about ways of avoiding bad positions by means of maintaining certain board strengths. At that stage, it is possible to verbalize general rules concerning types of configurations which should be avoided. According to Popper, even the laws of natural

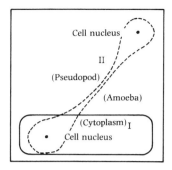

Figure 7.2 Shogi seen as a digital simulation of the analog pattern of phagocytosis by an amoeba. Digitally, a winning sequence of moves could not be found within the lifetime of the universe, but a practised Shogi player, using analog and intuitive techniques, can find a winning sequence of moves

science are rules of exclusion. Proof of the validity of a natural law is not possible; on the contrary, the scientific endeavour is to disprove hypotheses. A hypothesis which has resisted disproof is, by default, accepted as true, but only provisionally. For example, the law of the conservation of energy is accepted only because disproof of the non-conservation of energy has not been achieved. Popper argues that natural science in general is a word game about the ways in which logical inconsistencies can be eliminated.

7.4 THE CREATIVITY OF THE IMMUNE RESPONSE

The immune system is a mechanism for protecting the living body from invasion by foreign bodies. If the nervous system can be thought of as the contact point between the external world and the living body, the immune system is the front line of defence in contact with the 'internalized external world'.

Undoubtedly the greatest theoretical problem in explaining the mechanisms of the immune response is the fact that antibodies are produced in response to micro-organisms and chemical compounds which the organism has never before experienced. In other words, the similarity between these new external substances and substances which have previously been experienced is detected, but the new substances themselves have not been encountered previously and, indeed, may be artificially synthesized compounds which have not appeared in all of evolution. Today, immunologists argue optimistically that the organism produces antibodies to deal with all varieties of new molecules that might exist.

Once an antigen has been detected, it is 'remembered' by the immune system and, when experienced again – that is, its sameness is detected – it becomes the target of an aggressive response by the immune system. How the immune system can produce antibodies to all types of foreign matter – all substances that act as antigens – has been a long-standing puzzle in immunology, but the basic mechanisms involved are now fairly well understood (Tonegawa, 1983; Honjo *et al.*, 1983). From immunogenetic research using mice, it is known that approximately 10^7 antibodies can be produced. Furthermore:

1. The undifferentiated antibody gene has the ability to recognize antigens in contact with the long and short chains of antibody proteins and exist as several varieties of short segments of different physiological activity.
2. These segments join in various combinations during the process of differentiation from antibody genes to the formation of lymphocytes.
3. Even when the combination of segments has been determined, there are still variations in the strength of binding of the antibody to the antigen.
4. After completion of differentiation, there is a high rate of mutation at the level of the somatic cells.

In this way, a nearly infinite number of antibodies can be produced by combination of gene fragments which originally did not number more than a few hundred. Among these many antibodies, an antibody which will bind to virtually any antigen – including those never before experienced – is likely to be found.

It is indeed a remarkable finding that the random recombination of only several hundred genes can deal with unknown future antigens. This diversity from such a small number of original genes is reminiscent of Schrödinger's equations governing all atomic and molecular phenomena and Einstein's equations in which the same ten symbols suffice to express a plethora of phenomena. The finite grammar for combining gene fragments or mathematical symbols gives birth to a virtually limitless creativity in their interaction with the external world.

7.5 THE EVOLUTIONARY PRESSURE FOR THOUGHT AND VOLUNTARY MOVEMENT

Let us briefly consider the evolution of the vertebrate brain. As shown in Figure 7.3, the development of the neural tube between the spinal cord and the olfactory bulbs is the main stage of evolution. The control centres for vision and audition, motor activity and autonomic activity all lie here. The surface of this neural tube makes up the primitive origins of the cerebral cortex, thalamus,

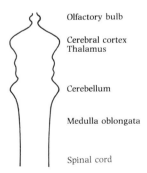

Olfactory bulb

Cerebral cortex
Thalamus

Cerebellum

Medulla oblongata

Spinal cord

Figure 7.3 The brain, ballooning between the olfactory bulbs and the spinal cord

midbrain, cerebellum and medulla oblongata. In this process of serial expansion, portions which have stopped evolving take on part of the functions of portions which have newly begun to evolve, so that the older parts of the brain are gradually given considerable powers of control over more primitive functions, while the parts of the brain which continue to evolve control less primitive functions (Bishop, 1960).

In *Chance and Necessity*, Monod considers that, in the distant past, an amphibian in an evolutionary soup realized its 'dream' of going on land through a combination of random chance and creativity. In order for this Lamarckian 'dream' to become an evolutionary pressure, it was necessary that a chance 'image' of some kind was 'fixed' in the central nervous system of the emerging amphibian – and that image activated and motivated the animal's subsequent behaviour, driving it to struggle onto land.

For this to happen, there is first the need for the animal to 'discover' its own upper limbs, that is, for the upper limbs to fall within its field of vision (Lorentz). That new information then needs to be used in the 'creative synthesis' of an image of the animal on land propelled by its own motor behaviour. Next, there must occur the partial release of motor activity from genetically determined spinal reflexes and the transition to voluntary movement. As expressed in terms of Figure 7.3, it is necessary for the lower regions of the neural plexus, which have already finished expanding, to hand over control of limb movement at least partially to the newly expanding, higher-level brain structures. Ultimately, this move away from the unconscious, 'mindless' reflexes of the spine to the more elaborate responses of the cerebral cortex results in the consciousness of higher vertebrates and the workings of the will.

In man, spinal reflexes and preconscious neural activity still control the autonomic activity of the internal organs, but the somatic musculature – particularly, the hands and the organs of speech – fall under voluntary control mechanisms. By means of such voluntary movement, we can use language in speech. 'Talking without speech' (Vytgotsky) and 'internalized speech' (Piaget) are thought.

In the early part of the talking stages in children, children can say sentences that they have not previously heard, using a vocabulary of but ten words and a uniquely human 'universal grammar' (Chomsky). In contrast to the idea of a genetically programmed human ability to acquire language, Piaget has argued that, since the number of the languages on earth is greater than the number of distinguishable races or blood types, language itself must have a self-organizing ability which is not under genetic control.

7.6 LONG-TERM MEMORY AND THE BIOLOGICAL VALUE OF INFORMATION

Human beings have two kinds of memory: short-term memory lasting from several seconds to several days, and long-term memory, which is semi-permanent. In the stimulus–response theory of the behavioural psychologists (B. F. Skinner and others) – where the human mind is thought to be essentially a blank sheet or *tabula rasa* (Locke) onto which natural laws are written through experience (Hume) – short-term memory is thought to become long-term memory through repetition or reinforcement. Such ideas became the guiding principles in the early days of AI and, indeed, from our own daily experience, we know that even a momentary image can become a permanent part of our long-term memory.

The characteristics of these memory systems have gradually been clarified in laboratory experiments on both animals and human beings. From experiments by psychologists such as Atkinson on multilingual subjects, it was learned that memory relies more upon the repetition of the meaning of events and phenomena than upon repetition of words and word phrases. Moreover, the emotional strength of the meaning is even more strongly encoded and more easily recalled than the meaning itself. Noble (1967) then showed that the 'strength of meaning' can be quantified by means of the number of words produced in free association to the original word over a set period of time.

In general, it is possible to measure the strength of a piece of information to a biological organism by the degree to which that information contributes to the maintenance of the organism or to the preservation of the species. For an animal with a strong sense of curiosity, such as a human being or a crow, however, the 'exploratory value' of information must also be considered. The 'newness' neurons of the frog also show some 'interest' of the frog in the unknown.

Figure 7.4 shows a classification of the biological value of information as regions on the surface of a sphere separated by lines of longitude – the 'sphere of the emotions'. Each value is associated with positive or negative emotions. The northern hemisphere has a positive biological value and the southern hemisphere a negative one. The strength of the biological value of the input information is greater at the poles, where strong reflex reactions are initiated. Information falling on the equator would be emotionally neutral, with little biological value.

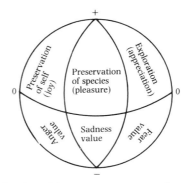

Figure 7.4 The biological value of the emotions expressed as a 'sphere of emotions'. The northern hemisphere represents the positive emotions; the southern hemisphere the negative emotions. The equator is neutral and without biological urgency

and would enter consciousness and short-term memory only transiently – after which it would be forgotten unless, within the interval of short-term memory, the information were given some emotional significance or associated with inform-ation with higher biological value. As a rule, it is easy to form associations between items of information near to each other on the sphere.

It is likely that the chemical neurotransmitter substances which are involved in each of the emotions around the emotional sphere will eventually be identified. The accuracy and stability of long-term memories which depend upon the specificity of those neurotransmitters would therefore be affected in precise ways by changes in the chemical balance of the neurotransmitters in a given individual. As one's chemical balance changed, one's ability to recall certain events would be altered.

7.7 MEMORY AND CONSCIOUSNESS

The limit on the input of sensory information to human beings can be estimated from the number of sensory cells as approximately 10^7 bits per second (this is about the amount of information contained on the screen of a television). From this large volume of information, the number of meaningful data which can be brought to consciousness, stored in memory and later influence behaviour is only 10–50 bits per second. This compares with about 40 bits of information per second which can be input during reading and 20 bits per second output during a piano recital.

If we assume that during a lifetime, a person is awake for about 50 years, the total volume of meaningful information received is only about 10^{10} bits – which is approximately the amount of information stored in the human genome. The bulk of this information passes through the brain with only transient effects, but some information in short-term memory has influence on planning and behaviour – and some information is stored as a permanent record in the brain.

The advocate of bidirectional communication theory, Hans Marko of Munich Technical University, has used a sophisticated mathematical model to show how short-term memory is connected to consciousness and long-term memory is related to the unconscious (Marko, 1965). For the interested reader not intimidated by autoregressive mathematics and computational techniques, Marko's models are a source of insight into the bidirectional transfer of information between any two entities which send and receive information. Although well known among workers in communications theory, his techniques have not yet been fully exploited.

Figure 7.5 depicts Marko's model of short- and long-term memories and how they relate to consciousness. The functional unit of the cerebral cortex (called here an 'association unit') is the seat of short-term memory and consciousness. Information input from the external world is immediately converted into response commands by means of genetically determined programs. Some information reaches the 'association unit' and calls up past records in long-term memory into

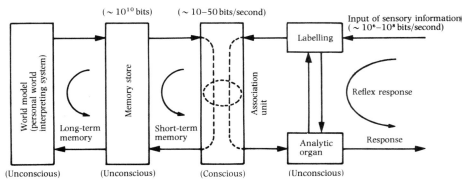

Figure 7.5 Extrapolation of Marko's bidirectional memory-consciousness model to include long-term memory. Some input information calls up stored information and is forgotten after being converted into a response (cognition of sameness and short-term memory). Other input information is used to modify the organism's world model and is stored in long-term memory (cognition of newness and long-term memory)

consciousness. Here, the 'input information' is the data concerning changes in the external world, and 'meaning' is the edited information with given causal relations.

Marko argues that, in the association unit, there is a process of 'stochastic matching' between the past memories and the current input information. Even if past memories are recalled, input information which is incompatible with them will be forgotten while the system waits for compatibility with a different memory, after the information has been stored temporarily as a short-term memory in the association unit and brought to consciousness.

7.8 THE BIOLOGICAL VALUE OF CREATIVITY

The cerebrum of the human brain is composed of three main components: the evolutionarily recent neocortex, the older limbic system and the still older basal ganglia. In light of their known functions, they are sometimes called the rational brain, the emotional brain and the reflex brain. Among these, it is the rational brain which has the functions of consciousness and language, and the emotional brain which is the seat of the emotions and many of the functions of the internal organs through the 'chemical language' of the hormones released from the hypothalamus. The reflex brain controls the instincts.

Karl Popper has argued that, while the rational brain is the seat of scientific thought and planning and predictions about future events, owing to the commands originating in the emotional brain and reflex brain, pre-verbal thought and behaviour are not subject to rational analysis or sensitive to issues of social acceptability. For this reason, only the neocortex contributes to our conscious world-view and our scientific ideas about the structure of the universe Popper and Eccles, 1977).

In contrast to the logical, analytic ideas of Popper, Paul McLean has argued that the human brain has an evolutionarily older, lower part which governs the emotions and reflexive behaviour and a newer, higher brain which stores experiences as memories and guides conscious behaviour (McLean, 1970). According to him, it would be the emotional brain, for example, which communicates the joy of scientific discovery – although the discovery itself may be due to the workings of the neocortex. When, however, a pianist forgets a musical score, but finds that the correct commands are none the less being sent to the fingers, it is the reflex brain which has taken control.

7.9 THE LANGUAGE OF BRAIN WAVES AND THE PLASMA MACHINE

Even though current computers cannot find for certain the path in a winning position in chess within the lifetime of the universe, virtually any human being who studies the game seriously for ten years can achieve such an ability. The search for a 'winning position' is a dynamic analog process reminiscent of phagocytosis by an amoeba (Figure 7.2).

In recent experiments using spoken verbal stimuli, differences in the spatial pattern of 'brain waves' (that is, the electrical activity of the brain measured as changes in voltage on the scalp) have been discovered in relation to the meaning of words or their usage as parts of speech (Chapman, 1980). Words with similar meaning also show similar spatial patterns in the EEG. For example, adjectives with similar or related meanings, such as 'good' and 'beautiful' produce similar EEG patterns, whereas phonologically identical words, such as 'red' and 'read' will produce distinctly different EEG patterns. There seems to be a 'language' of brain waves. Its decoding has remained a tantalizingly difficult problem, but progress over the last ten years bodes well for future research using this methodology.

If sentences instead of words are used as the stimuli, dynamic changes in the pattern of brain waves are observed. Imaging techniques allow visualization of the changes in voltage over the scalp in real time, and reveal amoeba-like flow and oscillation of electrical changes. These dynamic patterns have been called 'plasma waves' and might be decoded using the engineering techniques of plasma physics.

Let us look briefly at plasma phenomena which have been previously studied. In a plasma comprising ions with equal numbers of positive proton charges and negative electron charges, the following phenomena of interest have been observed (Davidson, 1971).

1. If an electromagnetic wave with a frequency near to the oscillatory frequency (the plasma oscillation value) characteristic of the plasma is introduced, a parametric induction of an ionic sound wave occurs (Figure 7.6).

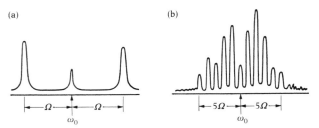

Figure 7.6 Parametric induction of ionic sound waves in a plasma owing to electro magnetic excitation (ω_0 is the plasma oscillation value, Ω is the ion sound wave oscillation value): **(a)** shows a narrow oscillation; **(b)** a larger oscillation

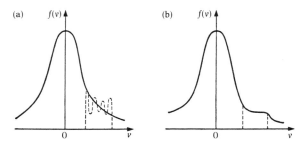

Figure 7.7 The function, $f(v)$, of electron velocities, v, in a plasma: **(a)** shows a plateau which is remembered as a stable waveform in **(b)**

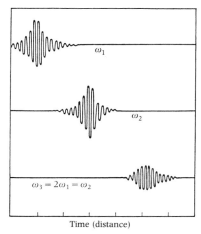

Figure 7.8 An echo (ω_3) produced by two previous waves (ω_1 and ω_2)

2. There is a plateau effect and 'memory' (Figure 7.7b) of the excitation added to the distribution of electron velocities (Figure 7.7a)
3. After the attenuation of the first electromagnetic wave (with oscillatory frequency ω_1), the addition of a second electromagnetic wave (with oscillatory frequency ω_2) brings about an echo (with oscillatory frequency ω_3; Figure 7.8).

These phenomena are well understood theoretically and may give insights into the grammar of the language of the brain waves.

Part Three

The general principles of biocomputers

8

Biodevice computers

8.1 BIOCHIP FEVER

Biochip fever began in the 1980s when the idea of electronic devices made out of protein molecules was first earnestly discussed and the labels 'biochips' and 'biodevices' were coined. It was realized that such devices could be as small as individual molecules, so that the scale of integration of integrated circuits could be decreased by several orders of magnitude. The memory of computers would then increase by something like 10 or 100 millionfold. With a plethora of technical problems still lying ahead, this realization was none the less the basis for the first wave of biochip fever.

With such memory size at least a theoretical possibility, the concept of a biocomputer no longer appeared to be science fiction – and together with the magic of words like 'biochip' and 'biocomputer', the concept of super-intelligent, carbon-based biocomputers has gained great popularity. The expectations for biochips has steadily increased since then, but the actual concept of the biochip has remained somewhat vague. Despite, or perhaps because of, the biochip fever, the circle of researchers on related topics has widened in Japan and elsewhere. While the difficulties of producing biochips are certainly acknowledged by all, instead of rejecting outright the early speculations concerning biochips, the idea of the fusion of the biosciences and electronics has been actively debated and the future directions for bioelectronics have been clearly expounded (Aizawa *et al.*, 1984).

What then is the background of the biochip? What potential significance does it hold? And what are the prospects for developments which transcend the early speculations?

8.2 TRANSCENDING SILICON TECHNOLOGY

8.2.1 The silicon wall

We are today in the middle of an era of ultra-large-scale integration. Starting with the integrated circuit, and passing through stages of LSI and VLSI technology, the miniaturization and integration of electronic devices is being pushed to its physical limits. The challenge of miniaturization has been based upon the technique known as lithography, which is a means of printing extremely minute electronic circuits on thin silicon wafers. Depending on how small the circuitry is, the beam used in lithography will be either visible light, ultraviolet light, electron beams or X-rays. Circuits have progressed from the micrometre range to the nanometre level.

What happens when silicon is cut this finely? Let us consider the physical limitations. If silicon atoms were handled individually, would it be possible to build circuits which still maintained electronic functions? No. The semiconductor characteristics of silicon would then be lost since the conduction of electrons depends upon the bulk properties of the silicon wafer. In other words, there is a smallest unit of silicon which can function in electronic devices – a physical limit the 'silicon wall', which poses an absolute limit to the miniaturization of silicon based electronic devices.

Let us therefore turn our attention to the possibility of electron flow in discrete molecules, rather than that in relatively large silicon crystals. Molecules are the smallest units of atoms bound together into stable structures. If a molecule is further broken into those atoms, it loses its molecular properties. In this respect silicon wafers and molecules are very different, since there is no minimal molecule-like unit of silicon.

8.2.2 Advocacy of the idea of molecular devices

The idea of designing a molecule which has a structure allowing it to carry out electronic functions is indeed a bold one. If such molecules could be constructed, it would be possible to go beyond the limitations of silicon circuitry. Such devices are generally known as molecular electronic devices or MEDs. Since, in a molecular component, the smallest functional unit is the molecule, an entirely different technological system for manufacturing such components is implied. For this reason, the challenge is not solely the theoretical one of determining whether or not the flow of electrons in molecules can be manipulated in a fashion similar to that possible in silicon circuits. There is also the manufacturing challenge, which will differ markedly from those of silicon technology.

In 1978, F. Carter of the Naval Research Laboratories in America first advocated the idea of molecular devices. Let us briefly examine one of his examples. He designed a molecule with three terminals. He argued that a charge density wave (soliton) could be made to flow between the first and second terminals. The third terminal would be located between terminals one and two. With such a structure, it should theoretically be possible to control the flow of the solitons by manipulating the third terminal.

Carter has designed a large number of such molecules and has chaired three workshops on MEDs in 1981, 1983 and 1986 (see Table 8.1). Interest in such devices has consequently grown, and the impact has been particularly great among organic chemists familiar with techniques for manipulating carbon-based organic molecules. If MEDs can be constructed, they will emerge from the laboratories of chemists.

Table 8.1 Trends in research on biodevices and molecular devices

Year	Researcher	Device/conference
1974	Abram	Molecular flow device
1978	Carter	Advocacy of molecular electronic devices (MED)
1981	Carter	First MED Workshop (Washington)
1983		STR Bioelectronics Symposium (Zurich)
	Carter	Second MED Workshop (Washington)
	Roberts	First International Conference on LB membranes (Durham)
1985		Second International Conference on LB membranes (Schenectady)
		International Symposium on new functional devices BED and MED (Tokyo)
		MED Conference (Strasbourg)
1986		Neural network computing
	Carter	Third MED Workshop (Washington)
		Start of MITI Future Generation Computer Project (biodevices)
		Start of the International Human Frontiers Project (biodevices)
1987	Mebius	Third International Conference on LB membranes (Göttingen)
		Bioelectronics Symposium (Budapest)

About the same time that Carter was first advocating molecular devices, ideas concerning biodevices and biochips (that is, bioelectronic devices or BEDs) were already in the air in America. Those ideas were concerned essentially with the construction of electronic devices using biological molecules, such as proteins, as the smallest functional unit. By means of the alignment of such molecules, it was thought that extremely small devices could be built – devices such as protein wires, molecular wires, interface molecules and so on.

The developments in this field, as outlined in Table 8.1 and Figure 8.1, are in fact little more than an expression of the hope of building components with molecules as the smallest unit structures. They do not indicate, for example, what molecular materials should be used to make a memory device or how such a device would be integrated with a large functioning system. Nevertheless, such ideas are of importance in indicating what areas of research might be beneficial, and for focusing criticisms of such possibilities.

It is in fact easy to criticize as mere speculation the idea of molecular devices and biodevices. Fundamental questions concerning their feasibility remain unanswered, but these ideas lead down a road which could have huge technological significance.

8.3 LEARNING FROM MOLECULAR STRUCTURES

Unlike the early research in silicon computing, research in carbon computing has an important teacher in the biological molecules already known to perform certain 'computing' functions. In the case of both biodevices and molecular

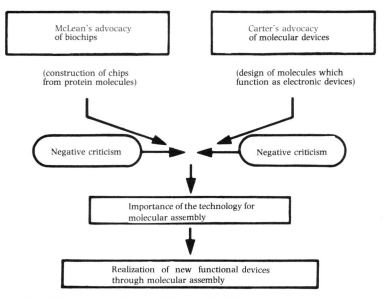

Figure 8.1 The ups and downs of the world of biochips and molecular devices

devices, the aim is to build functional devices by making molecules at the level of assembly commonly used in organic chemistry. While our aim is thus technological exploitation on a scale similar to that utilized in large chemical reactors, the origins of ideas concerning biodevices are clearly living organisms.

If we examine the origins of the functions of living organisms, the molecules and molecular aggregates which have definable functions all have definite and precise structures. It is appropriate to call these molecules 'functional molecular devices'. The large-scale integration and systemization of these molecular devices is the essence of what we call the 'life' of living organisms.

The possibility of modelling components after those found in living organisms is indeed the fascination of the molecular architecture. Let us take a look, for example, at the light conversion process undertaken by the light-sensitive bacteria. The molecule which receives the light is called 'bacterio-chlorophyll' (Figure 8.2).

A large number of such chlorophyll molecules are aligned together as a functional unit, but the main role is played by the so-called reactive-central chlorophyll. The surrounding chlorophylls act as antennas to focus the light energy on the central one. Let us refer to the chlorophylls which focus the light as D', and the central chlorophyll as D. When the latter is light-activated, an excited electron passes through intermediate molecules, such as prostocyanine (W_1 and W_2), and on to the quinone A molecule. The movement of the electrons transported from D to W_1 to W_2 to A occurs at a speed in the order of picoseconds to nanoseconds, but the time required for the reverse process (W_2 to D or A to D) is

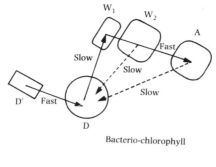

Bacterio-chlorophyll

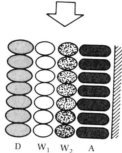

D   W₁ W₂   A

Figure 8.2 The structure of a molecular photodiode modelled after the mechanisms of bacterial photosynthesis

−6 orders of magnitude slower. This clearly indicates that a photo-excited electron moves unidirectionally with very good efficiency. This is an example of a fully known, naturally occurring photodiode.

The molecules corresponding to D, W_1, W_2 and A satisfy energy relations which allow the smooth transport of electrons. Needless to say, the arrangement of these molecules is important. A molecular device which is built with molecular architecture within it would be a true biodevice.

8.4 THE IMPORTANCE OF MOLECULAR PROCESSES

8.4.1 The LB method

Let us consider how we might realize the architecture of living molecules in an *in vitro* situation. It is first of all necessary to have techniques for combining and aligning various molecules in various configurations. Such a precise technology does not, however, yet exist, and there is not even a way of grasping a molecule as with an analogue of a pair of tweezers. The development of such methods is much needed as a fundamental technology in bioelectronics – and is certainly not beyond the ingenuity of today's organic chemists! Currently, the technique in widest use for aligning molecules is the so-called Langmuir-Brogette (LB) metho (Fukuda *et al.*, 1986).

The LB method entails placing molecules on an aqueous surface, increasing th surface pressure, thus producing a molecular membrane one molecule thick and then transferring that membrane to a solid surface. This is an extremely ol technique, but more effective methods have not been found. In fact, the L method has enjoyed something of a revival and is used by many group throughout the world today. One drawback of the LB method, however, is the fac that, in order to apply it, the molecules must have both a hydrophilic portion an a hydrophobic portion, which together are responsible for the alignment of th molecules on the aqueous solution. Although there is this limitation on th nature of the molecules which can be manipulated in this way, the LB metho allows the construction of single molecule membranes with the molecules aligne in a defined orientation.

How then might the molecular diode of bacterio-chlorophyll – as a model c molecular architecture – be constructed? There is unfortunately no mean known today for separately removing the D, W_1, W_2 and A molecules. Even if tha were possible, there is no way of gaining access to individual molecules an measuring their output. At the present stage, the shortest road to such structure is to produce molecular membranes of each molecule and then t stack them on top of one another. For such purposes, the LB method is indee an effective technique (Figure 8.2).

First there is the need to select the D, W and A molecules in light of their know energetic characteristics and known interactions. The W molecule is th molecular wire. Once appropriate molecules – with hydrophobic and hydrophili portions also present – are chosen, the LB method must be used to produce th necessary layers. The layers must then be placed on an appropriate substrate. photoelectron flow occurs when this structure is illuminated, we then have molecular photodiode built from organic molecules.

8.4.2 Molecular Diodes

It is important to note, however, that, depending upon the molecule chosen fo the D and A components, a variety of functional devices might be produced. Let u first consider the construction of a charge carrier. The notable feature of a charg carrier is clearly its conductivity. Bareau has produced such LB membranes i France and demonstrated their conductivity when doped with iodine atoms Kawasaki and colleagues in Japan, on the other hand, have produced a simila conductor which does not require doping – thus coming one step closer to th production of an organic wire.

What if an insulating molecule were placed between the D and A layers? Thi situation would correspond to a molecular diode. Let us refer to the insulatin molecule as I. It should then be possible, using the LB method, to produce D–I–A LB membrane with properties similar to those of the diodes nov produced using silicon.

A variety of molecules might be used as A and D components, but there are special merits in selecting organic molecules for those roles. Not only is carbon a plentiful atom, but if solely organic molecules are used, there is the possibility of using genetic engineering techniques to have bacteria produce the needed constituents without going through expensive and inefficient inorganic reaction steps.

Among the molecular devices proposed by Carter, most are devices with D and A components within a single molecule. Abram has shown molecular designs in which a single molecule – with a donor region, an acceptor region and an insulating region lying in between – has diode-like properties. It has been found, however, that the synthesis of the intended molecules is quite difficult and unintended properties are often produced. Using his own molecular design concepts, Fujihira has succeeded in synthesizing D–I–A molecules. He has reported that LB membranes using those synthetic molecules can be constructed on an electrode surface, and that they exhibit photoreactivity. Although this is not a device made of a single molecule, it is an LB membrane device containing subcomponents at the molecular level.

All of the examples up to this point have been designs for molecular devices based upon the relationship between the electron donor and acceptor portions of molecules, but there is no reason to confine ourselves solely to this kind of molecular interaction. Indeed, a wealth of design plans for molecular devices has been proposed and their theoretical properties worked out. Empirical demonstration of such properties is a more difficult task.

In addition to electrons and photons, the carriers suggested for molecular devices include ions and solitons. The organic molecules which show the conductivity of such carriers have recently drawn much attention as the raw materials for molecular devices. (Table 8.2. gives a brief history of research developments in this field.) Already in the early 1950s, the conductivity and charge-carrier properties of tetra-cyano-quino-dimethane (TCNQ) were dis-

Table 8.2 Trends in organic conductor research

Year	Research
1950	Early research on organic conductivity (Akamatu, Iguchi)
1958	Synthesis of polyacetylene
1960	Synthesis of TCNQ and demonstration of conductivity
1962	Conductivity of $(SN)_x$
1964	Little's model of high-temperature superconductivity
1971	Synthesis of polyacetylene film
1975	Superconductivity of $(SN)_x$
1977	Conductivity of polyacetylene owing to doping
1980	Conductivity and electrolytic polymerization of polypyrrol Superconductivity of $TMTSF \cdot ClO_4$

covered. The conductivity and even superconductivity of the so-called $(SN)_x$ macromolecules was also shown. Little was able to synthesize high-temperature superconductors using macromolecules and has become well known as the advocate of a theoretical model to explain such phenomena.

About the same time that the conductivity of macromolecules was becoming a topic of much discussion, Shirakawa and associates at Waseda University succeeded in producing a film of polyacetylene. In collaborative work with Pennsylvania University, they then showed that the conductivity of such a film can be remarkably increased by means of selective doping. Subsequent work along these lines has been extremely fruitful, with a variety of metallic elements being used in the doping of polyacetylene, polypropyl, polythiophene, etc. What most of these conducting macromolecules have in common is pi-electron bonds – suggesting that they are deeply involved in the phenomenon of conductivity. Of interest also is the idea that soliton transport is thought to depend upon a pi-electron mechanism.

8.5 BIOMOLECULES AND SEMICONDUCTOR COMPONENTS

8.5.1 Preserving the unique functions of biomolecules

It has been found to be quite difficult to construct biodevices using only the molecules of living organisms. There is thus a need to approach the problem from a somewhat different angle. Today, the idea being most actively pursued is that of inserting organic molecules into semiconductor devices, thereby introducing functions not normally found in silicon chips.

The unique feature of organic molecules is the ability to recognize specific molecules. An enzyme acts on a specific substrate, an antibody responds to a specific antigen, a hormone binds to specific sites on the cell-membrane and so on. It is not, however, an easy matter to synthesize molecules which have these recognition functions. Moreover, using semiconductor materials, such functions are not likely to be realized in the near future.

Although there are some prospects for building a molecular photodiode or molecular diode using biomolecular or biomimetic molecules, these devices do nothing more than reproduce the functions of previously known semiconductor devices. If that were all that is possible, there would be no reason to develop a new carbon technology to re-create that which is already possible in silicon. If however, it is possible to retain certain of the unique features of the biomolecules, then the connection of biomolecules to semiconductor devices promises to provide devices with genuinely new properties.

8.5.2 Bioelectronic sensors

The most noteworthy feature of biomolecules is the mechanism of molecular recognition – the ability of one molecule to distinguish among other molecules

Table 8.3 Trends in research on biosensors

Period	Research
1960s	Initiation of concepts of biosensors: advocacy of oxygen-sensing biosensors
1970s	Development of biosensors: practical applications of oxygen sensors advocacy of micro-organism and immune biosensors
1980s	The era of bioelectronic sensors advocacy of biosensors combining O_2 and FET advocacy of new biosensors combining electronic/opto-electronic devices with O_2 and antibody sensors

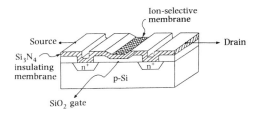

Figure 8.3 An ion-sensitive FET

An enzyme finds its substrate, an antibody its antigen, a receptor its hormone. Biosensors are molecular devices which exploit these functions.

Table 8.3 shows the trends in biosensor research over the last three decades. Oxygen sensors, in which O_2 molecules in membranes are detected by electrodes, were first made in the 1960s. Thereafter, a great many biosensors were designed, and some of them have become practical tools (Suzuki, 1984; Moriizumi, 1987). Among these developments, sensors using semiconductor material have been built – notably the ion-sensitive field effect transistors (ISFETs). This was the first success using a semiconductor sensor in a liquid solution. Today, ISFETs that do not have stability problems are used as sensors for detecting pH changes (Figure 8.3), and it has also become possible to build ion sensors using semiconductor materials.

The emergence of ISFETs was a dramatic event, but it has proved difficult to proceed as far as molecular recognition. For this reason, a hybrid approach, employing both semiconductor materials and biomolecules, has been used. That is, the ion-sensitive portion of the ISFET is used as a gate surface, at which an enzyme membrane is placed. In principle, this device is similar to previous biosensors, but it has the merit of complete compatibility with semiconductor

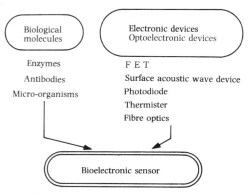

Figure 8.4 A bioelectronic sensor

process technology. It is truly a bioelectronic sensor (Figure 8.4). Future developments in this field are certain to be important.

In addition to ISFETs, other electronic devices such as thermistors, photodiodes and surface acoustic wave (SAW) devices have been developed.

8.5.3 Simultaneous multimodal sensation

Progress has also been made in the development of biosensors with multiple functions and in the increased 'intelligence' of such components. One particular target has been to integrate several sensor elements together and to add circuits for arithmetic functions within a single device. This is of course easily accomplished in semiconductor devices and will lead to greater intelligence for biodevices.

One of the important functions of living nervous systems is the ability to receive and process various kinds of sensory information. Not only do we see and hear, we also have subtle organs for touch, smell and taste. The inclusion of these other sensory modalities is relevant to biocomputing.

We have made efforts to develop biosensors with multiple sensory capabilities by putting LB layers with different selectivity on top of one another. In order to measure the sensitivity of such a device, we have used an optical technique which records changes in fluorescence. By utilizing differences in the wavelength of the emitted light, the nature of the information processing in the membrane can be manipulated.

The mechanisms of sensory information processing have been gradually clarified, but, despite such progress, mechanisms exploitable in computing have been few. Clarification of the simultaneous information processing of multiple molecular layers, based upon ideas concerning bio-architecture and bio-algorithms, will undoubtedly be a major theme of biocomputer research during the 1990s.

8.6 THE SEMICONDUCTOR–BIOMOLECULE INTERFACE

It has become possible to make many biosensors which are the product of a fusion between semiconductors and biomolecules. These biosensors do not, however, allow the exchange of electrons directly between biomolecules and semiconductors. On the contrary, when a biomolecule which is the target of measurement is detected, the changes therein are indirectly converted into the electron flow in semiconductor materials.

There remain doubts, therefore, about the utility of biomolecules in electronic devices, unless methods can be developed for inducing electronic changes in semiconductors or metals directly from biomolecules. In biomolecules, particularly in large macromolecules such as proteins, it is known that there are specific sites at which electron movement occurs and that elsewhere the electronic structure is rather static. This is the primary reason for current difficulties in achieving electronic transfer between biomolecules and semiconductors or metals.

We have therefore focused much of our own work on the construction of a biomolecular interface that will allow the smooth movement of electrons from biomolecules. Such interfaces are of two main kinds: electron mediators and electron promoters. Electron mediators are oxidizing-reducing substances which allow the direct transport of electrons. Typical examples are the ferrocene and quinone groups of molecules.

Electron promoters do not allow the direct transport of electrons. Instead, they maintain the 3-D structure of biomolecules such that electron transport can occur between other molecules. Hill, working in Britain, and Taniguchi, working at Kumamoto University in Japan, have found many electron promoters, many of which are sulphur-containing molecules. Moreover, Akaike and colleagues have reported that macromolecular electrolytic substances act as electron promoters. Our knowledge is still insufficient to allow the design of electron-promoting molecules, but the general structure of such molecules in nature is gradually becoming clear.

We have recently suggested that conducting macromolecules might be used as biomolecular interfaces. For example, we have been able to use polypyrrol membranes containing the glucose oxidase (GOD) enzyme to function as interfaces. Binding of pyrrol and GOD has been found to occur in an aqueous solution and a thin polypyrrol film containing the GOD molecules can then be formed. In the polypyrrol chain, there are double covalent bonds, and when appropriate dopants are added, the chains show conductivity. The polypyrrol membrane containing GOD has been shown to maintain its conductivity and can be called a 'conductive enzyme membrane'. What we have also found is that, in this membrane, there is electron movement from GOD to the polypyrrol chains. This indicates that the polypyrrol can act as an electron mediator.

Higgins and Hill have used the ferrocene inducer as a GOD electron mediator and have succeeded in constructing a new kind of biosensor in which the electron movement from the GOD enzyme is directly measured.

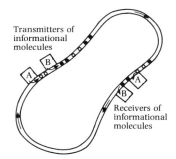

Transmitters of informational molecules

Receivers of informational molecules

Figure 8.5 Molecular communication

8.7 FROM NEURONAL COMPONENTS TO BIOCOMPUTERS

8.7.1 Neuronal devices and synapses

Biodevices have been the focus of much attention as the subcomponents in biocomputers, but, from the perspective of current research in biodevices, it is clear that the construction of computers using biomolecules is not the only application of biodevices and, in any case, is not yet a realistic possibility. Rather than concentrate solely on the development of new computers, research has progressed with the idea in mind of creating a variety of functional devices. There are of course a variety of approaches to these problems, all of which will accelerate developments in biocomputing itself.

In a comparison of the characteristics of biological and non-biological information systems, particularly noteworthy is the fact that living systems use chemical transmitters to convey information (chemical communication; Figure 8.5). Although the 3-D structure of the nervous system is extremely complex, at the heart of all neuron-to-neuron communications is the 10–30 nm synapse separating neurons. Since any one neuron is thought to have thousands or even tens of thousands of synapses, it sends and/or receives information to and from that many neurons. And, given a neuron count of some 10 billion in the human brain, the number of connections must exceed 100 trillion.

8.7.2 Devices modelled after the synapse

There are two main approaches to the development of neuronal devices. The first is the construction of the pre- and post-synaptic membrane pairs and the development of functional devices which mimic the synapse. The second is the simulation of the excitability of the post-synaptic membrane.

Functional devices which use informational molecules, as at the neuronal synapse, have not been heavily researched, but we have studied functional devices which resemble the pre-synaptic membrane. In order to use informational

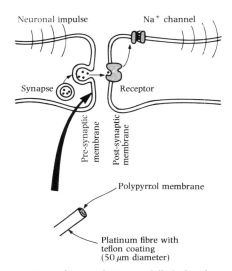

Figure 8.6 A neurotransmitter-releasing device modelled after the pre-synaptic membrane

molecules, these devices must be essentially liquid. The basic idea has been to produce devices which release neurotransmitters when subjected to an electrical pulse.

Many possibilities come to mind, but we have focused on the electrochemical doping of charged substances in conductive macromolecule membranes. For example, if a positive potential is applied to polypyrrol, the polypyrrol is oxidized and becomes positively charged. In order to neutralize this charge, the negative ions in the solution are taken up into the membrane. By controlling the parameters of the polypyrrol membrane synthesis, we have been able to produce the release of substances as a result of electrical stimulation – similar to that occurring at the pre-synaptic membrane (Figure 8.6).

8.7.3 The road to biocomputers

We have only begun to be able to construct neuronal devices, and success in the transfer of information by means of neurotransmitters has not yet been achieved. Once it has, the next stage will be the integration of neuronal devices and the construction of neuronal device networks. At that stage, it will also become necessary to study the plasticity of neuronal device synapses. Of particular importance is the fabrication of networks which respond to multiple sensory inputs. Needless to say, models of the bio-architecture of real brains and nervous systems will lie at the heart of such developments. Once we are well into the second stage of developments in the construction of neuronal devices, our image of the potential and practicalities of biocomputers will become much more clear. The target of subsequent stages will be the development of truly intelligent biocomputers.

9

Learning from the brain to build a computer

9.1 Introduction

The 21st century will be an era of man and information. Despite the many conveniences which the remarkable developments in science and technology of the 20th century have brought, the dark side of such progress has been the disruption and destruction of nature. The 21st century must therefore be one of human restoration of the balance and re-creation of the harmony between man and nature.

The world is rapidly becoming smaller, and internationalization continues apace in all respects. The rapid and frequent exchange of information between people and between societies continues to increase and there are growing needs for the appropriate handling of that information. The development of intelligent information processing systems is required, not only for industrial and financial purposes, but also for the proposed restoration of the harmony between man and nature in the 21st century. When information is exchanged between people or between cultures using computers, the inadequacy, inefficiency and inconvenience of data-processing by computers which are not truly intelligent are a great disadvantage to both man and society. This problem is what I consider to be a form of 'computer pollution' – not the pollution of the physical environment, but the clogging and slowing of channels of communication that should not and need not be hindered. In order to process information for human purposes, it is essential that computers function in ways which more closely resemble the processing which human beings themselves use. For this reason, an urgent topic for work from now until the 21st century is the development of new and genuinely intelligent information processing systems (Matsumoto, 1987).

In recent years, owing to developments in neuroscience, cognitive psychology, information science, information engineering and electronics, great advances have been made in the elucidation of the brain's processing and storage of information. A new field of engineering, 'biocomputing', has emerged, which, by exploiting insights from our new understanding of brain functions, is endeavouring to produce new information processing systems. Biocomputing is a field of engineering devoted to the development of computers which acquire knowledge through learning and therefore do not require programs. This contrasts sharply with the programming paradigm which characterizes the functioning of present-day computers, and is the same as the functional paradigm of living nervous systems. For this reason, the functions of biocomputers will closely approach those of human beings. Also being pursued for the development of new forms of information processing before the 21st century are systems which have capabilities that are not merely friendly to human users, but that resemble those of human beings. These capabilities are the most difficult ones to implement in computers and include perceptual capabilities similar to man's, the ability to process information rapidly even in complex and ambiguous situations, and the ability of pattern recognition, recursive inference and intuitive thought processes.

In the present chapter, we will review questions such as why the development of more human-like computers is essential for human welfare and how they might be developed. Starting from these topics, we will discuss the relationship between man and scientific-technical progress.

9.2 BRAINS AND COMPUTERS

The differences in information processing capabilities between the human brain and computers have often been pointed out (Matsumoto, 1983, 1987). It is well known that brains are superior to present-day computers in several respects. One is in the area of pattern recognition, which entails the input and virtually instantaneous processing of information, particularly of visual images and auditory sounds. We all know from personal experience the speed and efficiency of the pattern recognition capabilities of the human brain. Consider, for example, the speed with which we can recognize the one person among many whose voice we hear only for the brief moment of saying 'hello' over the telephone. It is not merely that we can identify the speaker, but we can also judge in a moment his or her mood. Current computers are simply not capable of obtaining this degree of information from such a simple voice pattern as 'hello'.

Another example of the superiority of the brain in information processing is in the processing of visual patterns. It is a simple matter for us to identify the face of an acquaintance from among a large number of people, but it is extremely difficult for a computer. In order to have a computer distinguish human faces, we must first give it a database concerning human faces, in which the characteristics of faces are recorded. Since information processing in current computers is extremely logical, feature analysis of human faces is also done in a logically consistent manner. In other words, the computer will extract the facial features – eye colour, size, shape, distance apart; nose shape, size, distance from eyes; and so on – and then analyse those features, describe the relationships between those features, and thereby determine that 'this is the facial data of person A'. Similar processing will be done for many faces, and a 'face database' will be constructed. If a human face were then shown to such a computer for recognition, it would again analyse the facial features presented and check through the database, comparing the current facial features with each and every one of those in the database.

Such an extremely logical judgement would easily lead to errors if a portion of the face currently perceived were suddenly to change its configuration. For example, let us assume that a man has lost most of his hair. Since the computer has stored information on the person's hair prior to balding, a strongly negative correlation factor with regard to hair would be generated, and it is unlikely that a correct answer would be obtained. In contrast, despite the fact that we may have information concerning our school friends that is several decades old, when we meet, we can recall who they are without error. It is clear that this recognition does not rely solely on logical information processing. Indeed, when asked what the basis was for determining that a certain face is that of Person A, it is surprising how vague our answers normally will be. We are even unsure whether or not Person A is wearing glasses. In contrast, if a computer has been able to identify someone as Person A, it will be able to answer in a logically consistent way what the basis for that judgement is. The judgements we make concerning visual information are simply not as logical as those of computers, but how then are we able to process pattern information in such a complex and rapid manner which is clearly superior to that of the computer?

There are two main reasons for producing new information processing systems, once we learn the information processing principles of the brain. The first is concerned with 'concepts and information which cannot be handled solely with logic' – that is, the kinds of information processing which are the forte of the human brain: pattern recognition, inference and language understanding. It seems unlikely that success will be achieved in this regard, no matter what kinds of innovation are appended to today's logical information processing systems (digital electronic computers) for these purposes (the processing of concepts and information which cannot be handled, or can be handled with great difficulty, solely by means of logic). Secondly, it could be inadequate, misleading or even harmful for us if computers cannot process detailed human information.

Today, there are many instances where, to make up for the insufficiencies of current computers in such information processing, it is we who make the compromises to make use of the conveniences of rapid computerized processing. Consider, for example, the results of using computers in education. Computers are used to quantify school performance and to determine the mean and standard variation of the abilities of children; they are used simply for the one reason that a large volume of test results can be processed rapidly. An inevitable consequence of the reliance on computers, however, is that only problems which are easily scored by computers are used. It is of course highly debatable whether or not it is really desirable to use computers to evaluate the abilities and talents of children when computers can evaluate only very roughly certain 'computer-friendly' aspects of intelligence. Knowing that there are differences between computer intelligence and human intelligence, would it not therefore be better to refrain from informing children directly of their positions in terms of standard deviations from the norm on tests which measure only a certain kind of intelligence, and leave such information simply for consideration by human teachers? And can it be said that the untapped potential of children is in any way measured by such an evaluation method? By giving high priority to the fact that computers make measurement easy and then evaluating the child on the basis of these extremely narrow, if easily quantified, measures, the use of computers in education can be of real damage to children with talents in areas not easily measured by computer. This problem of the reliance on computers where computerized measures have only limited validity is another form of 'computer pollution'.

It would of course be possible to list many examples of pollution in the destruction of nature and undesirable effects on the human body which are direct consequences of the electronics industry. Because 'computer pollution' has direct effects on the human mind and spirit and cannot be seen, it demands just that much more attention. The delinquency and misconduct of children have become a problem throughout the developed world, but it is difficult to maintain that such problems are unrelated to the problems inherent in the mechanical testing in children and the attempt to automate both education and career choices. Here, too, is a kind of computer pollution.

Until a few decades ago, before the time-lag between scientific-technological developments and their social and economic effects was apparent, it may have been meaningful to study science and technology as a completely separate academic discipline from the social sciences. Today, however, with our increasing understanding of nature, it has become important to warn of the influences on individual human beings and the effects on social and economic structures which accompany rapid technological progress. For this reason, it is important to analyse the ripple effects on man, society and economics, and come to an understanding of the directions of developments in science and technology. It is of particular importance to establish new academic fields which deal specifically with these problems and to nurture specialists with knowledge in both the social sciences and in the natural sciences and technology.

Human beings, too, are a part of nature, deeply involved in the alteration of nature and inevitably being changed by it. When such changes are so rapid that we cannot anticipate the implications of the changes we are initiating, pollution – in its wider sense – is the result. The new academic disciplines which deal with the sociology of technological progress must therefore consider three main areas.

1. Whether or not the pace of change is appropriate and how the pace can be maintained at a rate that we, as individuals and as societies, can accept.
2. How to achieve a scientific understanding of the human psyche – which, among the natural sciences, lags behind other sciences.
3. What is the relationship between the human psyche and scientific-technological progress?

Table 9.1 The road towards development of human-like computers

Research field	Artificial intelligence *(program required)*	Neurocomputing *(program required)*	Biocomputing *(program not required)*
Means of development	Using current computer technology and the creation of new computer architectures	By means of the learning done in systems made up of artificial neurons	Learning from the structure of the brain, and how that can be technologically reconstructed
Objective of development	Computers with human-like capabilities (such as inference, knowledge processing, pattern recognition natural language understanding, etc.) will be developed		
Current obstacles	The creation of new architectures; development of ways of handling information which cannot be handled logically	The creation of new learning algorithms; development of ultra-parallel processing computers	The elucidation and modelling of the learning algorithms of the brain: development of technological means of reconstruction
Current projects	MITI's 'Fifth Generation Computer Project' (in progress since 1982)	Research in progress at ATR, and many universities and private firms	MITI's 'Biodevice Project' and 'Biocomputer Project'

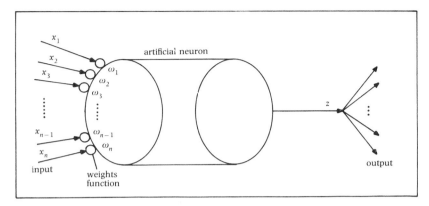

Figure 9.1 The engineering model of the neuron – the artificial neuron. The artificial neuron receives input signals from many other neurons. The connection weights of these input signals are summed (Σ), and the difference between that sum and the neuron's threshold (h) determines the output of the neuron, depending on its conversion function. The same output from the neuron is transmitted to many other neurons. The input signals from other neurons are taken as x_i $(i = 1, 2, \ldots, n)$, the weight of each input is ω_i the conversion function of each neuron, $f(p)$, is non-linear, and 1 if p is positive or zero and 0 if negative

9.3 BIOCOMPUTING

Artificial systems which process knowledge that has been acquired by means of learning are called 'biocomputers' (Matsumoto, 1983, 1987). So-called 'neurocomputers' fall within the field known as biocomputing, but are not identical to it (Table 9.1). That is, the neurocomputer can be defined as a network of interconnected simple units, so-called artificial neurons (Figure 9.1), which process information in parallel and are able to obtain 'correct' answers (those which we want produced) by means of the alteration of the weights of the connections among the neurons during a learning process.

A noteworthy, concrete example of a neurocomputer is the so-called NetTalk system (Sejnowski and Rosenberg, 1986). NetTalk is a machine which converts English words into their corresponding phonetic sounds and reads them aloud. It comprises a three-level artificial neural network. The neurons within each layer are not connected to each other, but to the neurons in adjacent layers (Figure 9.2).

The input layer contains 203 artificial neurons, which are divided into seven groups of 29 neurons each. The reason why there are 29 neurons in each group is that each corresponds to a letter of the alphabet, the full stop, the comma and the space. For example, when 'a' (or a space) is input, the first (or last) neuron in each group responds. Words made of a series of letters are sent to the seven artificial neurons in the input layer at specific time intervals. The letter

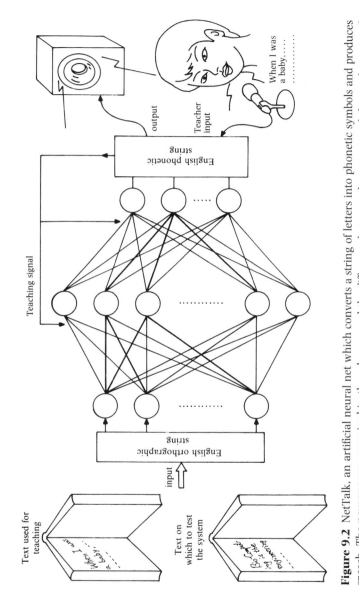

Figure 9.2 NetTalk, an artificial neural net which converts a string of letters into phonetic symbols and produces speech. The neurons are organized in three layers, and the difference between the output and the teaching signal is 'back propagated'. Learning occurs by the adjustment of the weights among the neurons. By acquiring knowledge in this way, it learns to produce the correct speech in response to written English (see text for details)

pronounced is that directly in the middle of the seven letters sent to the input layer neurons; the preceding and succeeding three letters are used for determining the changes in the pronunciation.

The output layer has 26 artificial neurons and represents the code of the sounds to be pronounced. When this code is put into a voice synthesizer, human-like speech is produced. By means of learning the rules of conversion, in the middle layer containing 120 artificial neurons, the input characters are expressed as the output pronunciation code. In other words, a comparison is made between the output pronunciation and the correct pronunciation, and, if there is a difference between them, the weights of the connections in the middle layer are altered.

This process continues until no difference remains. Since the weights prior to the learning procedure are assigned randomly, the first sounds are similar to the meaningless, continuous gurgling of babies, but gradually, as the learning progresses and the significance of the full stop, comma and space are understood, the sounds become discontinuous and it becomes possible for the computer to pronounce simple sounds. As the learning continues further, the rules of pronunciation are formulated in the middle layer and, for example, the 'a' in 'ran' and 'say' is pronounced differently, owing to the preceding and succeeding letters. Since the rules of pronunciation are represented as the weights within the network, even if it is shown words that differ from those in the English textbook used for learning, they can be read following the internal rules of pronunciation.

Such experimental successes have been one of the real attractions of neuro-computing for many people. There are in fact several other examples of useful neurocomputing – including the determination of the secondary structure of proteins from their primary amino acid sequence, the detection of metals on the sea-bed and the determination of the structure of half-hidden objects. Several obstacles, however, still hinder the application of neurocomputing techniques to larger and more complex problems. One problem is that too much time is required for the learning procedure. Although NetTalk contains only 349 artificial neurons, it is said to require about one week of constant learning in order to read correctly. In this case, the back-propagation learning algorithm was used (Rumelhart *et al.*, 1986), but if the number of neurons were increased, the learning time would increase significantly. Since it is essential that more neurons are eventually included in neural networks designed to handle more complex problems, it is important first of all to develop more efficient learning algorithms.

Moreover, since biological neural nets perform information processing in parallel, there are limitations when such nets are simulated on serial computers. Because the connection weights among the artificial units are computed serially, a delay in computation is introduced, and its approximation to parallel computing is limited. Clearly, there is a need to develop parallel computers designed for neural net computations. In such a case, it is important that, even if the computations to be performed by each processor (each artificial neuron) are simple, a large number of such processors (for example, more than 1 million) can then work simultaneously in parallel. This point differs from the developmental ideas behind so-called parallel computers and supercomputers which are essentially digital computers working in parallel.

Moreover, in a neural net made up of artificial neurons, regardless of the system's minimum energy state, it often happens that the system reaches a false stability (a quasi-stable state) in the process of minimization. No general technique for avoiding such a situation has yet been found. For the above reasons, when a neural net consisting of artificial neurons undertakes high-level information processing, the following three points are of importance.

1. The back-propagation algorithm must be speeded up by several orders of magnitude, or an entirely new algorithm with much faster learning capabilities discovered.
2. Parallel computers for neural net computations must be developed.
3. Neural net architectures must be devised which avoid the problem of false minima, or algorithms discovered such that, once a false minimum has been found, the system will rapidly exit from it.

Neurocomputing research is currently engulfed in these problems and completely surrounded by barriers. Mathematical and engineering ideas are being explored to overcome such difficulties, but it is also important that hints be obtained from the neurosciences. Biocomputing is research which is aimed at creating systems which acquire knowledge by means of learning, and then process that information (see Table 9.1). In other words, biocomputing includes neurocomputing.

9.4 RESEARCH IN THE NEUROSCIENCES AS SEEN FROM THE PERSPECTIVE OF THE INFORMATION SCIENCES

Let us briefly consider what direction research in the neurosciences should take from the perspective of research in biocomputing. It is well known that the neocortex has a layered structure (Itoh, 1980); the human cortex is a thin sheet of 1.5–5.0 mm thickness and has a total area of about 1000 cm^2. The neocortex containing the neuron cell bodies can be subdivided into four distinct layers according to their morphology. In general, there are many connections between layers and relatively few between neurons of the same layer. This is similar to the artificial neural network structures currently in use (Figure 9.2). It is not the case, however, that there is a uniform distribution of neurons in each layer, as assumed in artificial neural nets. Judging from the differences in morphology of neurons, the cerebrum contains at least 50 distinct varieties of nerve cell. Moreover, it is known that neurons are not simply the passive components which are assumed in artificial neural nets – where an output is implied whenever the input signal exceeds a certain threshold. The neuron is in fact a more active component, whose characteristics can change diversely, depending on how it is used.

Changes in the characteristics of neurons with use are due to various factors. The efficiency of information transmission at a synapse can change because of its own past history or input information at other neighbouring synapses. Moreover, the duration of this altered efficiency can be remarkably different depending upon the cell. The environment within which the neuron is placed can also alter its characteristics (for example, an excitatory synaptic site becoming an inhibitory site). Information is highly processed at the four layers of the cortex. For example, it has been argued that a Fourier transform is done on the retinal image information received at the primary visual cortex as the information is passed from layer to layer. Since the dynamic range of information which can be transmitted in neurons is extremely small, this presents an interesting technological problem. (The dynamic range is of the order of 10^2. This means that, if information is converted into frequencies and transmitted as the incidence of pulses, the recovery time of nerve fibres would be about 5 milliseconds, and it would be impossible to send more than 200 pulses per second.) We know that a wide dynamic range is required for a computer to be able to do an accurate Fourier transform on a signal. We also know that the spatial Fourier transform which would need to be performed between layers of the nervous system takes place in the extremely short period of several milliseconds. In other words, it appears likely that the neuronal layering or neural network either is functionally specialized to perform Fourier transform extremely efficiently or achieves its results completely without a Fourier transform. This property is seen at all places of the cortex and is not a special feature of only one small part of the brain. Let us therefore look more closely at the nature of the visual information processing which takes place at the primary visual cortex (Fujiwara and Okajima, 1987).

9.4.1 The flow of visual information processing

An outline of the flow of visual information in the brain is shown in Figure 9.3. Visual information enters the eye and undergoes photoelectric conversion at the retina. After the strength of the light is converted into a pulse rate, it is transmitted to the primary visual area of the cortex after synapsing at the lateral geniculate body. At the cortex, the processed visual information undergoes further processing along two main routes. One is a pathway to the inferior temporal gyrus where the processing of shapes mainly takes place. The other pathway is to the parietal lobe, where it is thought that the visual information is processed mainly to determine visual-spatial relations. The hypercolumn is thought to be the fundamental functional unit of the cortex.

Here we will consider the functions of the primary visual area from the point of view of information processing and discuss modelling of such functions. It is of course true that the mechanisms shown by this model are not yet proven to exist in the actual brain, but it is known to be a powerful working hypothesis, capable of accounting for a variety of physiological and psychological data from the perspective of information processing.

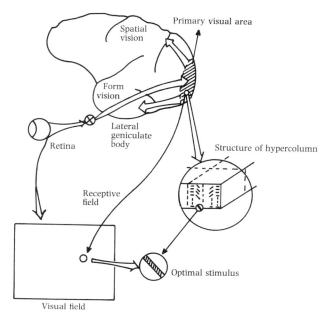

Figure 9.3 The flow of visual information and the structure of the primary visual area

9.4.2 Experimental facts concerning the physiology of the primary visual area

A great many facts concerning the visual cortex have been established since the early experiments of Hubel and Wiesel. The most basic findings can be summarized as follows.

1. The primary visual cortex comprises regularly repeating, modular structures called hypercolumns. Each module processes information corresponding to a specific region of the visual field (a receptive field), and the entire visual field is covered by hypercolumns of this kind.
2. Each module responds specifically to a bar with specific orientation shown to the corresponding receptive field and is made up of a regular arrangement of cells.
3. There are two main types of such cells: simple cells and complex cells. Simple cells respond to a bar of specific orientation at a specific site, whereas complex cells respond to a bar of specific orientation, but regardless of its position in the visual field (Figure 9.3).

It has previously been thought that such cells work to detect the characteristic features of bars, but here we will discuss the basic ideas concerning a model in which the hypercolumn is considered as a spatial frequency analysis apparatus.

For consideration of this spatial frequency analyser as a pattern processing function, the multi-channel hypothesis of Campbell and Robson is used. Based upon psychological experiments, they have argued that frequency-dependent channels exist in the visual system which perform spatial frequency analysis on visual images. The model to be described here uses these facts from experimental psychology and the above-mentioned physiological facts about visual cortex in suggesting how we can understand these phenomena from an information processing standpoint.

9.4.3 Structure of the model

The model is built upon the two following assumptions.

1. Images projected on the retina are broken down into small areas and hypercolumns perform spatial frequency analysis on them.
2. The spatial frequency analysis done in these hypercolumns is done by first converting the image into a 'tomographic display' (to be described below).

By means of these two assumptions, the visual information processing will have the following features. First of all, the spatial frequency spectrum of the pattern will not depend upon the position of the displayed pattern. As a consequence, within the receptive fields of each hypercolumn, strong processing can be done on the positional differences of the patterns. Secondly, the functions of the simple cells within hypercolumns are not thought of solely as detecting bars, but as devices used in the 'tomographic display' conversion of the visual image. Thinking in this way, it would be possible to handle input other than bar shapes in a similar way and, simultaneously, since it would be possible to process independently components with individual orientations, the Fourier transformation would be simplified. As a consequence, the neurological mechanism would be simplified.

Next we will briefly explain the 'tomographic display'. The principles of X-ray computerized tomography (CT) are shown schematically in the bottom of Figure 9.4.

In X-ray CT, a narrow X-ray beam is scanned in the direction t across the object under study and the absorbency of the object is calculated from the diminution in beam strength, in other words, the beam transparency. By slowly changing the angle of the beam and measuring over 180 degrees, it can be mathematically shown that the original object can be uniquely reconstructed from the series of data collected.

In the following model, instead of the density distribution of the object, the darkness of the visual image is handled in the calculations and the activity of the simple cells corresponds to the strength of the diminution in the X-ray beam. In other words, the alignment of cells within a hypercolumn which responds to bars of the same orientation (vertical alignment) would display a series of data when the image in the receptive field is scanned in a specific direction. It is thought that

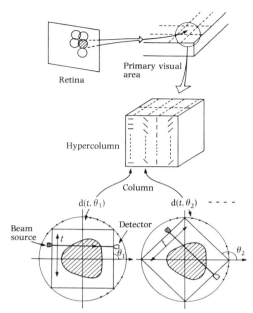

Figure 9.4 The principles of X-ray CT and the relationship with the model described in the text

the alignment in the horizontal direction would display a series of data when changed by an angle, θ (Figure 9.4).

The image of the receptive field corresponding to the hypercolumn can be uniquely reconstructed from the pattern of excitation of all of the simple cells in the hypercolumn. In order to perform the Fourier transform there, it is necessary to collect the level of activity in the simple cells responding to bars of the same orientation in a single cell. It is thought that complex cells may carry out such a function.

9.4.4 Analytic results of the model and its characteristics

Let us first consider what characteristic features this pattern processing apparatus would have.

First, as already mentioned, since the spatial frequency spectrum of the image is constant in relation to the position of the pattern, the output value of each hypercolumn is stable against positional movements of the input pattern. Calculations of the degree of similarity between two images (Figure 9.5) are shown in Figure 9.6 as a function of the shift. The degree of overlap with the original image is greatly reduced by the shift of several digits (Figure 9.6a), but after conversion using this model the degree of overlap shows large values over nearly the entire receptive field area (Figure 9.6b).

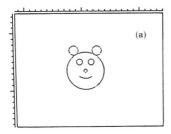 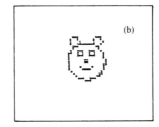

Figure 9.5 Images used for evaluation (image **[b]** is a discrete form of image **[a]**)

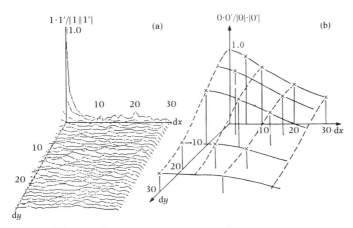

Figure 9.6 Stability to changes in the position of the pattern

In image processing technology, a method to increase the stability of an image to shifts entails making the image 'fuzzy'. Although stability to shifts is obtained, this method necessitates discarding components above a certain frequency, thus reducing the resolution of the image. In the model presented here, however, since the higher frequency components of the spatial frequency spectrum are preserved, there is no loss of resolution, and pattern processing which is also strong with regard to shifts is obtained. It is thought that this process occurs after the frontal visual areas and is the basis of the stability to spatial shifts which is obtained in higher-level pattern recognition functions.

Secondly, biological organisms often need to be able to recognize a shape – sometimes similar to that previously seen, and sometimes dissimilar. If the model described here is used, this function is also easily performed. For example, let us assume that there are two images, as shown in Figure 9.5. We can say that, at a macroscopic level, the two images show the same face, but microscopically it is possible that they appear to be completely different.

Let us calculate the degree of correlation between these two images when processed by this model. It is found that, when the higher-frequency components are suppressed (case 2), the correlation is 0.987, whereas when they are not suppressed the correlation is 0.523. In this way, by means of evaluation in the frequency domain, even if the images are the same (case 2) or different (case 1), they are calculable. Such functions could be easily realized by means of inhibition of the neurons handling the high-frequency components.

9.4.5 Conclusions about the model

In the primary visual area, information processing occurs over a small local area – a fact also apparent from the smallness of the neuron's receptive field. It is thought that functions of recognition and judgement of the entire visual field, where the information from local areas is unified into a whole, occur at higher levels beyond the primary visual cortex. It is undoubtedly the case that information is processed in the primary visual area into the form that is suitable for passing on to anterior visual areas.

For this reason, achieving an understanding of the functions of the primary visual cortex is equivalent to achieving an understanding of pattern recognition and is the first step towards realization of biocomputers capable of pattern recognition.

9.5 EXPERIMENTAL DEMONSTRATION OF THE MODEL

In order to demonstrate that the model outlined above is actually at work in the brain, it is necessary not only to investigate the details of previously obtained physiological data, but also to carry out new experiments to test the model. The model described here has so far been discussed primarily in terms of experimental results concerning the hierarchical processing of visual information. There is, however, both a hierarchical view of visual information processing and a parallel processing view. In the latter, it is thought that, even at the retina, visual information processing is functionally differentiated, after which processing occurs in parallel. In the actual brain, both hierarchical and parallel processing occurs, and it is likely that there is also feedback at every level of processing. Since the model described here accounts for one particular aspect of visual information processing, it is proposed as one working hypothesis which is likely to be effective in unravelling the complex workings of the brain. In any case, the model is thought to demonstrate that extremely high-level information processing can take place in a single layer of neurons.

We believe that in order for the brain to undertake some specific information processing, it is necessary to consider not only the wiring of the neuronal circuitry, but also the specific differentiation of the neuron itself for such information processing. That is, the neuron should be thought of not as a simple, transistor-like component which is the same wherever it is found in the brain, but rather as a complex LSI microprocessor. Moreover, such a microprocessor has certain memory functions attached to it. The reason why we say 'certain' memory functions is that the specific memory functions differ according to the type of neuron and the type of information processing to be done by the neuron. As a consequence, what needs to be clarified in the neurosciences for the purposes of biocomputing are the following two issues:

1. the properties of specific neuron types with specific memory functions working as VLSI microprocessors, and the mechanisms giving rise to those properties;
2. clarification of the nature of the parallel processing occurring in the circuitry of the neural net system.

It is known that various different kinds of information are processed at different sites in the brain, integrated at association areas and then output. Visual information entering at the eyes reaches visual areas, and processing of verbal information is done at language areas. After such independent processing at different locations, they are unified in association areas in the parietal lobe. Moreover, there is a 'computer' which unifies the output of the specialized parallel computers for each modality and makes judgements on that integrated information. In other words, the brain has a hierarchical structure in which the various levels work organically together and allow us to think and act. If we do not reach an understanding of the highest level of the hierarchy, that is, an understanding of the ways in which the various brain 'computers' unify their information, it is unlikely that we will be able to understand the ways in which the brain thinks and makes inferences. If the objective of biocomputing is, for example, information processing which allows fast and accurate pattern recognition, the neurons and neural nets will be the object of research for some time to come. Which of the brain's neural nets we will study will depend upon what type of information processing we are interested in. If we are interested in distinguishing between visual images, we must analyse the information processing done at the various levels of the neural nets involved in processing visual information.

Starting from the perspective that, since the information processing in the nervous system takes place by acquiring knowledge through learning, we believe that elucidation of the mechanisms of learning will contribute importantly to biocomputing research. For this reason, we have chosen the neural circuitry of the mammalian hippocampus for detailed study (Figure 9.7). It is not the case that the role of the hippocampus in the brain is already firmly established, but it is known that it is involved in both learning and short-term memory. That is, in patients with damage to the hippocampus there are marked deficits in serial recall (deficits in memory for recent events and recall), while memories for older events are not lost. Assuming that learning from experience results in relatively long-term change in behaviour, our main interest is, therefore, how and in what form external influences are preserved for storage in the hippocampus.

The ability of the brain to store external influences for the long term is known as brain plasticity, and it is becoming clear that the brain's plasticity is due to the connections (synapses) between neurons. In other words, the plasticity of the synapse is the basic process of learning and memory. Certainly, the characteristic

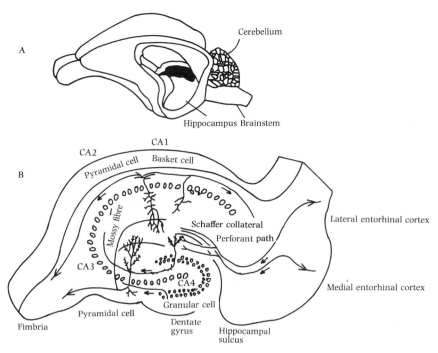

Figure 9.7 The guinea pig hippocampus. After removing the guinea pig cortex, a peanut shaped hippocampus remains **(a)**. The hippocampus is removed and serial sections are made orthogonal to the long axis of the 'peanut'. The internal structure of the darkened portion in **(a)** is shown schematically in **(b)** (the neural circuitry). Characteristic of the hippocampus are the two saddle-shaped neuronal aggregates which fit together like teeth. One of the groups is made up of granule cells, forming the dentate gyrus; the other of pyramidal cells. The pyramidal cells called CA4 are at the end of the narrow cell layer between the dentate gyri. This is continuous with CA3 and CA2 made up of large pyramidal cells and continues as CA1, which is a dense aggregate of small pyramidal cells. In this way, in the hippocampus there is a complete circuit: medial olfactory area → perforating branches → granule cells → mossy fibres → CA4, CA3 → Schaffer collateral branches → CA2, CA1 → hippocampal base. Input to the hippocampus originates from the medial olfactory area through the perforating branches, parahippocampus, etc. Output from the hippocampus goes to the parahippocampus and hippocampal base

feature of the interactions of the neurons of the hippocampus is that the long-term potentiation phenomenon can be seen at all of the main synapses (Figure 9.7). Long-term potentiation is an effect whereby a brief (for example, one second) high-frequency (for example, 100 Hz) stimulus to a synapse results in a remarkable increase in the efficiency of information transmission at the synapse (normally twofold or threefold), and this effect remains for a relatively long period (several hours to several weeks). The fact that such plasticity is a property of specially differentiated neurons and neural nets is indicated by the fact that, among vertebrate animals, such synapses are not found anywhere outside the hippocampus except between the granule cells and Purkinje cells of the cerebellum. (In the cerebellum, this effect leads to prolonged inhibition. It should be noted that recently long-term potentiation has been detected in the primary visual cortex and in peripheral nerves, but its physiological significance is still being debated.)

Our research objective has therefore been to discover the learning algorithm used by the hippocampal circuitry and to exploit it in the development of a human-like computer (Matsumoto, 1988). We must ask where in the cell the memory functions known as neural plasticity reside. And what are the specific characteristics of the neural net circuitry that allow learning? A great many researchers are actively involved in trying to answer these questions. Our approach has been to use a non-invasive technique where electrodes are not inserted into cells to measure their activity, but many points are simultaneously measured from hippocampal slices. Since the membrane potential of neurons changes during activity, our technique is based upon the prestaining of the neurons with a voltage-sensitive dye (a dye whose light absorption or fluorescence alters according to changes in the membrane potential). The neuronal activity is measured simultaneously as changes in light intensity. The principles of this method are outlined in Figure 9.8.

The method was first developed in America and used at several institutes for the simultaneous measurement of 100 sites (Cohen *et al.*, 1974). The system which we currently use can measure 256 sites simultaneously, but the photodiode pixel number is still insufficient to measure the changes in individual neurons. We are now in the midst of developing a system which will allow the simultaneous measurement of 32 000 sites.

Using our current 256 channel system on hippocampal slices, we have been able to make long-term observations of the temporo-spatial patterns of hippocampal activity before and after long-term potentiation, and have found that a variety of information can be obtained, in addition to that obtained from observations from a single electrode (Iijima *et al.*, 1990). By means of the physiological data obtained in this way, knowledge concerning the connections among neurons as seen under the electron microscope; biochemical knowledge concerning proteins, enzymes and other organic molecules; and information obtained using methods in cell biology, such as monoclonal antibodies and genetic engineering, it will be possible in the near future to clarify the nature of long-term potentiation in the hippocampus from the molecular level up. By elucidating the way in which learning occurs in the hippocampus (the learning algorithm), hints can be obtained and useful information applied to the field of biocomputing.

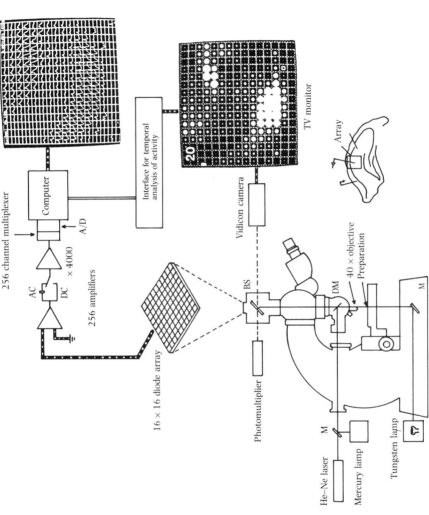

256 channel multiplexer

Computer

AC

DC ×4000

A/D

256 amplifiers

Interface for temporal analysis of activity

16 × 16 diode array

BS

Photomultiplier

DM

40 × objective

Preparation

M

He–Ne laser

M

Mercury lamp

Tungsten lamp

Vidicon camera

TV monitor

Array

Figure 9.8 The non-invasive simultaneous photon detector system for measuring neural activity using a 256 channel photodiode array. A hippocampal slice previously dyed with a voltage-sensitive dye is illuminated by a halogen-tungsten lamp. The image of the hippocampal slice is projected on the photodiode array, and the 256 pixels are amplified and sent to a computer. On the display is shown the

9.6 CONCLUSIONS

In this chapter, we have discussed the necessity of developing computers with capabilities closer to those of human beings, problems encountered in that developmental effort and relevant advances in research in the neurosciences.

The amount of contact between man and computer will increase massively in the future, and for this reason alone the development of more human-like computers is a necessity. There is also a need to achieve a better understanding of human beings themselves. No matter how advanced science may become, how thorough our understanding of nature and how human-like computers may someday be, the basis of human society must be the joy in acknowledging the existence of other human beings. We believe that the biocomputers which we are currently attempting to develop will be a tool contributing to the balanced development of such a society. In that process, the effort to obtain an understanding of the brain will also contribute to our understanding of man. Technological developments must serve human purposes and must contribute to the harmony between man and nature. The creation of biocomputers which approach the capabilities of the human mind is a desirable goal, particularly since computer technology has a direct bearing on questions concerning the psyche, and, in the process of developing such computers, we will undoubtedly learn much about man.

10

The creative computer

10.1 ARTIFICIAL INTELLIGENCE AND CREATIVITY

10.1.1 The ultimate aim of biocomputer research

The ultimate aim of biocomputer research is the development of a machine that has cognitive capabilities at least equal to those of human beings. In this chapter, we will first discuss the idea that, to be equal to human beings, a computer must be capable of some degree of creative thought, and then we will consider the problems involved in building a computer which has creativity. Here we have said capabilities 'at least' equal to human beings because – once biocomputers attain some degree of autonomous mental activity – they potentially could outstrip human capabilities. However that may be, we will only touch on this issue at the close of the chapter.

It is likely that many readers will respond to the assertion that 'Today's computers cannot think like humans' with the argument that current work in AI and the Fifth Generation Project will, eventually, result in machines that think like men. Here we must first clarify what it means to have human thought processes, so let us examine the basic structure of current expert systems which have so-called 'artificial intelligence'.

10.1.2 Human-like thought

Let us consider a topic such as medical diagnosis which a physician in the field of internal or cardiovascular medicine must undertake. Two methods of arriving at a diagnosis might be considered. The first is to review individually a variety of known disorders, the symptoms associated with each disease and the nature of the diagnosis which would be made in light of various clinical tests. The second method is to administer every possible test and to make a diagnosis on the basis of the test results. Of course, a combination of these methods is possible, but let us assume here that the first method has been chosen.

In such a case, the doctor's diagnostic logic can be expressed as follows: 'If the patient has symptoms $S(1)$ and $S(4)$, but not symptoms $S(2)$ or $S(3)$, then it is disease $D(X)$.' If we could get the doctor to write down the entire spectrum of such rules for the diagnosis of, for example, circulatory or metabolic disorders, we

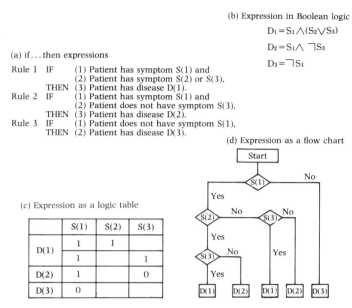

(a) if...then expressions

Rule 1 IF (1) Patient has symptom S(1) and
            (2) Patient has symptom S(2) or S(3),
      THEN (3) Patient has disease D(1).
Rule 2 IF (1) Patient has symptom S(1) and
            (2) Patient does not have symptom S(3),
      THEN (3) Patient has disease D(2).
Rule 3 IF (1) Patient does not have symptom S(1),
      THEN (2) Patient has disease D(3).

(b) Expression in Boolean logic

$$D_1 = S_1 \wedge (S_2 \vee S_3)$$
$$D_2 = S_1 \wedge \neg S_3$$
$$D_3 = \neg S_1$$

(c) Expression as a logic table

	S(1)	S(2)	S(3)
D(1)	1	1	
	1		1
D(2)	1		0
D(3)	0		

(d) Expression as a flow chart

Figure 10.1 Equivalent expressions for empirical rules in an expert system (modified from Shortliffe, 1976).

would have a collection of diagnostic criteria or rules which apply to all the possible diseases of the heart or other internal organs. Once we have an explicit list of the conditions which are found in a specific disease, it is a relatively easy matter to convert them into computer programs in various forms (see, for example, Figure 10.1).

The actual structure of knowledge for diagnosis is in fact somewhat more complex. For example, in the case of diagnosing a heart disease, X-ray photographs, electrocardiographic recordings (ECGs) and ultrasound techniques are normally used to obtain the basic data on the patient's heart condition. That analog information which is obtained, however, must first be 'read' and transformed into descriptive symbolic information, such as 'hypertrophy of the cardiac walls' or 'abnormal Q-wave' and so on. In light of a combination of such findings, ultimately a final diagnosis will be made. It can be seen, therefore, that the process of diagnosis has a complex hierarchical structure. As a rule, the diagnosis begins with information obtained using only the simplest (but often analog) equipment and gradually proceeds in stages toward detailed clinical tests – which employ more sophisticated techniques.

For each disease, there are certain known causes and the doctor is faced with the need to predict the future course of the disease – the prognosis. For these reasons, extremely complex models of aetiology, the natural course of the disease, symptomatology and outcome can be constructed for any given disease. The structure of diagnostic knowledge therefore implies a highly complex relationship between one set of rules relating to one disease and other sets of rules relating to other diseases.

How such knowledge structures can be expressed in computer programs is an important topic in software engineering and the focus of much current research. Although it is an important issue with regard to the efficiency of storing and later using such knowledge, we will not discuss it here for the one reason that questions of efficiency have little to do with the actual diagnostic power of the system itself. It would make no difference to the doctor or patient if the decision were arrived at after hours of supercomputer computations or immediately on a personal computer. The more important issues are whether or not computers can be of use here and whether or not accurate diagnoses can be obtained.

It would of course be desirable if the dialogue with the computer system could be as close to natural language as possible, and for data to be given to the computer in an easy manner, but again that kind of computer 'intelligence' has little to do with the essential work of medical diagnosis. The same can be said of doctors themselves: a gentle bedside manner and accurate diagnosis do not necessarily go hand-in-hand.

It should be clear that the 'artificial intelligence' intimated above entails no secret formulae of any kind. The usefulness of the computer is simply to hold a great volume of data and to apply systematically a wide range of rules to the entire database. The strength of computer systems – their ability to process a huge database systematically – is, however, related to their inherent weakness: the systematic search through a database is extremely rigid. They are systems containing rules which, in combination, provide diagnoses in response to specific answers to specific questions, but they cannot give meaningful answers outside the given specialized field. Moreover, no matter how many patients they 'experience', they get no wiser and, indeed, it is generally not an easy matter to add new knowledge to an existing expert system.

In current AI systems, if new clinical tests are developed, their relationship to the previously encoded rules of diagnosis must be appended individually by hand by the human programmer. Moreover, since the system does not handle the analog data obtained by human doctors by the direct observation of their patients, they are incapable of doing many things which experienced doctors are capable of – that is, intuitively grasping the essential condition and going directly to the relevant clinical tests which will provide an unambiguous diagnosis.

In order to bridge this gap between AI and medical specialists, several developments are needed.

1. The ability to formulate new diagnostic rules on the basis of past cases and to rewrite current rules using a recursive learning process.
2. For this purpose, such a system must have heuristic thought processes which will allow it to know what it should learn from which cases. In other words, it must have the meta-level control which will allow it to think autonomously.
3. It must be able to adapt to circumstances and rethink choices when confronted with unexpected phenomena and mistaken diagnoses.

4. Moreover, it would in fact be desirable if computers did not rely solely upon data which have been converted into numbers and symbols: they should have access to the wealth of analog data found in the real world. That is, AI systems require the ability to deal with the raw materials of diagnosis – the huge volume of analog information obtained through the five human senses by confronting patients in the clinic – seeing the colour of the patient's complexion and his or her emotions, demeanour, gait and general appearance.

Virtually every researcher in AI would welcome a computer system with these and other creative thought processes and indeed a variety of hardware and software mechanisms has been proposed. Thus far, however, methods for implementing creative thinking which have both specific consequences and generality have not been found. Let us briefly examine some of the representative methods which have been studied.

10.2 CREATIVE THOUGHT IN A MACHINE

10.2.1 Heuristics

Heuristics is a method devised by some of the earliest AI researchers involved in the construction of programs which play games. Since the rules of draughts, chess, Shogi and 'go' are in essence simple and the issue of winning and losing is clear cut, games such as these are easy topics for research. In a game such as noughts and crosses, the number of moves is quite small, and all possible outcomes can be easily calculated as soon as the first × has been drawn. The entire pattern of possible games is usually referred to as a 'tree', and the possible outcomes are often depicted as branches of different colours representing victory or defeat.

In order to write a program that will always win, first of all, all possible outcomes must be explored and colour-coded. This is easily done for noughts and crosses, but as the game becomes more complex, as in draughts or chess, the time required to explore every avenue of play increases explosively and soon becomes impractical. For example, in chess, even if it took only one-millionth of a second to examine one pathway to completion, it would still take 10^{90} years to examine all possibilities. Clearly, for even a moderately complex game, it is not feasible to use an exhaustive, mechanical search procedure.

What then is to be done? Rather than exhaustive examination of all possibilities, what was then considered by AI researchers was the introduction of certain methods for 'aesthetic' evaluation of the game board and the introduction of agreed-upon formulae to allow searches for partial exploration of search trees. Such techniques have already reached a certain level of success. Particularly well known are the methods devised by two workers at IBM during the 1950s and 1960s, the draughts-playing program of A. Samuel and the theorem-proving program of H. Gernder.

Unfortunately, not all real-life problems can be reduced to an appropriate search problem for which these techniques can be used, and it is often difficult to analyse a given problem on the basis of externally provided human knowledge. Despite those successes in the realm of game-playing, similar techniques have not been significantly developed subsequently.

10.2.2 Cognitive models

The fundamental idea behind the 'cognitive model' approach is that if the internal mechanisms of a computer were designed to resemble the workings of the human brain, the computer would then have human-like creative abilities. Clearly, this approach is similar to the thinking behind the development of biocomputers, in general. In fact, however, our ignorance of the 'mechanisms' of the mind is profound. Despite quite precise knowledge of many neuronal details, we do not yet know how the human brain is related to the human mind. Particularly with regard to higher-level information processing – such as memory, reasoning and language – the very fundamentals of the related neuroscience and physiology remain uncertain. As a consequence, researchers have developed quite divergent information processing models of the human brain based upon quite incomplete 'hardware' information.

Models developed in such a climate must be evaluated in two ways. One is to study whether or not human information processing actually occurs as in the model; this is a problem of the science of cognitive psychology. The second evaluation is in terms of whether or not such a model is useful; this is essentially a problem of computer technology.

If our ultimate aim is not to produce a 'humanoid' type of intelligence which would result simply in friendly robots to play with, but to produce an object which will do work, there is really no need to have information processing mechanisms identical to those of human beings. On the other hand, it is often the case that the brain's way of solving a problem is the only one we know of. So, we do not want to commit ourselves to slavishly imitating the brain when that may not be the easiest road to technological implementation, but we cannot afford to ignore the successful mechanisms which have emerged in biological evolution. In this regard, researchers in so-called 'cognitive science' are still having difficulty in defining their own position – sometimes emphasizing the importance of understanding the human brain and sometimes pursuing realistic possibilities for non-physiological implementations.

One of the classic problems in cognitive models is the 'monkey and banana' problem. Imagine that we have a monkey in a cage. Some bananas are hung from the ceiling, beyond the monkey's reach. In the cage, however, are a box and a stick, which an intelligent monkey will be able to use to get hold of the bananas. How well would a robot in a similar situation fare?

This problem has many of the features which are encountered by industrial robots. Their movements require a host of 'intelligent' actions – recognition of objects, background analysis, somatosensory and positional perception of the robot arms and fingers, planning of the combination and sequence of movements to reach an object, and so on. In order to achieve any given goal, a feasible model of the series of necessary information processes must be built within the computer. What is also required, however, is a general strategy for recombining robot actions to produce novel behaviour – to grasp the banana when not explicitly programmed to do so.

In a very different realm, similar 'models' must be implemented in computer systems for the purposes of natural language understanding and machine translation. In this field, both syntactic analysis and semantic analysis are required. Certain successes have been achieved in the realm of syntactic analysis, but less progress has been made in developing methods for mechanically grasping the meaning of words – that is, semantics. The reason for this disparity between the progress in syntax and semantics is very simple. Syntactic analysis involves only the conversion of one string of symbols into another string, starting with a finite number of such symbols in one language and a finite number of the allowed transformations.

For the understanding of meaning, however, a large amount of background knowledge is inevitably needed. Simply constructing that massive knowledge base is a huge and expensive problem, and it seems unlikely that completion of such a practical database will be completed even within the lifetimes of researchers currently working in the field of AI. With ultimate completion so far in the future, it is difficult to become motivated to begin the work. Given such a pessimistic outlook, it is no surprise that, Don Quixote-style, many researchers attack the problems of semantics making use of tools that clearly will not suffice for the job!

10.2.3 Deductive heuristics

Methods currently being researched by those AI researchers who favour formal theoretical methods include recursive inference and analogical reasoning. In general, it is difficult to implement mechanical processes for discovery and heuristic processes, but it is not categorically impossible. To understand this, it is easiest to consider a problem typically found in primary school textbooks. The problem is for the student to fill in the blanks with a single word to produce meaningful phrases:

river —————, ————— window, savings —————

In a test situation, there is no choice but to wait and see what ideas arise, but, given the opportunity, if nothing comes to mind a deductive dictionary search would be necessary. If we looked under 'river', a dictionary or thesaurus would provide a list of words that are used in combination with river: river boat, river bed, river bank, river pollution and so on. Among many such possibilities, only a few are likely to combine meaningfully with 'window' and 'savings'. In this case, 'bank' is clearly the correct answer. Even assuming that we were able to discover this answer immediately, most adults are quite unsure if they are then asked if there is a second word which can be used similarly.

A similar problem is found in arithmetic. Consider what answer is required when asked to fill in the blank:

$$3, 5, 7, \text{———},\ldots$$

If we assume that this is a sequence of odd numbers, the answer is 9, but if it is a sequence of prime numbers the answer is 11. It is simply uncertain which answer is required, and some conditions must be applied to limit the number of ways in which arithmetic sequences are generated. Conversely, if there are some conditions (limitations) imposed on the ways of generating arithmetic sequences, it may be possible to enumerate every relevant sequence quite rapidly. When a computer races through such a search procedure, it appears to us that the computer has discovered the answer in a flash, quite intuitively – but in fact the search procedure is a long, serial slog through all of the logical possibilities and without any spark of intuition. Computer searches are of course not limited to character strings and numbers, but can include mathematical functions, rules, relations and mathematical structures. Their apparent 'intelligence' may therefore be quite high, but then 'insight' remains nil.

The problem which remains is the same as that encountered with computer diagnosis of diseases. Even if we were to say that the computer is 'thinking', it is still the case that human beings must supply the relevant data (as well as the relevant algorithms used to process the data) beforehand.

Establishing the permissible range over which a search is to be done is a difficult problem. Taking an extreme example, it is often stated that, given enough time and paper, a monkey could eventually type out the complete works of Shakespeare. Certainly, that statistical possibility cannot be denied, but the real problem would not be the production of meaningful words and phrases in the monkey's writings, but their subsequent selection from a mountain of meaningless garbage. The problem of mechanically producing Shakespearean verse has perhaps been solved, but the entire issue has been transformed into one of the selection of such verse.

The problem of medical diagnosis by computer is not unrelated. For example, if the above-mentioned deductive reasoning methods were applied to a large volume of medical data, a great many meaningless medical hypotheses could be obtained. To sift through such a volume of possibilities in search of the probably correct hypothesis buried there would simply not be a task worthy of the effort.

Deductive methods of discovery can be useful with regard to problems with a small number of possible solutions, but today these methods are virtually powerless for dealing with real-world problems. This is because the bulk of our daily experiences cannot be formulated easily as the logical expressions which are suitable for computer manipulation.

If we were to imagine that symbolic manipulations and the techniques of modern AI are, in principle, effective and suffice for creative thought, they should first be successfully applied in the field of elementary geometry – where, like the world of games, the number of rules is relatively small and the objectives are clear cut. Here, however, genuine successes are rare indeed. In most cases, careful study of claimed AI successes in formal geometry shows that considerable human intelligence has been supplied externally and *post hoc* to allow the computer achievements. In conclusion, the methods of modern AI appear not to be as practical as their academic supporters would have us believe.

10.3 PRECONDITIONS FOR CREATIVE THOUGHT

10.3.1 Why can human beings think creatively?

Given the mechanical thought that computers are so good at, it is easy to understand that creative thought processes, insight and discovery are extremely difficult for them. Why then is creative thought even possible for human beings? Let us list what are admittedly little more than guesses why this is so.

1. There is a massive amount of highly complex data stored in the brain – the magnitude of which is beyond tabulation.
2. In addition to logical deduction on symbolic information, a large amount of analog information is used in any decision process.
3. All thought is handled by means of high-speed parallel and distributed (analog) processing.

These three factors may be the 'secret' to the creative thought processes of man. Even if we optimistically assume that there are no other unknown factors, it is none the less clear that current work in AI is being done without satisfying any of the above three conditions for creative thought. On these grounds alone, AI is still far from achieving creativity. Clearly, this is not to blame researchers in AI for failing to achieve higher-level cognitive capabilities because AI hardware systems do not provide the necessary basis for creativity, but it is an indication of the magnitude of the problems which remain to be solved.

It is worth pointing out that there is one more important factor, in addition to the above three, leading to creative thought (Figure 10.2). That is the simple fact that human beings are alive and, as a consequence, have the freedom and the ability to make value judgements. Thus, it is the autonomy of living beings which is probably more important than the actual means of logical operations in distinguishing man from machine.

It is frequently said that people are more emotional than rational and that emotions are in fact the motivating force behind thoughts. Love makes a man wiser and, when driven into a desperate situation, he can sometimes find previously untapped sources of wisdom. Similarly, scientists attracted to various problems are often driven by a sense of curiosity or desire for fame, and they do not shy away from the hard work then demanded. These kinds of factors simply do

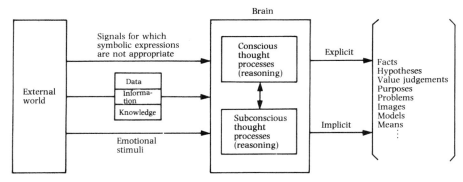

Figure 10.2 At the heart of creative thinking lie the mechanisms of subconscious thought (modified from Abu-Mostafa and Psaltis, 1987).

not come into consideration in current AI research. Although there has been some research on systems which are designed to mimic the workings of human emotion, no effort has been made to include such factors in research on ways to produce more creative thought processes. To integrate functions of a purely logical kind with a 'coprocessor' for emotional functions would be an interesting research theme, but how those two realms should be mixed and controlled is still a matter of speculation.

10.3.2 The process of scientific discovery

Several well-known scientists have written memoirs describing the psychology of their scientific discoveries. Poincaré's mathematical discoveries and Yukawa's idea about mesons are particularly well known. Such discoveries were theoretical insights in vastly different fields, but they have in common the fact that the problem at hand was first defined and consciously and thoroughly considered from all angles. In each case, a conscious decision was made to stop ruminating on the problem for several months. Then, after a certain lapse of time, the correct answer was hit upon with apparent suddenness. Many episodes of this kind have been related by well-known scientists and are not uncommon for more mundane problems in everyday life. This may well be a general rule for creative thought: first there must be a period of concentrated conscious reasoning, followed by an escape from the problem – during which the subconscious, autonomous wor-kings of the mind are allowed – and finally when consciousness is refocused on the problem, previous obstacles are found to have been resolved.

The earlier phase of creative thinking can be understood in models corresponding to the logic circuits in a computer and is at the heart of the best in current AI research, but the latter phase is quite different and cannot be explained without introducing some sort of chemical-reaction-like model. Since this latter phase is an important part of the creative process, we believe it is the key to implementing true creativity in computers (Figure 10.2).

However that may be, it seems unlikely that the gap between current computers and the brain's subconscious will be bridged in a single easy link. We can only proceed by groping ahead at what appear to be fruitful avenues.

Let us next discuss one concrete topic where some insights have already been obtained.

10.4 THE APPROACH FROM PRACTICAL APPLICATIONS

10.4.1 The challenge of new applications

Owing to widespread 'advertising' of expert systems, at least one misunderstanding has been fostered. That is the belief that research in AI – which for so long was thought to be little more than play – has at last entered an era of practical applications and is having significant impact on many areas of science.

It is instructive, therefore, to look at the underlying methodology which has actually been adopted. It is clear that the researchers in biomedicine and chemistry who first developed genuinely useful expert systems worked almost entirely independently of the AI research which was current at that time. In other words, they developed new and important techniques which were required by the applied problems in their own specialist fields – rather than taking the research results in AI and applying them to their own fields. The theoretical developments in AI which have proved useful were thus largely a result of the development of applied systems.

For example, the man responsible in the 1960s for the ideas behind DENDRAL, an expert system capable of determining the structure of organic molecules from spectroscopic data, was J. Lederberg, then of Stanford University and already well known for his work in molecular biology. The man behind the knowledge system LHASA – a system which includes the knowledge and aesthetic judgements of chemists needed for discovering organic synthesis pathways – was a leading chemist in organic synthesis, E. Cawley of Harvard University. With regard to the medical diagnosis systems developed in the early 1970s, C. Kurikowski, who developed the thyroid and glaucoma models which were later embodied within the expert system known as EXPERT, had until that time not been working in AI at all, but had been studying pattern recognition under Professor H. Watanabe at Hawaii University. The developer of MYCIN, E. Shortliffe, had graduated in applied mathematics from Harvard and had recently entered the medical school at Stanford. The present author, who developed an expert system for diagnosing cardiac disease, also had little knowledge of AI methods at that time. Finally, the developers of the UNITS system of the MOLGEN project – later to be connected with the KEE system – P. Freedland and co-workers – have said that they also were not students of current AI techniques when they developed their system.

Those who have most loudly advertised the successes of expert systems are in fact mostly those who entered the field in the late 1970s. But since then, there have not been any revolutionary developments in programming techniques and no new and powerful methods for breaking through the walls which these early prototype systems ran into. This is not to say that progress in AI has not been made, but it simply is not the case that the relatively minor hardware and software tinkering of academic research in AI has led to quantum jumps in the performance of expert systems.

These facts hold an important lesson for AI research in general. That is, what has repeatedly motivated and refreshed AI research has been researchers working in applied fields on real-world problems. For the fine-tuning of functioning systems, of course the specialists in AI with superior programming techniques have been important and contributed in significant ways to the development and/or refinement of usable and user-friendly systems. This historical fact also suggests that now, following the widespread acceptance of expert systems into scientific fields, it would be advantageous actively to pursue various applied problems which are likely to lead to the discovery of new AI methodologies. In other words, we believe that the time has come to accept the challenge of practical applications which will demand the development of new techniques in AI – techniques which transcend the current methodologies – and not wait for the emergence of disembodied technical advances before starting on practical projects.

Two premises which underlie the selection of such applied research projects should be mentioned. The first is that, even if computers cannot be made to be 'creative', it is important to acknowledge a preliminary strategy of building systems which will support and facilitate the creative thinking of people. The second is that a problem area should be chosen which, if successfully managed, will have a large and valuable impact on human existence.

10.4.2 Conversational graphics

Based upon current technology, one area in which developmental efforts would certainly produce valuable results is the realm of high-level conversational graphics. Current image displays and graphics techniques are primarily techniques for displaying artificial, highly-simplified images. Typical examples are the animation sketches, various computer-aided architectural designs and the dynamic screen displays in games such as 'flight simulator'. More sophisticated uses of image capture, image display, image analysis and pattern recognition are being developed. On their own, they do not constitute computer creativity, but, when skilfully used, they can certainly aid human creativity.

The greatest advances in this direction have been the graphics packages which are used to produce 3-D displays of selected molecules. Molecular graphics packages are not, however, designed solely to display molecules, but are in fact tools of use in the understanding of the structure and function of molecules.

Particularly for the complex structures of the molecules of life – with their diverse and complex interactions – computer graphics are not an amusing luxury, but are heavily relied on for giving researchers insights into molecular mechanisms.

Unfortunately, current molecular graphics packages utilize primarily static displays, and are incapable of dynamic views without expensive additional hardware. This is a notable shortcoming: for many of the important molecules of biology, coordinated movement of portions of the molecule plays an important role in their biological usefulness.

The 3-D movement of an image greatly aids our recognition and understanding of it. In fact, our eyes themselves are in constant motion for this purpose. When using a microscope, we also exploit this fact when we move the lens up and down near to the point of focus in order to improve the observation of the 3-D structure of the object under study. In other words, movement aids perception and our ability to discover relationships among three-dimensional objects. Dynamic visual display is therefore a matter of high priority and requires means of effectively dealing with a large volume of data.

Sufficient study has not been done, however, concerning the problem of what kind of dynamic display is most appropriate for what kind of problem. Such research will require functions similar to those of professional flight simulators, but today those systems cost millions of dollars. As mentioned in Chapter 2, the development of various parallel processors and their manufacture as single chips are progressing rapidly, so that sophisticated dynamic display systems and research on human perception and creativity can be expected to proceed significantly in the near future.

10.4.3 The structure of massive and complex knowledge

Operations on knowledge using inference systems have become popular in computing. But, relative to the number of pronouncements concerning 'knowledge acquisition', 'knowledge representation' and theories concerning the 'structure of knowledge', the number of actual working examples is quite small. Although the methodologies have blossomed, the number of systems applying such methods has remained small.

In fact, the structuring of knowledge is not an easy problem. One reason for this is that, previously, all knowledge was collected and organized under the presumption that it would be used by human beings. It has thus turned out that reorganizing that knowledge for machine-based logical operations is a major undertaking. In contrast, the structure of massive amounts of data or knowledge stored in computers as symbolic knowledge (or facts) is extremely simple. For example, in a system used to search for chemical substances, Chemical Abstract Service (CAS), some 7 million substances are recorded, but the system does not have any means for dealing with that information except in symbolic form.

Let us look at an example of the use of such a database with regard to a specific problem concerning cancer. Every year, a huge volume of experimental data and reports are published in a variety of fields related to cancer – including immunology, clinical medicine, pharmacology, toxicology, chemical biology, etc. Structuring of that raw data for use in a unified way in computer systems has not yet been achieved. Particularly for knowledge in the field of cancer research, the structuring of the known facts in a way that makes them easily accessible would greatly reduce duplication of research and waste of resources. The mechanical processing of such knowledge would raise the possibility of discovering truths which are already deducible from known facts, but which are hidden from sight by the volume of unorganized information on cancer-related topics.

The organization of knowledge structured with its utilization by computers, in mind from the outset, will soon become a necessity in the neurosciences, as well, where the growth in research is exponential. For elucidating the complex workings of the brain, computers will need to be exploited to the full, and a strategy followed in which research is pursued while organizing the relevant facts.

A large-scale knowledge system for use in the life sciences is not a small undertaking, but rather is comparable to the construction of particle accelerator facilities in fundamental physics. Its construction will require the collaboration of a large number of people and, ideally, use the resources of more than one country. Much of the work involved cannot be said to be directly scientific research, but would be concerned with the infrastructure. If work on such a mammoth intellectual tool were begun, it would be welcomed by a great many people and eventually used by many more.

It is worth noting that this kind of intellectual tool may be fundamentally inconsistent with the current 'publish-or-perish' system of evaluating academic researchers, but would none the less be an objectively valuable contribution to science. Particularly in the neurosciences and cancer research – where the significance of scientific progress can be profound – the exploitation of a computer-based research strategy and the structuring of knowledge in these fields should be pursued. Efforts in this direction are also likely to lead to the emergence of new computer methodologies with diverse applications.

10.4.4 A right-hemisphere-like database

The human brain is divided into left and right hemispheres, whose functions are sufficiently different that the labels 'left brain' and 'right brain' have come into use. The left hemisphere is logical and works in a computer-like fashion; the right hemisphere is more intuitive and emotional and is superior at image processing.

Without relying too heavily on this particular characterization of the cerebral hemispheres, it is worth asking how a right-hemisphere-like image processing computer could be constructed. As mentioned in Chapter 2, this question returns us to the problem of how to measure the similarity or dissimilarity between two sets of analog data. This is essentially a pattern recognition problem, and it would be desirable to be able to process the data in parallel. Developments in optical computing are most promising here. Let us emphasize here that if a significant, concrete, applied method in this field were found, it would undoubtedly become the technological basis for a new generation of computing.

10.4.5 Unified intelligent systems

Above, we have subdivided thought processes into categories such as planning, insight, induction and deduction, but actual thought processes are undoubtedly more complex and less clearly categorized. For example, although theorems and inference rules are needed for deduction, deductive conclusions are often discovered inductively, and their correctness is emotionally or intuitively evaluated before the formal deductive steps have been taken.

Similarly, if one examines inductive thought processes, it is found that they contain many deductive conclusions within them. In other words, inductive and deductive thought are intertwined and mutually dependent. In this respect, the isolated computerization of induction, deduction, creativity, planning, etc. is highly unnatural. Moreover, the often-used word 'association' can be thought of as partial correspondences between bits of knowledge or data. In order to achieve computer systems which can serve as flexible aids to human thought processes, it will be necessary to achieve an organic unification of various databases, knowledge bases, planning programs, visuo-spatial graphics which aid creativity, logical inference systems and data analysis systems which include the processing of analog data (Figure 10.3).

In principle, the development of such computer systems is not impossible, but it does not yet in fact exist. Some ten years ago, we began the development of such a

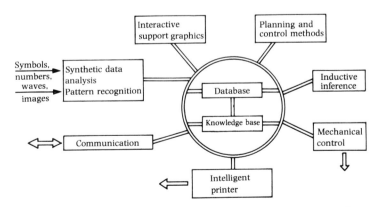

Figure 10.3 A computerized assistance system with functions relating to human needs (Kaminuma, 1988)

unified system for use as an aid in research in the field of biomedicine, but the flow of information in such a system proved to be overwhelmingly difficult.

One reason why the development of such theoretically possible systems is not further advanced is because the number of fields in which such a system is needed is surprisingly small. One field would be cardiovascular medicine. After inputting the patient's subjective complaints and the results of clinical biochemical tests, such a system would need to be capable of accepting X-ray photographs, ECG traces, ultrasound pictures and other forms of analog data. The construction of a system which could produce a quite detailed diagnosis is in fact technologically feasible. The software for such a system would, however, be expensive to develop and the hardware alone would well exceed several hundred thousand dollars. Although of extreme importance for a small number of cardiac patients, the economic usefulness of such a system would, therefore, be very limited. From a business perspective, its development does not make sense and, in any case, maintenance costs could be very high. The problem of such a system is of course but one example, but, for similar reasons, the development of potentially useful systems within narrow specialist fields has not proceeded with the pace that would be desirable.

Whatever might be said about current AI, it is clearly an experimental science. If such systems are not constructed and tested for various uses, new and valuable capabilities will not be developed, and the possibility of hitting upon exciting new techniques and methods with much wider applicability will be lost. As mentioned earlier, however, since the capabilities of individual computer components are rapidly increasing and prices decreasing correspondingly, the road toward high-speed local area networks which coherently combine such facilities is wide open and begging for adventuresome travellers!

Such unified AI systems will therefore undoubtedly emerge over the next decade. The applied themes mentioned above will in fact indirectly nurture the development of research in biocomputing. Conversely, the construction of computer systems which can efficiently absorb the results of the diverse findings of the life sciences will undoubtedly be required for technological applications in the development of biocomputing. In other words, these complex intelligent systems will simultaneously be tools employed in biocomputer research and products benefiting from insights into biocomputing.

10.5 COMPUTERIZING THE SUBCONSCIOUS MIND

10.5.1 Discovering the workings of the subconscious mind

In order to produce a truly creative computer, it will be necessary to understand the workings of the subconscious mind. The subconscious is a mental force which, by definition, cannot be brought to conscious awareness, and it cannot be easily explained in the terms we commonly use to explain the dynamics of the conscious mind. As a result, many introductory books on creativity use a variety

of literary and poetic expressions to describe the subconscious and its characteristic features without explicitly defining them. Such descriptions, however, are of
little use to the computer engineer.

Our greatest interest is of course in the implementation of digital electronic
circuitry of the subconscious mind. Since the era of McCulloch and Pitts, it has
been known that the brain has an electrical network-like character, and progress
in neuroscience has since clarified many of the structures and functions which
real brains contain. Important among these are the findings of the existence of
neurotransmitters at the neuronal synapse, the role of external stimulation in the
formation and alteration of neuronal networks in changing the strengths of
neuronal connections, the electrical potentials associated with brain activity and
so on.

We must ask what kind of model will be appropriate to relate, in a consistent
way, our knowledge of brain 'hardware' and the workings of that part of the mind
known as the subconscious. We can perhaps begin to answer the question with
current technology in terms of pattern matching and parallel processing in
imitation of right-hemisphere-like image processing. There is, for example, a
holographic theory of memory. The principles of holography are not
complex – requiring only the Fourier transformation of an image, as mentioned
earlier, and the nature of computations on such transformed data has long been a
topic of study in the field of image processing. For limited purposes, therefore, a
holographic memory system could in fact be built today (Figure 10.4).

As discussed in Chapter 9, the new Hopfield-style memory model does not
imply a unidirectional flow of information from lower to higher levels, as in the
perceptron, but implies a 'looping' of information within the network. In such a
model, information is not stored at specific addresses, so that a content-
addressable system is possible. Neural nets of all kinds show great potential for the

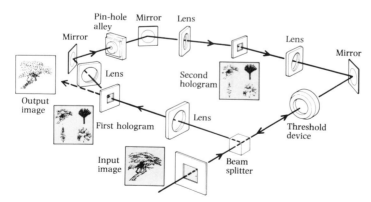

Figure 10.4 A prototype experiment of the 'optical neural computer' of Y.S. Abu-Mostafa
at Caltech. With this kind of system, the direct matching between images is possible (after
Abu-Mostafa and Psaltis, 1987)

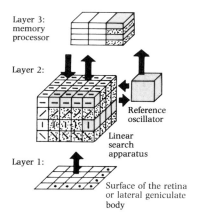

Layer 3:
memory
processor

Layer 2:

Reference
oscillator

Linear
search
apparatus

Layer 1:

Surface of the retina
or lateral geniculate
body

Figure 10.5 Schemata of the 'holonic computer', advocated by H. Shimizu (1985) in the Creative Science Inference Project

elucidation of the subconscious in so far as, for example, hidden layers have a structure or connectivity that strongly influences the output, but is not identical to it.

The workings of the subconscious mind can also be viewed as more like a chemical reaction than an electronic circuit. Moreover, sudden insight and flashes of intuition are reminiscent of the points of stability in non-linear systems. The non-linear oscillations of chemical reactions may thus provide a better model of the subconscious mind than an artificial addition of 'emotional' algorithms onto an otherwise deductive inference system. Of interest in this regard is the work of Hiroshi Shimizu and colleagues at the Department of Pharmacology of Tokyo University. They are exploring the possibilities of an information-generating computer which utilizes non-linear oscillations from the viewpoint of the 'holonic computer' and the 'synergetic computer' (Figure 10.5).

10.5.2 A three-layer model of the brain

Many years ago, Alan Turing, the inventor of the 'paper computer' – the Turing machine – proposed an unstable chemical reaction system as a model to explain the ontological development of living organisms. Thereafter, chemists discovered the so-called Jabochinsky reaction in which a spatial concentration pattern changes with time. It is said that, today, Soviet researchers are exploring the use of such chemical reaction dynamics in computer components, but clear-cut progress has not yet been reported.

M. Conrad of Wisconsin University has proposed a so-called double-dynamic system which combines digital circuitry with chemical reaction circuits (Figure 10.6). Biosensors are used for the interface between the opto-electronic circuits and the chemical reaction circuits. The opto-electronic circuits can be

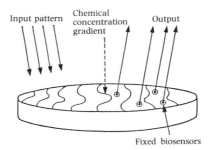

Figure 10.6 An example of a device proposed by M. Conrad (1985). Within the disk are a concentration gradient and several fixed biosensors receiving and outputting signals. The input is an analog signal; the output is converted to a Von Neumann digital signal

programmed, but the chemical reaction circuits are allowed to work semi-autonomously.

We believe, however, that the brain is more naturally modelled as a three-layered, rather than two-layered, system. The first layer is a neural network which resembles 'classical' electronic circuitry, the second layer is a chemical reaction circuit modelled after the workings of the neurotransmitters, and the third layer is a potential field, similar to that of the electromagnetic activity recorded from living brains (Figure 10.7). Of course there must be a close coupling between the neural circuits and the chemical reaction circuits, but that entire system would then be embedded in a potential field and bound to it in a non-linear fashion.

Speculation about this kind of model of course comes easy, while obtaining concrete and significant results is a more difficult matter. The first step is therefore to simulate models of this kind, and if new functions can be demonstrated in simulations, then it is enough to manipulate the simulation program without

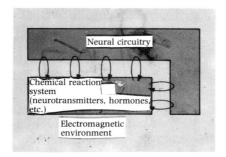

Figure 10.7 A new image of the brain – not seen solely as an electrical circuit, but coupled with an informational system dependent upon chemical transmitters and embedded within an interacting electromagnetic field

having to build a new computer. Real problems for simulation remain, however, in so far as it is difficult to simulate realistically in current computers either chemical reactions or potential fields. Moreover, since non-linear systems are as yet imperfectly understood, this type of research remains an interesting challenge for the future. In any case, biocomputer research must begin by narrowing the gap between experimental techniques and theoretical methods.

10.6 CREATIVITY AND FREEDOM

10.6.1 The essence of life is the pursuit of freedom!

Professor (Emeritus) S. Watanabe of Hawaii University – known primarily for his work in theoretical physics, information science and the philosophy of science – has argued that the essence of life is the pursuit of freedom (Watanabe, 1980). Although the lowly bacteria does not engage in particularly intelligent tasks, it has properties which even supercomputers cannot emulate, for it holds the secret of the possibility of evolution to human or even supra-human form. This is not to say that the bacteria around us today will evolve to that level of complexity, but it seems certain that bacteria-like organisms of aeons ago did in fact evolve in such a way.

In contrast, computers work by following programs. Living organisms, on the other hand, acquire programs by themselves. No matter how remarkable the task carried out by computers, the computer itself has a finite existence. In contrast, living beings have limitations on what they can now do, but there is no intrinsic limitation on their future possibilities. This difference in the potentiality of living organisms marks a great gap between organic life and inorganic, silicon-based computers.

If a computer were truly creative, it is natural to think that it must acquire a freedom similar to that of living beings. There are, however, very real limitations on how human-like we can get computers to be simply by means of innovations in software. It is not simply a matter of teaching computers how to go fishing – a difficult enough task – but we want to give them the ability to learn on their own how to go fishing!

10.6.2 Freedom and Play

The expectations we have for computers which 'think like human beings' are of machines that think autonomously and adapt to changing situations, for it is simply not possible to predict future circumstances by means of deductive reasoning, and not possible to write programs which cover all possible future circumstances.

For these reasons, researchers in AI also put great emphasis on the learning process, but a wide gulf still separates the learning of biological organisms and that of machines. For example, a computer technologist will always think with a certain objective in mind, but neither man nor animal is born with such strongly developed teleological capabilities. On the contrary, the ability to learn is acquired from the experiences called play during childhood. The ability to handle completely new circumstances is thought to be particularly nurtured in this way.

Let us assume that, some day, we will have succeeded in synthesizing life. Let us further assume that this artificial life form has a certain level of intelligence and, if given appropriate energy (nutrition), will proliferate like natural living organisms. How then would such a life form increase its intelligence? This problem is inseparable from both problems of learning and of evolution, and directly related to the age-old question of the relative importance of nature and nurture in the determination of the level of intelligence. Let us simply note that, for the development of biocomputers, this problem must be explored from a technological-engineering perspective.

There is a deep relationship between creativity, on the one hand, and play and humour, on the other. Moreover, since 'love makes men wise', the feeling of love and even religious emotions may also need to be acquired. A learning process may also be needed which is comparable to the human 'culturing of sentiments'. Thoughts such as these sound foolish or as pointless as science fiction to many engineers, but in fact serious research is being conducted today on the process of implementing such mental processes as programs, if not yet for the nurturing of artificial life forms.

Human feelings and emotions would not exist without the storage of the masses of analog data received from the five senses and recorded in the brain. The nature of that information is well beyond the capacity of current computers to store, much less process, so that attempts to give current computers emotions and feelings is little more than inserting 'conversational stories' into computers. In other words, they are not the integration of emotional processes with logical cognitive processes, but a completely independent subroutine, which may be of interest from the perspective of human psychology, but has little to do with the natural emotions.

If we are intent on developing truly human-like computers, we cannot avoid the problem of creativity, and so we must ultimately produce learning/evolving machines which have the autonomy of living organisms. Human-like intelligence is inextricably linked with actual life and is not simply an abstracted, cold and logical information processing system. The same reasoning is behind Watanabe's advocacy of a new type of computer which manipulates paradigms in a Platonic sense as symbols, combining concepts and actual objects (Watanabe, 1985). It is therefore inevitable that the ultimate aim of biocomputing becomes the development of a form of artificial life and the development of an ultra-intelligent machine which will someday transcend human intelligence.

Part Four

Plans for biocomputers and society

11

The road towards realization of biocomputers

11.1 THE INCREASING INTEREST IN BIOCOMPUTING

11.1.1 An uncharted technological continent

In Part Two of this book, we introduced several areas in the life sciences which constitute the basis for biocomputers, and in Part Three we discussed the corresponding engineering approach to such functions. We none the less believe that we may not have succeeded in communicating to the reader a sufficiently clear image of what precisely the biocomputer is and can become.

We have mentioned several times already that there is indeed no single definition of biocomputers. For convenience, we have defined it as a computer containing features characteristic of living organisms, but it must not be said that biocomputers are simply the nth generation of computer technology. On the contrary, it is probably more appropriate to speak of biocomputing as a synthetic technology emerging from the fusion of two great sciences/technologies – that is, the life sciences and computer technology or, alternatively, biotechnology and electronics.

From the bonding of these two technologies will be born many new technologies. There can be little doubt that a multitude of subtechnologies will emerge as a direct result of efforts in biocomputing: the development of organic molecules with new functions never before technologically exploited, a technology of molecular arrangement and modification, extremely large-scale circuitry, chemical sensors, high-resolution optical electronic visual sensors, parallel processing chips, molecular mechanical machines, interfaces between living organisms and electronic components, technological means for precise measurement of brain and nervous system activity and, finally, design principles (architectural principles) for exploitation in computing at levels extending from the molecule to the brain itself.

Some researchers – particularly those involved in the development of biodevices – think of biocomputers as computers built of biodevices. This indeed is one valid approach. There are others who view the biocomputer as a kind of so-called neurocomputer – a computer with an architecture similar to that of the human brain. That also is a valid approach, but we believe it best not to restrict our concept of the biocomputer to the neurocomputer or to the biochip computer

Certainly, the idea of biodevices has had impact of biocomputing, but virtually no researcher today takes the dramatic announcements of the more aggressive advocates of biodevices at face value. A mixture of optimism and scepticism i. essential. Moreover, as discussed below, the concepts of molecular devices biodevices and the biocomputer itself have already been the topics of fierce debates. Rather than a clear victor emerging from such discussions, the validity o various approaches has become clear. It has also become entirely evident that a neurocomputer containing an architecture which is revolutionary in design has not yet appeared. On the contrary, new designs have mostly been limited to variations on the multiple-processor Von Neumann configurations. Redesign from first principles on the basis of insights from the biosciences has not been achieved. Nevertheless, despite some reservations, a spirit of challenge through out the world to design computers which contain biomolecular/biochemical components and architectures which embody the known characteristics o brains and nerves is rapidly becoming apparent.

What then are the sources of such interest? The first motivation that comes to mind is a feeling of crisis concerning the maturation of semiconductor technology. Semiconductors have fortunately not yet become the source of major international, particularly Japanese–American, trade conflicts, but the growing maturity of the semiconductor industry suggests potential problems – such as those experienced over textile fibres, steel and automobiles. While a technology is still young and rapid developments are taking place, any group that can produce something new will stand a good chance in the market-place. Once the fundamental technology has matured and the bulk of the obvious, first-order applications have been tried, the advantages of bold creativity decrease, and those of corporation power increase. The potential for international trade conflicts increases correspondingly.

With regard to the interest in applied technologies, AI remains much in the news, but current AI techniques still rely heavily on the knowledge of experts to be laboriously transferred to computers. A re-evaluation of AI was therefore inevitable – and efforts were made to circumvent what has proven to be a difficult bottleneck in all expert system applications, that is, the collection and codification of expert knowledge. Many would indeed argue that both theoretical develop ments and innovations in hardware within the realm of AI have slowed to a virtual crawl.

A second source of interest in biocomputing stems from the inevitable development of biotechnology from electronic technology. Therefore, regardless of whether or not biodevices and biocomputers themselves are a target for commercial development, planning for the evolution of current techniques into fields of biotechnology is essential for survival, especially of small private enterprises. The move towards biocomputers can therefore be seen as one aspect of the restructuring of business organizations for future research and develop ment. In other words, even with some vagueness remaining with regard to the concept of biocomputing, these business and commercial considerations are the basis for involvement in biodevice and biocomputing research as a part of the growing competitiveness in biotechnology among the developed nations.

We have made use of the working hypothesis that the biocomputer is essentially the fusion of computer technology and the life sciences, but, above all else, we believe that the most important attitude for those in biocomputing is to be able to look with a fresh eye at the phenomena studied in biology. Because of the relative youth of the computer sciences, radically new thinking is not uncommon, but the maturity of the life sciences has brought with it traditional ways of thinking which could be obstacles to new developments. Particularly in view of the fact that a fundamental understanding of many of the central phenomena of life has not been obtained, there is room for a great many new ideas and eventual testing of those ideas.

11.1.2 The gap between the fifth and sixth generations

The combined project of computing and brain science is sometimes referred to as the Sixth Generation Plan. We ourselves are not deeply impressed with the generational labels for the various stages in the development of computers, but, based upon previous experience in computing, it is apparent that a considerable technological gap remains between the so-called fifth generation of machines capable of mechanical inferences and biochip computers or, in a broad sense, biocomputers.

We are trying to attract interest in research aimed at the development of biodevices and biocomputers and especially to entice young and talented researchers into this field, but we do not believe that there will be an easy transformation of research from the fifth generation to the sixth. In the present chapter, first we introduce developments in biocomputing in various countries and then we try to outline a research scenario in this field. In view of trends in computer research in general, however, we are worried by the dramatic break with current work in AI. Great efforts will be required to fill this gap between current trends and future hopes. This topic takes us beyond the scope of the present book, but because of its importance we briefly present our own thoughts on this topic towards the end of this chapter.

11.2 RESEARCH TRENDS

11.2.1 Trends in America

What interest is there outside Japan in biocomputing and related fields?

In 1974, A. Abram and M. Ratner at IBM pointed out the possibility that molecules could be controlled such that their electrons would flow unidirectionally. In the late 1970s, F. Carter of the US Naval Research Institute advocated the idea of molecular electronics devices (MEDs), and suggested a variety of specific components. Together with ideas concerning biochips, this led directly to increased interest in and funding for research in molecular devices and biodevices (Carter, 1982, 1984; Haddon and Lamola, 1985, *Molecular Electronics*). Those ideas have been central to current expectations for the practicality of eventually developing biocomputers. Carter himself has stressed that his own interests are in MEDs, as distinct from biodevices, but the essential point of all such molecular components is that they are orders of magnitude smaller than the semiconductor circuitry which is at the heart of current computer technology and yet potentially identical in terms of functional capabilities.

In this respect, a computer built of such molecular devices would conceptually be no different from current computers. Although the molecular components would in fact be organic materials based upon the carbon atom, such a computer would have no particular relation to living organisms. After advocating the concept of a so-called soliton switch, in which a molecular soliton acts as a molecular signal, Carter has become involved in its experimental verification.

In contrast, Maclea, the man responsible for the current boom in biodevices, formed a company, Gentronics, which, with military funding, has continued research on topics such as organic semiconductor lithography, biochips and the art of culturing neurons on semiconductors. This also is an example of venture capital being invested in the US in the fusion between biotechnology and computer science.

The man who made 'problem engineering' a fashionable phrase, K. Ulmar, moved from the Genex Corporation to Maryland University and became the leader of a biological devices research team within the Physicochemical Research Institute's International Frontiers Research System. He is researching techniques to make two-dimensional arrays in lipid bilayer membranes.

For this purpose, it is necessary to reconstruct artificially a portion of a natural protein. The actual technique employed is genetic engineering, by means of which a portion of the amino acid sequence of a protein is replaced by a different sequence. This technique is of an extremely general nature and is, in principle, the same as that which, for example, could allow a particular artificially altered enzyme to have a capability several hundred times stronger than the natural enzyme. In other words, it has gradually become possible to 'design' proteins with the desired structure and function. As research in this direction proceeds, it will accelerate developments in biocomputing and biodevice computing.

It is worth noting, however, that Ulmar himself has since left the National Bureau of Standards and again set up his own company, so it appears that it is not necessarily the case that all is proceeding according to plan! Prior to Ulmar's work, K. Drexler of MIT (1981) pointed out the importance of applications in protein design (see Table 11.1). He has repeatedly stressed the possibilities of not only MEDs, but also molecular mechanical devices (MMDs) (Drexler, 1982; see, for example, Figure 11.1). Moreover, he has pointed out that, in living organisms, there is indeed a wide variety of molecular machines at work.

Table 11.1 Relations between engineering technology and molecular devices (modified from Drexler, 1981)

Engineering	Function	Analogous device at the molecular level
Pillars, framework	Support	Microtubules, cellulose
Cables	Maintaining tension	Collagen
Fasteners, glues	Binding of objects	Intermolecular forces
Solenoid	Movement of objects	Morphological changes in molecules, protein, actin/myosin
Motor	Transmission of torque	Flagella
Bearings	Support for rotating objects	Σ bonds
Containers	Containment of liquids	Vacuoles
Pipes	Transport of liquids	Tubules
Pumps	Mobilization of liquids	Flagella, membrane, proteins
Conveyor belt	Movement of objects	Movement of RNA in ribosomes
Clamps	Immobilization of tools	Binding site of oxygen
Tools	Various functions	Metal complexes
Production line	Construction of complex objects	Oxygen systems, ribosomes
Numerical control system	Storage and reading of programs	Genetic system
Fuel, electricity	Source of energy	ATP

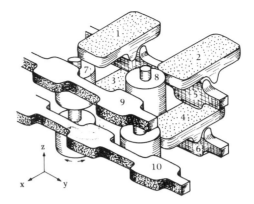

Figure 11.1 One example of Drexler's hypothetical molecular mechanisms, a random access memory (Drexler, 1984). Mobile sliders [1, 2, 3, 4] move along the x-axis. Mobile selectors [9, 10] move along the y-axis, and mobile rods [5, 6] move along the z-axis

Other researchers with somewhat more realistic goals, such as R. Metzger of Mississippi University, have been investigating organic conductors and organic semiconductors. If organic substances, which were once thought to be strictly insulating materials, can be made to act as conductors or semiconductors, possibilities would open up with regard to new computer materials and new electronics materials.

M. Conrad of Wayne State University envisages still more revolutionary computers with features characteristic of living organisms. He has emphasized the need for a global perspective for progress in this field and indeed has fostered collaborative research with Soviet researchers. The emphasis on international collaboration is a perspective which we fully endorse. Among other research efforts in molecular devices and biodevices, notable are those at the Research Triangle Park of North Carolina and the Crump Medical Technology Institute at UCLA. Carnegie-Mellon University has recently established a Study Center for Research in Molecular Devices and Arthur D. Little of think-tank fame now includes biodevices as one of his topics of research.

Bell Labs of AT & T have long been known for, among other things, neuronal research on snails, but the greatest single contribution from Bell Labs to biocomputing may well prove to be the neural net model of Hopfield and Tank – which has initiated a wave of research in related neural net models. Also of possibly profound importance is the culturing of neurons on VLSI chips, undertaken at Bell Labs by L. Jerninsky and colleagues. J. Rosen of Stanford University Medical Center is engaged in similar research, and it is likely that giant corporations such as IBM, GE and DuPont are already at work on molecular devices, biodevices and biocomputing in anticipation of commercial applications. TRW Corporation is among those computer manufacturers involved in neurocomputer research and may well be engaged in such work in relation to current efforts behind the Strategic Defence Initiative (SDI).

1.2.2 Trends in Europe and the Soviet Union

Turning our attention to Europe, most noteworthy is the fundamental research done in the United Kingdom. Let us not forget the long tradition of research there. The discovery of the helical structure of DNA took place in Cambridge, and the tradition of research in molecular biology remains strong there. Particularly noteworthy is the Medical Research Council's (MRC) Molecular Biology Research Unit, headed by S. Brenner. For more than 20 years, he has contributed to research on the ontogeny and morphogenesis of multicellular organisms, primarily that of the *Nematoda*. Also of importance have been the work in protein engineering done at Imperial College in London and that in lipid bilayer research done by G. Roberts and colleagues at Durham University.

Recently, under the auspices of University College, London, an interdisciplinary team for the design of computers modelled after the brain has been organized (Fagen, 1986), and, in direct response to the Fifth Generation Project in Japan, a new research agenda called ESPRIT was formulated in Europe. More recently, in recognition of the limitations of current symbolic processing and expert systems design, a newer project, ESPRIT II, has been advocated and awaits government funding.

In France, as well, considerable efforts have been made to advance computer research at many levels. Partially reflecting the French tendency to follow a uniquely French path, they have invested heavily in strategic industries, including nuclear power, computing and ship-building. At the Institute Nationale pour Recherche d'Industrielle et Automatiques (INRIA), they have, since the late 1970s, been researching sandwich devices containing layers of semiconductor and organic, membrane-like structures.

While retaining unique national perspectives, the advanced nations of Western Europe have continued to deepen international collaborations in high technology. Best known is, of course, the particle physics research at CERN (Geneva) and the molecular biology research at EMBL (Heidelberg). More recently, a 'European Technology Fund' has been suggested for collaboration in various aspects of information science and biotechnology throughout Europe.

As evident from the above, the interest in new technologies throughout Europe is considerable, and it is shown both by private industries and federal governments. The strength of both Europe and America remains in the fact that so much progress has already been made over the past decades in fundamental life science research. The advances in molecular biology in particular (to which, until recently, Japan had contributed so little) give Europe and America a real advantage in future developments in biocomputing. There is no greater tradition than a tradition of successful creative thinking!

11.3 PREVIOUS EVALUATIONS OF BIOCOMPUTING

11.3.1 The conclusions of the UCLA Conference

Thus far, technological developments in Japan have succeeded primarily by formulation of a clear-cut goal and the organization of a large team which can be motivated to work with enthusiasm towards a particular goal. In the developing race for biocomputers, however, there are countless possible targets, and the focus needed for such a strategy is missing. What is therefore of importance is not the final goal, but the approach itself, even if the actual target is not fixed and final.

In Japan, there are many researchers who work efficiently in stages towards a goal which has been determined by others, but there are far fewer independent researchers who set their own worthwhile goals and develop their own approach towards those goals. Without question, research in biocomputing will not proceed simply as an exercise in technological development, but will require much creative research. At least in Japan the distinction between scientific research and technological development is often vague. Certainly, technological development can proceed to some extent under the guidance of a superior management team showing typically Japanese talents for 'management', but the management of scientific research requires different sensibilities and talents. In this sense, involvement in biocomputing will require genuine changes in the structure of management itself. Moreover, management will need to survey and evaluate previous projects with care and examine opinions critical of Japanese management in other areas. The essential issue is whether or not previous techniques will suffice for the development of a new technology during its early, creative stages. Of course, once the fundamental technology has matured, then tried-and-tested styles of management are likely to be reliable, but it is less clear that those same techniques are optimal for a technology in its explosive early days.

An important evaluation of molecular devices, biodevices and biocomputing can be found in a 'Report of a Conference on Molecular Computing' held at the Crump Institute for Medical Engineering, UCLA, in October 1983. The conference was organized by Eugene Yates and funded by the US National Science Foundation. Although some years have passed, its main conclusions are still of relevance today.

1. There are as yet no proven, fundamental, quantum mechanical or thermodynamic limits on computation. Theoretically, computation can be logically reversible and both non-dispersive and non-dissipative (thermodynamically reversible) with respect to energy.

2. There are practical physical limitations on erasing answers, on getting answers out of computers, on validating computations, and on extreme miniaturization of silicon-transister-based binary switching networks. However, current technology has not come close to those limits. The planned further miniaturization is feasible.

3. The so-called 'fifth generation' of digital computers will be based on silicon (or germanium or gallium arsenide) technology and will operate with logics and switches similar to those now used, though the new 'chips' will be faster, far more densely packed, and arranged in the newer architectures favouring more parallel processing and non–Von Neumann tree structures or ring-like data flow architectures. No single architecture will be universally suitable for all tasks.

4. Not all analog computation can be efficiently imitated in present-day digital computers. There are classes of problems for which analog computation is inherently superior (at least in speed, if not in accuracy). It is only for this class of problems that chemically based computer designs ultimately might be technologically interesting and useful. Problems for which analog computation might be, at least in some respects, inherently superior include the following:

(a) pattern recognition
(b) correlations
(c) convolutions
(d) context-dependent decisions
(e) solutions based upon incomplete knowledge or information
(f) efficient use of resources in parallel processing
(g) computation combined with microscopic chemical-sensing
(h) reliability in the face of component error or failure
(i) self-repair
(j) evolvability
(k) learning

(At the molecular level, 'analog', and 'digital' may not have clear referents.)

5. Shortcomings of analog computation include the following facts.

(a) Analog computers are not structurally programmable in the powerful sense that digital computers are.
(b) Analog operations do not execute a two-valued logic (which is the only logic we understand well mathematically). Analog computation depends on the dynamics of the computer instead of on simple, binary information as used by digital computers (whose switching dynamics are suppressed). This dependence on dynamics makes analog computation potentially more difficult to understand and less accurate than digital computation, because analog computation may be based upon very complicated dynamic or kinetic unit processes.
(c) Contemporary commercial analog computers are not well miniaturized, and a large stock of spare parts is required.

6. Chemically based analog computers will not compete effectively with

current or foreseeable digital computer technology with respect to computation for which digital computers are already well suited.

7. The brain is an analog computer. It invents two-valued logics, Turing machines, switching networks and digital computers, but resembles none of these in its own mechanisms or operations. Digital computers are biological artefacts (as are all machines); they differ from all other machines because they can imitate all other machines (except perhaps some analog computers – see above), including machines of their own class.

8. There may be an advantage (for special purposes) in using inherently three-dimensional (> 2-D) computational elements (e.g. the active site of an enzyme, or the recognition site of a cell membrane receptor, or a cellular microtubule) for analog computation. However, no clear examples were found, and many or most operations in > 2-D can be treated in lower-dimensional processes in simulations. Thus, the advantage of higher dimensional elements is not clear for digital computation. Furthermore, digital computation will continue to emphasize two-valued logics and obtain the gain in reliability attendant on the use of two-dimensional arrays of devices limited to only two stable states. The circuits on digital computer 'chips' are now only accidentally three-dimensional and operationally might be said to be 2- $+\varepsilon$-dimensional. (There are some designs using 3-D lattice structures in computer networks.) In contrast, however, new analog computers could, in principle, use dynamically rich elements having multiple states or which are describable by continuous functions, and some of these elements will depend intrinsically on their three-dimensionality for computation. The carbon-based world of biochemistry already provides numerous examples of extremely effective miniaturization and computation using mechanisms that are intrinsically three-dimensional, but these may be represented in simulations of lower dimension. The biological operations are not necessarily continuous, and discrete-time (or even discrete-state) simulations may be closer to the original than usually thought.

9. Any proposed design for a new computer architecture, based upon new materials or new styles of analog computing, ultimately must pass a fabrication test, i.e. eventually we must specify the means of constructing the device. Designers and digital computers now meet the fabrication test, and anyone proposing a chemically based analog computer will have to do the same.

10. 'Molecular electronics' has at least three different aspects.

   (a) Use of crystalline or semicrystalline materials, some of biological origin (e.g. proteins, nucleic acids) as monolayer films deposited on silicon or other suitable substrates as masks for exceedingly fine-grained photolithography of otherwise conventional binary switching computer networks. (This approach is perhaps more properly designated 'molecular technology'.)

(b) Use of carbon-based (or transition-metal-based) chemistry to create molecular switches, wires and logical gates that would serve as microscopic elements in an otherwise standard digital computer. The chemicals would take advantage of three aspects of electromagnetic phenomena: electron flow (or, perhaps, wave propagation of charge by solitons); molecular (electron cloud) conformational changes that can produce mechanical or informational effects (as in the case of allosteric enzymes that adjust their dynamic, catalytic action according to whether or not a ligand different from the substrate is bound at a 'recognition', control site different from the catalytic site); and quantum mechanical electron tunnelling.

(c) Use of electronic, conformational changes such as those of microscopic biochemical operations as new kinds of elements in a novel analog computer.

Item (a) above – molecular technology – can be tested on its merits, case-by-case, as part of conventional silicon-transistor technology. It needs no special attention here. Item (b) presents some new ideas, including proposals for the synthesis of new carbon compounds. This activity should be considered as basic science, not yet as applied science, and should be supported as such. After certain demonstrations are made (such as the reality of soliton propagation of charge down conjugated carbon chains in a nearly non-dissipative fashion), then this aspect of molecular electronics may be ready for a major investment as applied science technology. It is not yet that mature. Such work could become important in the future, and the basic science aspects need support now, in the fashion of the usual support for basic science – cautious but hopeful. Item (c) presents the greatest challenge, perhaps, and may appear farthest from realization. But this situation could change with the maturation of various emerging technologies such as immobilized enzyme techniques.

11. Biological systems have some operations that are astounding from an engineering, technical viewpoint. These serve as proofs that carbon-based, chemical analog computation does work. However, we are so far from understanding how to domesticate biological operations at the subcellular, cellular or multicellular organism level (except crudely, as, literally, in milking cows, or, metaphorically, in 'milking' recombinant *E. coli*, yeasts or mammalian cells in culture) that we cannot now or in the near future expect to use biological materials or components or whole organisms regularly as analog computers in a technological setting. The recombinant DNA organism and the hybridoma cell are the new domesticated organisms, and they perform analog operations (dynamic functions), given a technologically inspired, carbon-chemical, informational input. We program the recombinant organism (rewire its patch board) and have a modest understanding of how it then executes its dynamic operations. We know how to harvest some of the output. In this case, we are using the recombinant

organisms as factories to which we can give orders, but we cannot build the factories or specify all their internal operations. (Neither do we understand the endocrinological and metabolic basis of lactation in cows. It is not trivial that technological advances can occur without full understanding of underlying processes and mechanisms. Thus, a chemically based analog computer design could arise before we know what we are doing in detail).

12. Biological systems represent the chief inspiration for chemically based analog computer designs. If a technologically useful analog computer ever arises based on chemical processes, it will probably arise out of advances in biochemistry, molecular biology or cell biology. It may even consist of the first synthesis of a proto-organism in the laboratory. Whoever does that will probably not claim that he has built a chemically based computer (though that is what he will have done). In any case, that achievement will most likely occur just for the fun of it – not out of a desire to beat digital computers at problem solving.

11.3.2 Conditions for the practical use of new devices

Even assuming that molecular devices, biodevices and the resulting construction of a biocomputer are technologically possible, it is impossible to say today whether or not such systems would be a practical possibility. In this regard, it is of some relevance to consider the comments of researchers who had some contact with the development of the Josephson devices at IBM's Watson Research Institute some three decades ago.

There are two phases of development of such devices. The first is the stage in which the operational principles involved are confirmed. The second, more practical stage is to enter quantitative production. In this phase, there are three conditions that a new device must satisfy. First, at the future time when such a new device will be ready for production, it must be more capable than present-day (in this case, silicon-based) devices. The second condition is that the new devices can be partially integrated with current technology. Since a new technology cannot simply replace all current technology, it is essential that it can be combined with the accumulated successes of current technology. The third condition concerns how the new technology will contribute to improvements in the capabilities of entire systems. Even if a particular device is extremely rapid, if it must wait for slower, established technologies in order to work, i.e. if it cannot be integrated into the whole 'package', its contribution will be small.

Probably the single most commonly expressed doubt about biocomputing is that, when devices are reduced to an ultramicroscopic level, it will still be necessary to join them to the relatively macroscopic devices of current computers. Indeed, current ideas concerning the interfacing problem are far less developed than those concerning the devices themselves. Similar comments could be made concerning the architecture of biocomputers, and it should not be forgotten that current computer technology stands on the shoulders of massive contributions to computer software. A radically new computer architecture, such as the biocomputer, must somehow be joined to the already existing body of hardware and software successes. In other words, in order to make good progress in fundamental research for new technological developments, it is necessary not to develop a single technology, but to have a balanced and strategically organized management of such developments.

11.3.3 The relationship with competing technologies

Research in biocomputing is of course an attempt at realizing the ultimate goals of future computers, but there are in fact other, competing technologies also under development. First of all, there are the so-called 'post-silicon' semiconductor devices, some of which, such as the gallium arsenide semiconductors, are already in use, and others, such as Josephson devices using ceramic superconducting materials, are the focus of feverish activity. Clearly, for the further utilization and exploitation of current computer technology, these developments using inorganic semiconductor chips have an inevitable superiority to biodevices. There is, quite simply, no interfacing problem.

Secondly, there is optical computing. Again, seen from the perspective of materials and devices, optical computers do not require a major change from today's electronic technology. Electronics and optical technologies are first cousins, or perhaps even complementary to one another. For this reason, it is unlikely that there will be serious compatibility problems between today's electronic computers and tomorrow's optical computers. Starting with the laser, research in photonics has been and continues to be robust. Significant future progress can be expected, and there is a high probability that optical devices containing sensors and massive parallel computing capabilities will come into use, particularly for SDI-style detection, discrimination and attack of military targets. Such technology – in both military and civilian contexts – will soon be at a level for practical applications.

In contrast to the above technologies, those of the biodevices, biochips and biocomputers, and especially the molecular devices, are of a completely different character when it comes to the manufacturing process. For this reason, when biodevices and biochips eventually hit the market-place, the fact that they deviate from the basic principles of silicon and even post-silicon technology means that some time will be required before they can be incorporated into functional computer systems.

Even if we were to assume that biodevices will emerge within ten years, at the beginning it will probably be possible to combine them with current computer technology only in rather limited ways – for example, as artificial sensors. Therefore, as the technology of biocomputing matures, its greatest impact will probably first be in areas other than computing itself, such as in the development of medical products and therapeutic technologies.

The significance of these anticipated developments in biocomputing is that, at least with regard to short-term developments in hardware, biocomputing is not a technology which will compete directly with post-silicon semiconductors, superconducting devices or optical computing. Moreover, from the viewpoint of computer architectures, research in biocomputing (specifically, neurocomputing) is likely to precede and act as a guide to architectural developments in optical computing and new inorganic semiconductor chips. In biocomputer research, the question 'How do living brains compute?' is of extreme importance, and answers to that question will have great influence not only on the design ideas behind biochip computers, but also on all other future computers.

11.4 A MAP OF RESEARCH DEVELOPMENTS

11.4.1 Multiple goals

A distinctive feature of biocomputer research is the fact that it has several goals. Because it is perceived as an uncharted technological continent, several outposts must be established and future developments cultivated from there. A rough map of the terrain is therefore needed, but clearly a complete map is impossible since little exploration of the continent has yet been completed. Let us draw a crude map of possible progress in biocomputing and then try to draw up plans for the growth and proliferation of the many themes within biocomputing.

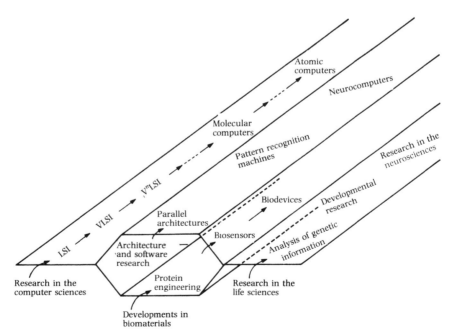

Figure 11.2 The road to realization of biocomputers. Biocomputers will gradually emerge from the convergence of four main streams of research: computer science, life science, architecture/software research and developments in biodevices

As can be seen in Figure 11.2, between the two fundamental pathways of technological development lie the goals related to biocomputing. On the right of the biocomputing pathway lie the developments of high-density, large-scale integration within electronics. On the left, lie the developments in the life sciences. Along both the electronics and the life sciences pathways there lies a variety of midway, short- and medium-term objectives. The exchanges between these stations in the two pathways is the region defined as biocomputing. Biocomputing is not only the interdisciplinary intersection of the life and computer sciences, however; it is also their complex web of possible connections. In other words, as one research objective is reached, its results penetrate throughout the entire technological network and influence the realization of other research objectives. Both researchers and managers must focus on specific objectives and strategies by having an unobstructed view of their own goals within this complex network of future technologies.

Let us briefly speculate about a possible scenario of biocomputing research.

11.4.2 The road to higher-density LSI

The main pursuit in computer developments thus far has unquestionably been the competition for higher-density semiconductor LSI, i.e. greater capabilities of individual computer chips. The sequence of developments has been from large-scale integration, to very large-scale integration, to ultra-large-scale integration – a continuing increase in the density of electronic components per square centimetre of chip. Let us abbreviate the future of this trend as V^nLSI.

As LSI densities increase, the width of the macroscopic physical connections among chip components naturally decreases, and there is a physical limit to the degree of such decreases. This 'wall' is not dependent upon limitations in technological cleverness, but is a limitation inherent in the physical basis of matter. Before reaching that absolute barrier, however, there are technological challenges at different levels, ranging from the techniques needed to increase the size of crystal growth to methods for producing molecular devices whose theoretical structure is understood, but whose realization remains problematical. At whatever level, as the scale gets smaller, there emerges a need for the appropriate technology for the design of molecules, and their alignment, assembly and control.

For such technology, answers to various questions must be found. Will there be a need for the controlled synthesis or construction of linear informational sequences, such as are found in proteins and the nucleic acids? Or will it suffice to rely on a physico-chemical process, such as that involved in the formation of lipid bilayer membranes? Will the approach of molecular devices be similar to that of biodevices? There is also the need to study the question of whether or not, for the integration of a certain kind of molecular structure, the interaction of molecules with specificity for one another, such as is seen in the immune response, will be effective.

By whatever path taken, progress in V"LSI will be based upon lithography techniques – but the reduction of the dimensions of current lithography methods will probably not suffice. Revolutionary techniques are required. Nevertheless, in so far as lithography is used, there is no conceptual discontinuity between current semiconductor technology and the world of MEDs. On the contrary, this is the inevitable direction of technological progress in semiconductors.

Already there has been speculation concerning the possibilities for sub-molecular devices that would transcend those at the molecular level. In 1985, the theoretical physicist, Richard Feynman, emphasized his belief that there are in fact few physical limitations to the speed of computations. At an invited lecture entitled 'Computing Machines of the Future' in Japan, he argued the following.

1. One bit of information can be stored in one atom.
2. Since there is a constant relationship between the energy loss associated with computation and the time required for computation, the heat efficiency can be increased indefinitely.
3. There is only the limit of the speed of light in transmitting signals. Feynman pointed out that, although it is of course true that such theoretical speculation has no impact on today's technology, nevertheless from the perspective of natural laws, there is considerable scope for the continued miniaturization of computers. So, following an era of molecular devices, it is natural to consider the possibility of 'atomic devices' and 'atomic computers'!

Let us reiterate that no one is seriously proposing the development of atomic computers next year, but the important message that Feynman has conveyed is that the conceptual boundaries which most of us have implicitly assumed may well be illusory. Developments in the direction of atomic computers and biocomputers depend as much on conceptual freedom as on technological breakthroughs.

11.4.3 The pathway of the life sciences

Within the life sciences, there are two intertwined pathways. The first is the technology which makes use of living organisms as 'structural models' (in Japanese, *mono*, literally, 'thing' such as a physical object). One example of such research is the use of the cytochrome electron transport system and bacterio-rhodopsin as photoelectric conversion devices. If we define biodevices as information devices which have biological molecules or similar molecules as their basic material, then they all fall within this general trend. The same can be said for the molecular mechanical devices.

The second pathway is the technology which utilizes biological organisms not as physical objects, but as 'functional models' (in Japanese, *koto*, literally, 'thing' such as a conceptual entity). In other words, this is learning about the mechanisms of biology for technological utilization, that is, bio-architecture. Triggered largely by Hopfield's neural net model, this is currently a topic of great interest. The neural (neuro-) computer is one example of developments along this path. Such models are easily simulated on today's computers and hardware built with equivalent electronic circuitry.

No matter how complex the brain is, if it is indeed an informational system which can be described in terms of the flow of signals in a network, then – questions of efficiency aside – it can be fully simulated on today's computers. It is possible to consider it as a massively parallel cellular automaton machine.

We have some doubt, however, whether it is wise to think of the 'physical object' and the 'informational model' aspects of living organisms in complete isolation. For example, if we wish to include some of the most important features of living organisms – such as self-organization and growth – then we certainly must study developmental biology and the morphogenesis of biological organisms. The interaction between energy and information is of the utmost importance.

The distinctive feature of the 'computations' undertaken by living organisms is the fact that a uni-dimensional signal sequence is used to control its three-dimensional development. In contrast, a computer functions essentially as a uni-dimensional signal sequence in control of a uni-dimensional sequence of actions. This difference is the difference between an organic information machine and an inorganic one. Once we have fully understood the essence of this difference, it may well become possible to add growth and developmental capabilities to today's computers. This is an exciting possibility which should not be dismissed out of hand. It would indeed be a breakthrough into biocomputing! Conversely, without this dimensional approach, the functions of a biocomputer could be simulated reasonably well by current computers – again neglecting issues of efficiency and massive information storage. Therefore, it is extremely unlikely that such a uni-dimensional 'biocomputer' would be capable of performing functions which serial, silicon computers cannot.

It follows that the ways in which a linear sequence of information is transformed into a three-dimensional structure and reflected in functions operating in four dimensions must be studied at various levels in biological systems. Such research must include:

1. investigation of how the uni-dimensional information of DNA is expressed in the structures and functions of three-dimensional proteins and their functioning in time;
2. study of how the regulation of uni-dimensional information in the process of ontological development is translated into the three- and four-dimensional structures of cellular aggregates;
3. particularly, investigation of neuronal and brain development allowing for language and purposeful movement.

11.4.4 The development of high-level computer systems

The computer itself is an extremely important tool for the study of living organisms as information machines. It first use is for research into the structure and dynamics of macromolecules and of the molecules which interact with macromolecules. Computer systems designed for this purpose are referred to as molecular graphics or molecular modelling systems, and have already become one of the basic tools of research in chemistry.

For the molecules of life, however, what is of importance is not merely the three-dimensional coordinates of their atoms – as obtained in X-ray crystallography – but the sequence of the information stored in the molecular structure. The sequence of nucleotide bases, which is the fundamental unit of information in DNA, constitutes the genetic information, and the sequence of amino acids, which is the fundamental unit of information in protein, determines the three-dimensional shape and function of proteins. In recent years, the techniques for determining such so-called 'primary' sequences have advanced rapidly, and valuable data of this kind have begun to accumulate.

For the administration and effective use of such data, a different type of computer has also become an essential tool: a relational database with the capability for statistical analysis. Current developments include pattern recognition, dynamic programming and inference techniques which can be applied to the fundamental sequence data.

In research on the ontology and morphogenesis of the nervous system, computer graphics and simulations will undoubtedly prove effective (see Figure 11.3). For example, it is thought that graphical display of cellular aggregates – similar to those available for molecular structures – will be useful in the discovery of the rules of structural aggregation of cellular components.

Similar to such techniques, there are also methods for reconstructing the three-dimensional structure of macromolecules and organelles from electron microscopical sections. One of the pioneers of molecular graphics, S. Leventhal of Columbia University, has developed a computer system which deduces the higher-order structure of protein molecules from their primary sequences. He is also investigating the three-dimensional reconstruction of nervous tissue using the same system. T. Fujida of Kyoto Medical University is also involved in the construction of a graphics system for studying the anatomical development of the brain.

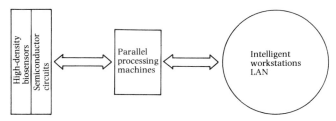

Figure 11.3 Will the first step towards the biocomputer be a parallel computer system capable of processing huge amounts of data by means of high-density protein biosensors?

Computers have long been used for the simulation of neural nets and the modelling and time series analysis of biological signals, such as the electroencephalogram. In the former case, the simulation is not based upon known principles of neuronal activity, so much as on a mimicking of the final result. In other words, the macroscopic phenomenon is simulated, not the microscopic one. In the near future, however, it can be expected that simulation of neuronal circuitry, the structure of which is empirically known, will begin.

For the development of high-level computer systems, such as outlined above, the close cooperation of specialists in the life sciences and the computer or information sciences is essential. Chances for such collaboration are also chances for further progress in defining the scope and meaning of 'biocomputing'. That is, the computer is simultaneously a powerful tool for studying the information processing of biological systems, and the further development of such tools provides opportunities for further dialogue between specialists in disciplines related to biocomputing.

11.4.5 From AI to biocomputing

Time is needed before sharp definitions of biocomputers and how they differ from current computers are obtained. Indeed, we believe that one significant step forward for biocomputer research would be the clear establishment of the cross-over points between life science research, on the one hand, and the high-density circuitry of semiconductors, on the other.

A second need is to establish research objectives which would bridge the gap between biocomputer research and AI research, which today remains extremely active. With regard to the latter need, the following themes are of importance.

1. The technology to follow expert systems: for example, network AI, the VLSI of an inference machine, creation of AI techniques for pattern recognition.
2. The higher-level processing of visual information: for example, high-resolution visual sensors and real-time data processing, flexible pattern matching search techniques (which will allow acoustic and visual patterns stored as analog data on optical disks to be rapidly searched), holographic search techniques, means for rapid input and output or partial information concerning a three-dimensional object.
3. Ultra-high resolution and flexible mechanical control which approaches that of biological systems, interfacing techniques for biological objects and electronic devices, and sensors which can be embedded in living organisms.
4. There may be no immediate need for computer systems that can fully understand natural language, but there is a definite need for computer systems which are in greater harmony with the needs of man – for example, visual displays which do not induce eye fatigue and electronic materials which allow recycling or pollution-free disposal.

11.4.6 High-quality analog devices

The next step will perhaps be the development of high-quality analog devices which can handle the data provided by biosensor devices. If we assume that a biodevice is simply a signal conversion apparatus, a high-quality analog device is merely a circuit which allows computers to use that information in their central processing units and store it in memory. This device would differ from current inorganic devices in that it would be made of organic molecules, would have extremely high density and would produce little or no heat. We also have hopes for self-detection of faults, self-repair and even self-organization, but such capabilities remain in the distant future.

It is also unlikely that complete computer systems will be made of biodevices. We should probably first consider the development of 'intelligent sensors' which handle large volumes of information from biosensor devices.

Even if it proves possible to build computers using such biodevices, it will not be possible at the start to design a computer which works like the living brain or nervous system. At the best, we will be able to build computers which have certain characteristics which resemble real brains in terms of parallel, asynchronous, distributed processing. We will probably have to wait for the next generation of computers to follow for the emergence of an actual biochip computer which has genuine biological features owing to the functioning of biodevices.

11.4.7 Artificial life and artificial intelligent life

Looking a further generation ahead, the development of artificial (and artificial intelligent) life forms will require considerable progress in the life sciences to obtain an understanding of the phenomena of ontology and morphogenesis. Comparable advances in the synthesis and control of the nucleic acids and proteins (or their artificial counterparts) will also be needed. Such understanding may well lead to artificial systems which are capable of autonomous, high-level self-assembly from fundamental units following a masterplan, similar to the self-assembly and self-replication of multicellular animal organisms. This would properly be called 'artificial life'.

Once the development of artificial life which resembles organic life forms has been achieved, then, by means of simulations which reproduce the long history of biological evolution artificially in a short period of time, it may be relatively easy to push the primitive artificial life forms in directions appropriate to their development of higher intelligence.

What becomes an important problem here is the role of the environment. It is uncertain, in the case of man, how great a role the environment has played in the rapid evolution of intelligence, but it is a factor which cannot be ignored from the outset. In other words, the living forms we know today may have become the way they are not merely because of dramatic changes in the genetic information they contain, but because of a complex interaction between that information and the external world which impinges on the organism – the influences of both nature and nurture. If the mechanisms of such interaction were known, it would be possible to control living forms, lead them through an accelerated 'evolution' of their own, and discover ways to raise the intelligence of artificial life. If this can be accomplished, we will have techniques available to guide evolution and to improve existing life forms to future forms, as well as to accelerate the development of intelligence in artificial life forms.

Clearly, the ultimate form of the fusion between the computer and the life sciences will have extremely important consequences for humankind, but it is impossible to know if this will be realized in the 21st century or even several centuries later. If the age of biocomputing is in fact several hundreds of years away, then current speculations about atomic devices and atomic computers, as well as artificial life, artificial intelligent life, and techniques for simulating evolution, must be looked upon today as little more than intellectual games. Nevertheless, if the electronics industry were to get seriously involved in fundamental research in the life sciences for such purposes – perhaps merely as a means of survival in the competitive atmosphere of commercial business – there are real possibilities for such roads to open quite rapidly.

11.5 THE NEW STYLE OF RESEARCH DEVELOPMENTS

11.5.1 Equal partnership

Research developments in biocomputers are of a fundamentally different nature from previous computer technology projects. Where other projects might be compared with urban redevelopment, biocomputing is the exploration of a new continent. What this means is that, instead of building on the basic techniques and human resources which have produced computer progress thus far, it will be necessary to establish a new style of research. In this sense, it may be necessary for the researchers and research organizations which will be involved in biocomputing to experience a kind of 'culture shock'. Instead of falling back on the methodologies and the 'old boy network' of today's computer technology, a difficult but essential fusion with the life sciences and biotechnology must be achieved.

The existing 'cultural divide' between computing and biology is easily pointed out, but less easily bridged. Deep and serious exchanges between these two disciplines depend ultimately on people willing and able to think in both worlds. Today, the people who will participate in the emergence of biocomputing are few in number; they can be found in only two disciplines: computer specialists who are in fields related to the life sciences, and life scientists who are affiliated with computer institutes and departments. Unfortunately, there is as yet no truly 'cosmopolitan' discipline or even academic conferences in which both the life and computing sciences are given equal emphasis.

For example, in Japan there is the Medical Engineering Society, which meets annually and discusses topics at the boundary between medicine and engineering. There, computer and electronics equipment is displayed as tools for medical diagnosis and treatment and, as a consequence, reports of research results are primarily concerned with medicine, subdivided according to medical discipline. There are, however, no themes of common scientific interest and no explication of potentially unifying technological methodologies. On the contrary, such conferences are designed for dialogue between engineers who make (and sell) tools and medical doctors who use (and buy) them.

In general, for medical doctors and biologists, computers are still seen as convenient tools which (may) help in their own work. On the other hand, for computer specialists, computers are objects to be sold and used by others for various applied purposes. Clearly, in this field there is nothing which approaches 'equal partnership' of scientists; it is only the relationship of the user and the used or the buyer and the seller. If the challenge of biocomputing is to start in earnest, this traditional relationship between biology and computing cannot be prolonged. A new partnership of collaboration – both as a science and as a technology must be born. Indeed, establishment of such a partnership may well be a necessary prerequisite for meeting the challenge of the biocomputer continent.

11.5.2 Strategies in computing

We have already discussed the fact that in approaching biocomputers from the life sciences, a 'support system' for advanced computer systems – including pattern recognition, AI, high-resolution graphics and so on – will be needed. In other words, the successes and failures of research will depend heavily upon how such computer systems and the specialists who use them are developed. Unfortunately, most of the universities and public research institutes in Japan do not yet have a clear vision of computer systems for support of strategic research developments. Here, private enterprises – particularly in the pharmaceutical and chemical industries – are further advanced, and sophisticated computer systems are rapidly being installed. But it does not necessarily mean that the education and promotion of the specialists and theorists needed to maintain, develop and utilize such systems are being pursued with sufficient vigour.

If such specialists were given the opportunity for 'equal partnership' research, we could anticipate a faster rate of growth in both the life sciences and biotechnology. For example, we might then expect the emergence of an understanding of the molecular switching mechanism which controls genetic information and the interrelationships of nucleic acids and proteins. Our understanding of the chemical computer of life phenomena would also undoubtedly advance.

There are indeed increasing numbers of examples where the participation in the life sciences of theoreticians in computing, biophysics and chemistry has been welcomed. But it is unfortunately the case that the participation of scientists coming from the computer end of biocomputing is often sought for service to the scientific ends of the life sciences, and they are not considered to be fully equal partners.

11.5.3 International cooperation

Both the MITI Biodevices Project and the New Devices Project of the Ministry of Science and Technology presume the participation of private industry. These types of organizations for research and development, which include public and private organizations, research institutions, and universities, are likely to play a larger and larger role in biocomputer developments. Corresponding increases in the freedom of thought and action of researchers and reductions in the number of bureaucratic rules, regulations and red tape are also needed. Rules are therefore needed to free researchers from as much of the time-consuming paperwork as possible, and to keep capable researchers involved directly in research activities. With regard to the proposed evolution of research as well, the participation of people outside established institutions would be of value – to open the discussion of ideas as widely as possible.

The development of international collaboration is as important as the collaboration between private industry and public institutions. Already, researchers from abroad are involved in Japanese projects, and this should also be possible for biocomputer research as well. Bolder efforts in this direction are, however, needed. For example, funding of research groups abroad that are involved in basic biological research should be considered, as well as the sponsoring of international conferences on biocomputing. Conversely, with regard to the technology of the developmental phase, it should be possible to get foreign industries to participate and invest in this Japanese project. With regard to the research environment, so-called 'research parks' are clearly the ideal.

Seen in this light, the research and development of the biocomputer may provide an opportunity to introduce a new style of management into Japanese industry – where experience has shown that the Japanese tend to cluster into exclusive, tightly knit groups which often realize well-formulated objectives, but tend to shun cross-talk and input from circles outside those immediately concerned.

11.6 THE EFFECTS OF LARGE-SCALE PROJECTS

11.6.1 Ideas on larger-scale international collaboration in science and technology

We believe that research in biocomputing must proceed in parallel with basic research as its trunk, and the applied research which uses the results of that science as its branches and leaves. What can be difficult here is determining what basic research is and whether or not it has an appropriate position in relation to developmental research with clear objectives and timetables.

At the Twelfth Summit Meeting of the developed nations held in Tokyo in May 1986, Japan advocated ideas concerning the international collaboration in large-scale science and technology for the 21st century. At the heart of these ideas was the feeling that mankind must make significant strides in basic science on man and nature in order to strengthen the technologies which will allow survival in harmony with nature.

The scale of this specific research project was 100 billion yen over a period of 12 years, with Japan paying half that amount. In addition to this project, MITI announced the Human Frontiers Project, and the Ministry of Science and Technology announced the Man–Nature Science Project. Within these projects the elucidation of the human nervous system and brain, and its technological exploitation is an important theme.

Although the ultimate aims of the Human Frontier Project have since become somewhat less clear, if such a large-scale project proceeds with its stated goals, it should have a large influence on the direction of research in biocomputing. Because the various disciplines within the basic life sciences will interact with one another, progress in one area will inevitably have beneficial effects in other fields. The problem then is mainly one of efficiency and, here, even with a large financial commitment, it is hard to be optimistic.

11.6.2 Deciphering the human genome

An idea that was suggested at the time when the Human Frontiers Project was formulated was the deciphering of the entire human genome. This idea has since become a target for debate not only in Japan, but also in North America and Europe. At issue are both the practicality and the significance of such work. The two basic perspectives on how to approach the human genome are the top-down approach and the bottom-up approach. Would it be better first to construct a map of each chromosome individually, and then to undertake the sequencing of the individual genes? Or would it be better to construct a library of gene fragments (by cloning techniques) and proceed bottom-up to reconstruct whole chromosomes? In terms of significance, again views are polarized. Some maintain that the project is politically and scientifically important, while others argue that it has virtually no scientific meaning.

It is currently estimated that the total work involved in such a project entails about 30 000 man years of work. At the US Department of Energy, 5 million dollars have already been set aside for mapping three human chromosomes, and the Department anticipates the completion of a rough map of all 24 chromosomes within a period of five years. One argument against this endeavour, as expressed by K. Ohno, is that some 98% of the human DNA sequence is known to be meaningless, so that the complete mapping task means a great deal of labour and only a small return.

11.6.3 The merits and demerits of large projects

Engineers and especially scientists have an instinctive fear of scientific research that has been brought into the political arena. If it is a technological problem, even an objective such as sending a man to the moon, scientists know that a sufficient investment of human and financial resources will lead to its achievement, but the same confidence does not always apply to problems that are purely scientific, rather than essentially engineering.

No matter how idealistic a national plan may be, there is no guarantee that, for example, even a single mathematical equation can be solved. But once the science is understood, the technology will follow directly. And for this reason the textbooks in physics do not even mention Thomas Edison, the developers of the atomic weapons or the planners of the Apollo mission. The great science which made those technological achievements possible preceded them and was undertaken by a different group of people.

In America in the 1960s, the Apollo Project to send a man to the moon was devised; in the 1970s a plan to conquer cancer in ten years was also drawn up and heavily funded. It is no accident that the former plan succeeded, whereas the latter failed – for the scientific foundations for attacking cancer at that time were simply too weak. Particularly with regard to technological developments, it is a historical fact that large-scale projects have often been carried through according to plan. In the 20th century, there are abundant examples where a large amount of manpower has been mobilized for scientific/technological purposes, leading to significant breakthroughs.

One such project was the Manhattan Project to develop the atomic bomb. This not only lit the fuse to the nuclear arms race, but also opened the road to the use of nuclear energy for peaceful purposes. Another such project was NASA's Apollo Project to reach the moon. This involved the twin technologies of landing on the moon and development of the ICBM to carry nuclear arms – both of which grew out of the rocket technology project of Nazi Germany. That same technology is today an essential part of the global communications network of artificial satellites. Provided that we are talking about technological development from a firm scientific foundation, there is historical proof that, with sufficient money and manpower, goals that might not have even been imagined until recently can be reached. In this perspective, it is clear that the mapping or sequencing of the human genome is a technologically feasible objective. The question then becomes one of the validity of the objective and the selection of the best means of achieving it.

The same questions must be asked of biocomputing.

12

The impact of the biocomputer

12.1 THE RIPPLE EFFECTS OF RESEARCH DEVELOPMENTS

12.1.1 The disappearance of the gap between computers and living organisms

In this chapter we will consider the influences of biocomputers on society. Let us first discuss the ripple effects of research developments in biocomputing. Throughout this book, we have taken the position that biocomputers can be usefully defined as computers which have certain characteristics of living organisms. Depending upon what one considers to be the characteristic features of life, however, one's ideas about biocomputers will differ considerably. In this sense, our definition of biocomputers has remained extremely vague, but the essential point is that, with regard to any given biological characteristic, engineering implementations can be gradually developed and biological functions realized within applied computer systems.

Science in the 20th century has demonstrated that biological organisms are a kind of chemical computer, but the science and technology of the 21st century will undoubtedly open the road towards engineering implementations of such chemical computers. Once we have obtained the know-how to manipulate these chemical reactions, the question of whether they should be called computers or living objects will become nothing more than a matter of personal preference. Computers and living beings have in common the fact that they are machines with internally stored information. But it is also self-evident that living organisms have quite different properties from those of computers. In spite of those obvious differences, as the characteristic features of life are defined with molecular precision and artificial implementations devised in the 21st century, we believe that it will gradually become more and more difficult to enumerate what their differences are.

That difficulty has nothing to do with the question of whether or not biocomputer research leads to applied biocomputer systems; it is simply a manifestation of the general trends of technology. So we must ask what concrete form will the closing gap between computers and biological objects take and what larger effects are implied? Let us look at a few possibilities.

12.1.2 What kinds of ripple effects?

The first ripple effects are those possibilities opened up by bioelectronic materials. They are likely to facilitate developments in medical therapeutic devices that need to be attached to or embedded in the human body – in various medical sensors, in artificial organs and support equipment. These techniques are also related to robot technology which maintains crucial biological characteristics. They will lead to the development of compact robots with integrated, high-level functions of lighter weight and greater flexibility. Such robots are less likely to be used as autonomous beings capable of doing human work than to be used as mechanical aids that are capable of facilitating human work.

The next possibilities that come to mind are those made possible by developments in neuroscience, brain science and developmental biology. The problem of cancer is of course an important one. The abnormal development of cancerous tissue is, in many respects, the inverse of normal developmental processes, so that any progress in understanding normal development will inevitably lead to better understanding of cancer, and vice versa. Progress here may lead to new therapeutic techniques for organ regeneration – an interesting theoretical possibility which remains beyond our current understanding. Re-growth of lost or injured organs may well strike us today as science fiction, but there is tremendous potential in this field. Not only can such lowly creatures as the water lizard regenerate tissue, but even man has some capacity for regenerating liver and bone tissues. More significant regeneration of other tissues is conceivable even for the higher organisms, but key insights into the developmental process must be obtained.

If it becomes possible to wield precise control over specific genes, it might then be possible to regenerate hair and teeth, and even organs which have been lost in accidents or surgically removed. Indeed, the regrowth and reconnection of severed or necrotic nerve cells is a medical topic of growing significance.

The problems of ageing are also deeply involved in problems of development. As the populations of the nations of the developed world continue to age, the diseases of the elderly will become an increasingly greater problem – particularly brain diseases which appear to incapacitate the elderly in a highly uneven fashion. While some suffer from rapidly deteriorating motor control or sensory deficits, others lose cognitive functions seemingly before motor and sensory functions are affected. Why ageing should be so uneven is not understood and many aspects of the ageing process remain a mystery, but insights into development and the ontogenetic process will bring insights into the failures of development and ageing.

Techniques in tissue and organ culture are not unrelated to biocomputing, but most of the early applications will probably fall within botany. One important development in botany would be the harnessing of photosynthetic functions. If an 'artificial plant' can be placed on a biochip, fine control of energy flow would be possible and new energy sources could be realized – through photoelectric conversion or hydrogen gas production.

In the light of developments such as these, it is clearly unnecessary to confine our conception of biocomputing to the world of digital information processing. For example, the age-old dream of an artificial muscle might be one result of such technology, with numerous applications in macroscopic and microscopic robotics.

12.2 THE IMPACT ON COMPUTING

The central issue of biocomputers is of course computing, and developments within the realm of 'What can be computed?' are likely to be among the most exciting. First of all, we can anticipate the emergence from biocomputing of high-density, high-resolution sensors as peripheral apparatus. Next, large-scale integrated memories and parallel processors will emerge. Although not a central issue concerning computers *per se*, one factor which is extremely important for the widespread dissemination of such computers is the development of display apparatus that causes no strain on the human eye, but still provides crisp images. If that long-standing problem can be solved by means of biosensors, computers can be expected to be used in significantly more applications.

Moreover, with developments in high-density, low-energy memories, paper literature will at least partially become electronic literature. Finally, we can anticipate a computer materials revolution such that discarded machines will be largely biodegradable. Particularly desirable would be the development of casing materials and biochips which would be as degradable as proteins, and which would replace elements currently in wide use, such as arsenic, which should not be discarded into the environment. If the interface with biological organisms proceeds in the directions already evident in the biocomputer revolution, it is likely that new possibilities currently undreamt of will emerge.

That is a small list of anticipated changes in hardware, but what is likely to appear more rapidly and with more definitive influences on future computing are developments in computer architecture and software. Algorithms for pattern recognition are one example, and techniques for searching through analog data for pattern matching – a crucial topic in which current AI researchers have shown little interest – are another. For example, many uses could be found for a computer system capable of searching through a large volume of sound patterns or visual images for a particular melody or image. This could be said to be a computer that accomplishes right-hemisphere-like tasks.

In order to get a foothold on the technology needed for such capabilities, it will be necessary to strengthen the associative capabilities of computers and gradually to implement a limited degree of creativity. This will probably not mean that computers will be able to think as flexibly as human beings. As long as the 'freedom' aspect of autonomous living beings is not realized in computers, it will remain impossible to implement true creativity. For this reason, while huge quantitative increases in computational capabilities are likely, it is as yet difficult to predict when a computer capable of autonomous thought processes and, therefore, free manipulation of language will emerge.

12.3 WILL BIOMACHINES DO HUMAN WORK?

With the development of sophisticated biocomputers, will such machines actually do the work of human beings or even take on the managerial tasks now solely the responsibility of human beings? Science fiction authors often introduce robots which look just like human beings, and are extremely human in both form and function. Realistically, however, there is no real need to produce robots which have a particularly human form.

The old image of a robot was essentially a mechanical doll – that is, a mechanism which is capable of doing work and a doll which is the object of play and simulated human interaction. Fortunately, the work function is certainly dominant in the modern concept of the robot, and the idea of a quasi-human robot which is the playmate of a bored humanity lies firmly in the realm of science fiction.

To be sure, in comparison with machines, living organisms have many superiorities in terms of both structure and function, but those structures and functions have emerged in evolution for use within a natural, biological setting. They have not necessarily been designed for optimal efficiency. What we require in the design of biocomputers capable of reproducing human, or at least biological, talents are only the functions which do specific tasks (and the associated structural characteristics). For this reason, there is no need to produce a completely faithful replica of the shape of living organisms. What we seek are the essential organic mechanisms which produce certain results. Once they are known, those same mechanisms can be assembled within a 'robot', the shape of which will depend solely on the infrastructure which those mechanisms require.

Included in the concept of the robot is the idea of automation – or the automatic undertaking of work tasks. However, if we look at the history of automation, it is clear that many of the successful cases were not achieved simply by replacing the human worker by a robot, but by redesigning the work itself such that it could be mechanized. Greater efficiency in automation in future technologies is also likely to depend upon the redesign of work such that human work can be mechanized. If this is the case, then – more important than a robotic machine which resembles the form of man or other living entity – the central issue becomes the development of a 'work-specialized, ultra-biological machine' which internally contains biological features, but which externally does not resemble any known life form. It may eventually be possible to construct a machine which resembles living forms, but such a machine, even if technologically possible, is likely to be a robot of only limited utility.

Similar statements can be made with regard to the realm of intellectual work. When computers first appeared, the image of an 'artificial brain' was firmly implanted in the minds of all people. Certainly, the workings of the human brain are wonderful in many respects, but it has many defects owing to the fact that it was not originally designed for flawless work. We easily forget details, lose our train of thought and make mistakes. In these respects, the human brain is not the ultimate goal of biocomputing! On the contrary, it is just the essential cognitive functions which we desire to implement, not the entire, wonderful, but fallible brain. What then are the goals of biocomputing?

One answer may be to scout ahead of the evolution of the human brain. Once the principles of the previous evolution of brains are known, it may be possible to predict and, most importantly, to facilitate its further evolution. It may also be possible to predict the future of other living forms and to design computers on the basis of such future organisms.

Another approach may be to determine precisely what kinds of work need to be computerized and then to develop computers specifically for those purposes. Whichever the case may be, we can anticipate a greater interdependence between human brains and computers. For example, if certain kinds of work are completely handed over to computers, we can expect no further natural evolution in that direction of neural structures to handle those functions. That is, as soon as we take the evolutionary 'pressure' off certain developments, their spontaneous arising will become that much more unlikely. Tinkering with evolution in this way is something which we must not undertake lightly, but a closer working together of organic brains and artificially constructed biocomputers will undoubtedly lead to this stage.

12.4 THE TECHNOLOGIES WHICH SOCIETY CHOOSES

The first computers were developed some 40 years ago. Since then, the computer has surpassed all predictions of its originators and has spread throughout modern society in unanticipated ways. As the various technologies implied by the word 'biocomputer' become realized, the computer will find still deeper and wider applications. Progress in computing continues to be rapid, and the end is nowhere in sight. However, a certain maturity has begun to cast a shadow on computer developments. One sign of that maturity is the fact that virtually anyone can get a computer. In the developed countries of the world, one does or does not use a computer depending solely on one's interests and talents: it still requires some time and dedication to achieve interesting graphics and musical results, but within ten years those capabilities will be fully absorbed within standard and conventional computer systems.

What may then become a problem is what one will do with such sophisticated computers. Just as it is today the case that, despite the availability of artistic and musical equipment, not everyone becomes an artist or musician, so it is that no matter how available computers become, their use and influence on society are limited.

The world of computing has until recently been a seller's market. The manufacturers have offered computer systems with certain capabilities, and buyers have obediently taken what was an offer. But the relationship between buyer and seller has gradually begun to reverse itself, with new developments in computing slowly shifting because of the buyer's demands. This change is clearly one for the better, in so far as the configuration and capabilities of future computers will be less dominated by the technology available and more by the facilities buyers demand from the manufacturers.

Biocomputers will open up many technological capabilities not possible with today's computers – with ramifications for fields as diverse as the artificial construction of life forms neuroscience, brain control and developmental biology. There is inevitably, therefore, some anxiety over the effects of such technology and its possible misapplication at large. In this regard, we remain cautiously optimistic, because the final choice concerning such technological developments lies with the conscience of society itself. Thus far, this kind of checking mechanism seems to have worked fairly well. If there are doubts about the successes of this checking mechanism, then attention should be paid to the fact that previous technologies – from nuclear power to genetic engineering – have had quite awesome potential for causing terrible disasters, and yet the worst of the scientific nightmares have so far been avoided.

This fact should not be a cause for complacency, but the fact remains that, even in the realm of serious science fiction, the technological realization of such disasters is unexpectedly difficult. For example, in George Orwell's *Nineteen Eighty-four*, the dictatorial control mechanism referred to as Big Brother watched over all human activity by means of visual and auditory recording of all of society. But in order to process such a mass of information, the number of human beings required to do the watching would undoubtedly exceed the number being watched. For that reason, that form of control over society is unlikely to be an effective political weapon – despite the existence of some of the requisite technology.

The opposite scenario is the rose-coloured world of near-omniscient home computers, doing nothing but aiding people in their constructive and peaceful ends. For many years, there has been talk of computers that could create nutritious menus, do home finance, and diagnose our health and exercise needs. There is in fact no technological obstacle preventing the development of such computers. But, if only menus – not the cooked result – emerge from such computers, there are few human beings who would follow such recommendations. Moreover, if there is a considerable saving of time with computerized home finance and no increase in income, then computerized finances involving the small sums of most homes would not make many people particularly grateful for the computerization.

Even if computers analyse our condition of health or unhealth and prescribe appropriate exercise, detailed measurements of cardiac functions, for example, are not easily accomplished even when employing dedicated systems designed specifically for patients with heart problems. It may be more feasible to construct a training 'menu' for athletes with a specific athletic record in mind, but for most people a computer is simply unnecessary to point them in the direction of more healthy living.

What about computer systems for testing the intelligence of children and adults, and then providing them with an appropriate study regimen? In fact there are already considerable mechanical means for determining abilities and aptitudes – and such results are already widely collected and analysed by computer. However, choosing a specialization for study and selecting course materials do not require the complex quantitative processes which demand the use of computers. Since a fully computerized program of this kind ignores most of the psychological and all of the physical dexterity aspects of development, the use of computers for this purpose is also probably an unattainable dream.

Policy concerning the ageing of society will become a serious problem in the near future – including issues of medical therapy and nursing, rehabilitation, health maintenance and psychological counselling. Such problems require more than technological developments, but the combination of the computer sciences and life sciences promises many new possibilities. Of particular importance are research in vision and organ regeneration, which could lead to prevention of visual impairment and tooth decay, and the functional maintenance of the circulatory system into old age. Moreover, the introduction of small and flexible bioelectronic and biomechanical devices into all aspects of nursing and adjunct therapies will be a silent and almost invisible development, but one which will considerably soften the crises of an ageing society.

Ultimately, it is impossible to anticipate in what ways bicomputing will enter modern society. We believe that, rather than replacing and making obsolete current computer technology, biocomputing will develop together with and complementary to traditional computer technologies. In any case, biocomputing itself does not inevitably imply either a rose-coloured future or a future filled with technological nightmares. The nature of biocomputing is for us to decide.

12.5 IMPLICATIONS FOR OUR UNDERSTANDING OF MAN AND NATURE

Perhaps the single greatest impact of biocomputing will not lie in the development of a particular technological artifact, but in the increased insight it will give into man and nature itself.

The extremely special nature of 'life' in the natural world is evident from the complexity of its design plans, the DNA. So far, however, we can read only a small part of the plans. It appears that the fundamental alphabet of life – the genetic code – has been deciphered, but we know only a relatively small number of words, and none of the sentences and short stories written with that alphabet. Of course, even if we assume that there is a Grand Designer behind life, it does not necessarily follow that we would know the intent of the Designer by reading his plans! Just as, in order to learn a language, it is not enough merely to hear the

We have much pleasure in sending the accompanying book for review.

It will be published on: **January 1991**

priced at: **£24.95**

We shall be glad to have a copy of the review when published.

Chapman & Hall
Scientific, technical, medical and
professional publishers

2-6 Boundary Row, London SE1 8HN
Tel: 071 865 0066
Fax: 071 522 9623
Telex: 290 164 CHAPMAG

words of the language, but, in addition, we must also use the words ourselves in speech and writing, similarly, in order to understand the design of nature, analysis may not be enough. Synthetic, technological methods may also be required – not solely for the technological benefits, but also for the increased understanding which the act of synthesis will give us. That is, as a consequence of the various efforts to incorporate biological characteristics within computers, we will gain a deeper understanding of life and nature, and indeed of human existence itself.

Life is a complex web of matter and information. Relying solely on the world-view of the physics which has shaped 20th-century science will not allow the unravelling of the puzzle of life. In addition to the laws of thermodynamics provided by physics and chemistry, the new dimension of information provided by information science is also necessary. Information science gave birth to and has been the central axis of computing, but essential parts of information science remain today undeveloped and uncultivated. That some progress has been made is witnessed by the rapid growth of computer science, but little work has been done to integrate the energetics of physics, on the one hand, with the information of the brain and computer sciences on the other. Let us not forget that, in the living systems known to science, there is no dichotomy between energy and information – they are both inherent in the control of living systems.

Science of the 21st century will be a dichotomous science including both matter/energy and information. This new science has the potential to revolution-ize our current understanding of nature in integrating these two realms within a unified framework. It is already clear that the future of the universe, including the existence of intelligence, cannot be predicted solely on the basis of the inorganic laws of nature. So one of the dominant themes of the science of the 21st century may well be consideration of the relationship between the intelligence found in organic life and the inorganic universe around us. It seems unlikely that there are two interpenetrating 'fluids' – one of intelligence and life and one of inorganic physics – but what then is at the root of this apparent dichotomy?

Intelligence tries to control its environment. In line with current astronomic predictions, one day earth will no longer be a suitable environment for life as we know it. Indeed, that is true of the entire universe. In a world in which extinction is the final and inevitable outcome, why are living beings born and why do they have the will to try to survive?

One possibility is that intelligent beings have the ability to control the universe through the power of intelligence. Nuclear energy, computing and genetic engineering are technologies used specifically with such control purposes in mind. Some people will undoubtedly feel some hesitancy with regard to biocomputing as a form of artificial life, but it seems certain that mankind will someday need such technology. Indeed, it may be that man is not merely a traveller on a one-way trip through an inorganic universe.

13

Recent developments in biocomputing projects in Japan

Owing to the rapid technological development of Japan, where economic effeciency has been given a high priority, the country has become a major economic power over the last few decades. As a result, Japan has often been criticized for making use of fundamental scientific research and basic technology at essentially no cost to herself, while reaping a disproportionate share of the profits. It has thus become essential for Japan to put greater emphasis on fundamental research and to advance, in both applied and basic science, in directions which are uniquely Japanese.

One manifestation of this need has been the Human Frontiers Science Programme (HFSP), which was first proposed by Japan at the Economic Summit Meeting held in Venice in June 1987 and officially welcomed by the member countries at the Toronto Summit Meeting in June 1988. In order to establish this programme, scientific-technological policy was organized with the cooperation of various ministries of the Japanese government – principally the Ministry of International Trade and Industry (MITI) and the Ministry of Science and Technology, but also including the Ministry of Foreign Affairs and the Ministry of Culture.

The programme's main objective is the promotion of basic research for the elucidation of biological functions through international cooperation. The following basic principles are thought to be essential to the programme and its implementation.

1. The programme should provide unique activities with a distinct identity in supporting research that transcends national boundaries.
    (a) The programme should serve as a stimulant for the promotion of inter-national cooperation among scientists in the fields included.
    (b) Many advances in basic research depend on originality, innovation, fresh ideas and insights. The programme must allow for the expression of individual ability and initiative.
    (c) Importance is attached to the training and support of young researchers, who are expected to play an important role in originating and pursuing creative research.

(d) Interdisciplinarity should be stressed since different ways of thinking and approaches play important roles in arriving at new ideas and discoveries.

(e) Flexibility should be allowed so that improvements in the programme's operation can be made whenever deemed necessary.

2. Proposals should be reviewed on the basis of scientific merit as the primary criterion. Internationality, especially intercontinentality, and interdisciplinarity ought to be significant points in the evaluation of proposals.

3. Research results must be published in internationally recognized scientific literature.

4. The programme's organization will not claim the intellectual property rights that will be generated through the research activities conducted under the programme. The attribution of the intellectual property rights will be determined on an equitable basis among the parties undertaking the research (and/or their institutions).

5. Bioethics must be given due consideration according to the guidelines of the country where the research is conducted.

The priority research areas are to be selected from among the following two areas: basic research for the elucidation of brain functions, and basic research for the elucidation of biological functions through molecular level approaches at the implementation stage in order to make the best use of limited resources and to identify promising research subjects most efficiently.

Since basic research on the elucidation of biological functions is in the midst of dynamic development, such priority areas should be reviewed annually in order that the latest trends be reflected.

Priority research areas are as follows.

1. Priority research areas for the elucidation of brain functions:

    (a) perception and cognition
    (b) movement and behaviour
    (c) memory and learning
    (d) language and thinking

2. Priority research areas for the elucidation of biological functions through molecular level approaches:

    (a) expression of genetic information
    (b) morphogenesis
    (c) molecular recognition and responses
    (d) energy conversion

The programme began in 1990 and continues to solicit appropriate themes for support.

One other manifestation of the emphasis Japan is now placing on fundamental research lies in the field of computing – that is, MITI's Next Generation Computer

Table 13.1 Research themes in the biodevices project and the related research organizations

Subtheme Name	Research Category	Organization
Elucidation of bio-architectures and research on technological modelling of them: research on learning and memory mechanisms	Research on bio-architectures: research on the neural circuitry of rat hippocampal slices, particularly on the clarification of the phenomena of long-term potentiation and suppression	Electrotechnical laboratory: Molecular and Cellular Neuroscience Section (Group Leader: Gen Matsumoto)
	Construction of visual information processing models	NEC Fundamental Research Institute (Group Leader: Shozo Fujiwara)
	Construction of cerebellar information processing models	Fujitsu International Information Social Sciences Research Institute (Group Leader: Kazuhiro Matsuo)
Research and development of biodevice techniques	Research on the fundamental technology of biodevices	Electrotechnical Laboratory: Molecular Functions Research Laboratory (Group Leader: Michio Sugi) and Chemical Technology Laboratory (Group Leader: Yasujiro Kawabata)
	Development of optical information recognition model devices using antibody proteins	Hitachi Corp.: Fundamental Research Institute (Group Leader: Yozo Odawara)
	Development of high-level information processing devices utilizing electron-transport proteins	Mitsubishi Electric Central Research Institute (Group Leader: Mitsuo Maeda)
	Development of visual information processing devices utilizing light-sensitive proteins	Sanyo Corp: Tsukuba Research Institute (Group Leader: Atsuo Minagami)
	Development of neural-like devices using organic macromolecules	Matsushita Technics (Group Leader: Shiro Asakawa)
	Development of perceptual information processing devices using organic macromolecules	Sharp Corp: Tokyo Research Institute (Group Leader: Tadahisa Katsuta)
	Development of photoelectric conversion devices by means of the design and synthesis of organic macromolecules	Mitsubishi Chemicals. Central Research Institute (Group Leader: Konoe Miura)

roject to develop 'biodevices'. This project has already passed through a two-
ear preliminary study stage (1984–5) and was established as a ten-year MITI
esearch project starting in 1986.

This project has two virtually independent aspects. The first is the elucidation of
io-architectures' and the technological research and development of related
memory and learning mechanisms. The second is the research and development
f the technology of biodevices.

Aspect one involves research on the methods used by the brain in learning and
n the development of engineering systems which can learn, process and store
nformation. Three distinct organizations – the Electrotechnical Laboratory
within MITI, and the NEC and Fujitsu Corporations – are participating in aspect
ne, with each establishing its own subthemes for research (Table 13.1).

The second aspect involves the development/improvement of a technology for
ne two- and/or three-dimensional organization of organic molecules or proteins.
ear the completion of the project, it is anticipated that it will be possible to
emonstrate such a basic device with functions of information transmission and
rocessing.

In addition to MITI's Electrotechnical Laboratory and the Chemical Tech-
ology Research Institute, six private firms are also participating in the project
Hitachi, Mitsubishi Electric, Sanyo, Matsushita Technics, Sharp and Mitsubishi
hemicals). Since the start of the project in 1986, the financial support of
esearch continues on schedule (Table 13.2).

Completely independent of the 'biodevices' project, the recent surge in interest
n research on neurocomputing has led to plans to begin a new large-scale project
o commence under the auspices of MITI at the completion of the Fifth Generation
roject. This new project is aiming for the 'technological creation of a system
which processes information in ways resembling human intelligence'. A two-
ear survey, which started in 1989, has been initiated. Continuing after the Fifth
eneration Project, this project is planned as a Japanese national project of the
ame scale as the Fifth Generation Project. During the two-year preliminary study
tage, various issues will be decided, such as the detailed contents of the project,

Table 13.2 Examples of research funding (millions of yen) in the
biodevices project (research at the Electrotechnical Laboratory on
bio-architectures and on basic techniques for constructing biodevices within two of the ten groups summarized in Table 13.1)

	1986	1987	1988	1989	1990...	1995
Matsumoto Group	27	26	33	41	–	–
Sugi Group	19	20	29	36	–	–

the make-up of the private companies and their participation in various themes, the organization of groups in the project, and so on.

The Ministry of Science and Technology has been advancing the Human Frontiers Research Project, based at the Physico-Chemical Research Institute. In this project, research centering on bioelectronics began in 1986, and research in the neurosciences began in 1989. Judging from the average of Japanese research funding, it can be said that this work is receiving generous support.

Professor Masao Karube and his group at Tokyo University's Leading-Edge Science Research Institute are actively pursuing research in biosensors. Many groups in private industry, independently or in collaboration with universities, are being heavily funded in research fields such as molecular electronics, bioelectronics and biosensors.

As may be seen from this brief review of the field of biocomputing, a desire to leave behind the old style of Japanese research and development, which was 'light on research, heavy on applications', and embark on a new style which is based on rigorous fundamental research can be read not only in the content of the research projects funded by MITI and the Ministry of Science and Technology, but also in the rapid development of projects originating in private industry.

Even if one were to question the ultimate value of Japan as a major scientific technological nation, it can none the less be said that the number and scale of projects such as mentioned above will undoubtedly have influence on research in other fields. They reflect a recognition by the Japanese of the beauty of science as one aspect of modern culture. Finally, let it be said that the biodevice project sponsored by MITI is a noteworthy step in this direction and will remain a monument to the renaissance of fundamental scientific research in Japan.

Literature references

TRANSLATOR'S PREFACE

Cook, N. D. (1986) *The Brain Code*, Methuen, London, New York (Kinokuniya, Tokyo, 1989).

Kaminuma, T. (1985a) *Biocomputers*, Nippon Keiei (in Japanese).

Kaminuma, T. (ed.) (1985b) *Biochemical Devices and Biocomputers*, Science Forum (in Japanese).

Mizoguchi, F. (ed.) (1990) *PROLOG and its Applications*, Chapman and Hall, London, New York.

Nagao, M. (1989) *Machine Translation: How Far Can It Go?*, Oxford University Press, Oxford, New York.

CHAPTER 1

Kaminuma, T. (1982–6) *Business Communication Series*, Feb. 1982 to March 1983, Dec. 1985 to Dec. 1986 (in Japanese).

CHAPTER 2

Aiuchi, K. and Hirose, T. (1984) *The Plan for Fifth Generation Computers* (in Japanese) Kaimei Publ., Tokyo.

Kawaii, K. (1985) *The Challenge of Supercomputers*, Iwanami Shoten (in Japanese).

Shaw, D. E. (1987) *Artificial Intelligence*, **332**, 151.

von Neumann, J. (1958) *The Computer and the Brain*, Yale University Press.

CHAPTER 3

Birkhoff, G. and Bartee, T. C. (1970) *Modern Applied Algebra*, McGraw-Hill.

Caianiello, E. R. (1961) *Journal of Theoretical Biology*, **1**, 204.

Dyson, F. (1979) *Disturbing the Universe*, Harper and Row, pp. 194–202.

Eigen, M. and Winkler, R. (1975) *Das Spiel – Naturgesetze steuern den Zufall*, Piper Verlag.

Haken, H. (ed.) (1989) *Springer Series in Synergetics*, Springer.

McCulloch, W. S. and Pitts, W. (1943) *Bulletin of Mathematical Biophysics*, **5**, 115.

Minsky, M. and Papert, P. (1969) *Perceptrons*, MIT Press.

Ohno, S. and Ohno, M. (1986) *Immunogenetics*, **24**, 71.

Rosenblatt, F. (1959) *Proceedings of a Symposium on the Mechanization of Thought Processes*, HMSO, pp. 421–56.

Thom, R. (1975) *Structural Stability and Morphogenesis*, Benjamin.
Turing, A. M. (1952) *Philosophical Transactions of the Royal Society of London*, **237**, 37
Wiener, N. (1956) *I am a Mathematician*, Doubleday.
Zeeman, E. C. (1977) *Catastrophe Theory*, Addison-Wesley.

CHAPTER 4

Alberts, J. *et al.* (1983) *The Cell*, Garland.
Garlick, P. B., Radda, G. K., and Seeley, P. J. (1977) Phosphorus NMR – studies on
    the perfused heart, *Biochemical and Biophysics Research Communications*, **74**, 1256.
Ingvar, D. M. *et al.* (1977) *Acta Neurologica Scandinavica* (suppl. 64), **56**, 14.
Kagawa, Y. (1968) *The Cell Membrane*, Iwanami Shoten (in Japanese).
Kagawa, Y. (1982) *Current Topics in Membranes and Transports*, **16**, 195–213.
Kagawa, Y. (1984) *New Comprehensive Biochemistry, Bioenergetics* (ed. L. Ernster), Elsevier
Kagawa, Y. (1985) *The Cell Membrane and Bioenergetics*, Tokyo University Press (in
    Japanese).
Kagawa, Y., Nojima, H., Nukiwa, N., Ishizuka, M., Nakajima, T., Yasuhara, T., Tanaka, T.
    and Oshima, T. (1984) High guanine plus cytosine content in the 3rd letter of codons of
    an extreme thermophile. *Journal of Biological Chemistry*, **259**, 2956.
Karube, I., Tamiya, E., Murakami, T., Gotoh, M., and Kagawa, Y. (1987) Microbiosensor
    based on silicon fabrication technology. *Annals of the New York Academy of Science*, **501**
    256.
Koppenol, W. H. and Margoliash, E. (1982) *Journal of Biological Chemistry*, **257**, 4426
Koretsky, A. P. *et al.* (1983) *Proceedings of the National Academy of Science* (USA), **80**, 7491.
Ulmer, K. M. (1983) *Science*, **219**, 666.

CHAPTER 5

Hedgecock, F., Cullot, J. G., Thomson, J. N. and Perkins, L. A. (1985) Axonal guidance
    mutants of *C. elegans* identified by filling sensory neurons with fluorescein dyes
    Developmental Biology, **111**, 158.
Kaminuma, T. (1986) *WAVE*, Nov., 76 (in Japanese).
Miwa, J., Schierenberg, E., and Miwa, S. (1980) Genetics and mode of expression of
    temperature sensitive mutations arresting embryonic development in *C. elegans*.
    Developmental Biology, **76**, 160.
Schierenberg, E., Miwa, J., and Vonehrenberg, G. (1980) Cell lineages and developmental
    defects of temperature sensitive embryonic arrest mutants in *C. elegans*. *Developmental
    Biology*, **76**, 141.
Sulston, J. E. (1983) The embryonic cell lineage of the nematode *C. elegans*, *Developmental
    Biology*, **100**, 64.
White, J. *et al.* (1986) *Philosophical Transactions of the Royal Society, London Ser. B*, **314**, 1.
Yamaguchi, Y., Murakani, K., Furusawa, M., and Miwa, J. (1983) Germline-specific
    antigens identified by monoclonal antibodies in the nematode, *C. elegans*. *Development,
    Growth and Differentiation*, **25**, 121.

CHAPTER 6

Fujita, M. (1982) Adaptive filter model of the cerebellum, *Journal of Biological Cybernetics*,
    45, 195.

Gilbert, C. D. (1985) *Trends in the Neurosciences*, April, 160–5.
Houser, C. R., Vaughan, J. E., Hendry, S. H. C., Jones, E. G., and Peters, A. (1984) GABA neurons in the cerebral cortex, in *Cerebral Cortex* (E. G. Jones and A. Peters, eds), vol. 2, Plenum Press, pp. 63–89.
Ito, M. (1980) *The Design of the Brain*, Chuo Koron (in Japanese).
Ito, M. (1984) *The Cerebellum and Neural Control*, Raven Press.

CHAPTER 7

Chapman, R. M. (1980) *Brain and Language*, **11**, 1.
Davidson, R. C. (1971) *Nonlinear Plasma Theory*, Academic.
McLean, P. (1970) *The Neurosciences*, Rockefeller University Press.
Marko, H. (1965) *Kybernetik*, **2**, 6.
Popper, K. and Eccles, J. (1977) *The Self and Its Brain*, Springer.
Tonegawa, S. (1983) Somatic generation of antibody diversity, *Nature*, **302**, 575.

CHAPTER 8

Aizawa, M., Akaike, I., and Sakube, H. (1984) *Bioelectronics*, CMC (in Japanese).
Amari, S. (1986) *Biocomputers*, Iwanami (in Japanese).
Carter, F. (ed.) (1987) *Molecular Electronic Devices*, Dekker.
Fukuda, K., Sugi, M., and Sakube, H. (1986) *LB Membranes Electronics*, CMC (in Japanese).
Kaminuma, T. (1985a) *Biochemical Devices and Biocomputers*, Science Forum (in Japanese).
Kaminuma T. (1985b) *Biocomputers*, Nippon Keiei (in Japanese).
Moriizumi, T. (1987) *Bioelectronics*, Kogyochosakai (in Japanese).
Suzuki, S. (ed.) (1984) *Biosensors*, Kodansha (in Japanese).

CHAPTER 9

Cohen, L. B., Salzberg, B. M., Davila, H. V., Ross, W. N., Landowne, D., Waggoner, A. S., and Wang, C. H. (1974) Changes in axon fluorescence during activity, *Journal of Membrane Biology*, **19**, 1.
Fujiwara, M. and Okajima, K. (1987) *Computers Today*, **4**, 47–52 (in Japanese).
Itoh, M. (1980) *Design Plan for the Brain*, Chuokoronsha (in Japanese).
Matsumoto, G. (1987) In, *Man in Transition*, Vol. 1, *Life*. (eds. H. Uzawa *et al.*) Iwanami Shoten, pp. 221–39 (in Japanese).
Matsumoto, G. (1983) *Elekiteru*, 8–10, 25–8.
Matsumoto, G. (1987) *Computers Today*, **4**, 35–45 (in Japanese).
Matsumoto G. (1988) *Future Generation Computer Systems*, **4**, 39.
Sejnowski, T. J. and Rosenberg C. R. (1986) *Johns Hopkins University Electrical Engineering Technical Report* JHU/EECS 86–01, 1.
Rumelhart, D. E., Hinton, G. E., and Williams, R. J. (1986) Learning representations by back-propagating errors, *Nature*, **323**, 533.

CHAPTER 10

Abu-Mostafa, Y. S. and Psaltis, D. (1987) *Scientific American*, March, 67.
Conrad, M. (1985) *Communications of the ACM*, **28**, 464.

Kaminuma, T. (ed.) (1988) *Biotechnology and Computer Uses*, CMC, Chapter 5 (in Japanese).
Shimizu, H. (1985) Creative scientific inference, abstract of a talk given at the Mizuno Bioholonics Project Research Meeting, March (in Japanese).
Shortliffe, E. H. (1976) *Computer-based Medical Consultations: MYCIN*, Elsevier.
Watanabe, S. (1980) *Life and Freedom*, Iwanami Shoten (in Japanese).
Watanabe, S. (1985) *Nippon IBM Reports*, **66**, 75 (in Japanese).

CHAPTER 11

Carter, F. L. (ed.) (1982) *Molecular Electronic Devices*, Marcel Dekker.
Drexler, K. E. (1981) *Proceedings of the National Academy of Science* (USA), **78**, 5275.
Drexler, K. E. (1982) Molecular machinery and molecular electronic devices, paper presented at the Second MED Workshop.
Drexler, K. E. (1984) *High Technology*, June 8.
Feynman, R. (1985) The computing machines of the future, *Nishina Kinen Koen*, 9 August.
Haddon, R. C. and Lamola, A. A. (1985) *Proceedings of the National Academy of Science* (USA), **82**, 1874.
Kaminuma, T. and Suzuki, I. (1989) *Molecular Graphics*, Keigakusha (in Japanese).
Molecular Electronics: Beyond the Silicon Chip, Technical Insights Inc.
Olsen, A. J. *et al.* (1983) *Journal of Molecular Biology*, **171**, 61–93.
Sakube, H. (1987) *Gakushin Kyokaiho*, **47**, 17 (in Japanese).
Yates, F. E. (ed.) (1984) *Report on the Conference of Molecular Computing*, The Crump Institute for Medical Engineering, University of California.

Index